# *Praise for* Reading in the Wild

"Each chapter reminds us of an important ingredient in the 'making' of a reader who, well, reads! From time to choice to quality . . . each disposition a reader must develop is captured gracefully and artfully and purposefully."

—Patrick Allen, fourth-grade teacher, Douglas County Schools, Colorado, and author of *Conferring: The Keystone of Reader's Workshop*

"Donalyn Miller's *Reading in the Wild* is the guide we need to understand the complexities of leading readers. She knows books, she knows kids, and she knows teachers. This book gave me new ways to think about a personal literary canon and the limitations of lexile levels. If you've hesitated about conferring with readers, *Reading in the Wild* will get you started with a new sense of purpose and the tools for diagnosing non-reading habits that you need. Donalyn's honest portrayal of the challenges of building reading lives is inspiring and practical."

—Penny Kittle, high school teacher and professional development coordinator, Conway School District, New Hampshire, and author of *Book Love: Developing Depth, Stamina, and Passion in Adolescent Readers*

"Where *The Book Whisperer* was a road map for powerful and empowering reading instruction, *Reading in the Wild* is a foot placed firmly on the accelerator. Donalyn Miller once again challenges the inner workings of our classrooms—and her own—and asks, 'If students were truly independent readers, why do they still need a teacher to orchestrate their reading lives?' With Susan Kelley, Donalyn redefines what it means to read 'independently' and draws on research and classroom practice to help every child become a bona fide wild reader."

—Chris Lehman, international speaker, consultant, and coauthor of *Pathways to the Common Core*

"This book is the perfect follow-up to *The Book Whisperer*! Not only do the authors expand upon the ideas for awakening the inner reader in every child, they also truly guide teachers at any level of experience to provide opportunities for their students to become Wild Readers. If you are looking for a book that will inspire all teachers and administrators to help students become reading tribe members, sit down and enjoy *Reading in the Wild*!"

—Marsha Thauwald, education consultant, Key Connections for Learning

"In *Reading in the Wild*, Donalyn Miller and Susan Kelley have crafted a book rich with possibility and authenticity. I feel as if they have genuinely seen my classroom, heard my questions, anticipated where I would stumble, and know my students well enough to lead me to see them in a new way. This is a unique book that acknowledges, validates, and encourages teachers. Built from the authors' own master-practice and inquiry, this is a book that nudges, models, and authentically supports teachers in elevating their practice when taking student readers from meaningful in-class experiences to cultivating the true habits and identities of 'Readers in the Wild.' Miller and Kelley are lead readers and visionary teachers who set the bar high, expecting students to grow from compliance to achievement, not because of limited school measures but because real readers have purpose, community, and identity. This is the kind of book we will pass amongst our colleagues, gift to those new to our field, and return to again and again. It evokes (and feeds) our own wild reading."

—Sara Kajder, eighth-grade teacher, Shady Side Academy,
Pittsburgh, Pennsylvania, English department chair, and author
of *Adolescents and Digital Literacies: Learning Alongside Our Students*

"In her inimitable way, Donalyn Miller has written another gorgeous book about relationships: relationships between teachers and children, relationships among children, and the intimate relationships wild readers have with books. She acknowledges the imperative of emotion and connection if we hope to engage students in reading that will impact their lives. Wild readers, she shows us, make time, assert choice, and find 'comfort' and 'a center' in books and conversation with each other. *Reading in the Wild* is brimming with children's voices and practical solutions to common obstacles. Instead of leading us further into the wilderness, it orients our professional and ethical compass to a perfect true north."

—Ellin Oliver Keene, staff developer, and author of *Talk About Understanding*

"Picking up where *The Book Whisperer* left off, *Reading in the Wild* extends the instructional conversation beyond the classroom to get students thinking about their reading lives outside the scaffolds we present during the school day. Straightforward, honest, and—above all—pragmatic, *Reading in the Wild* is as sensible as it is timely. Whether you're a fan of *The Book Whisperer* or you're just meeting Donalyn Miller through this newest book, you'll find a motivating friend whose realistic, you-can-do-this voice is both thought provoking and refreshing at the same time."

—Terry Thompson, instructional intervention teacher consultant, and author
of *Adventures in Graphica: Using Comics and Graphic Novels to Teach Comprehension*

"This book is special. Miller puts into practice what she offers from the pulpit. It's about connection, celebration, and choice. It's about readers and books."

—Paul W. Hankins, high school teacher, Silver Creek
High School, West Clark Community Schools, Indiana

# Reading
## in the Wild

# Donalyn Miller

*with* Susan Kelley

# *Reading in the Wild*

The Book Whisperer's
Keys to Cultivating
Lifelong Reading Habits

Foreword by Teri S. Lesesne

SCHOLASTIC INC.

ISBN 978-0-545-65202-5

12 11 10 9 8 7 6 5 4 3 2 1                                    14 15 16 17 18 19/0

Printed in the U.S.A.                                                             23

First Scholastic printing, January 2014

Cover design: JPuda
Cover images: (boy reading) © Stuart Stevenson photography/Flickr/Getty Images; (forest) © Dirk Wüstenhagen Imagery/Flickr/Getty Images
Miller photo courtesy of Jennifer Wynne
Kelley photo courtesy of Anna Tyson

All photos by Donalyn Miller and Susan Kelley

# Contents

*To Sarah, our wild reader. —D.M.*

*To Helena, Marisa, and Hazel. —S.K.*

# Foreword: Living the Wild Life of a Reader

THE SMARTEST ANSWER I ever heard to the question many authors face, "How long did it take you to write this book?" was this: "It took me all my life up to this point." Yes, the physical act of putting words to paper might have occurred in a discrete period of time, but the heart of the book, the soul of the book, was a lifetime in the making. And so it is with Donalyn Miller's remarkable *Reading in the Wild*. Donalyn brings together here her lifetime of reading, being a wild reader, being a member of various reading communities, and her passion for books and reading.

From the moment Donalyn began to talk about this book, the excitement has been there. I have watched eyes light up in a workshop as she talked about the concept that underpins *Reading in the Wild*. I saw firsthand how this idea resonated with educators. This idea of how we read when we are free to read is so essential, so basic, so fundamental that we have to ask, "Why has it not occurred to someone to write about it before now?" The answer is simple: this book is the product of Donalyn's unique perspective. We first saw it in *The Book Whisperer*—her approach to inspiring and igniting a passion for reading among her students. As Donalyn talked about her approach, heads of teachers nodded in agreement as if to say, *Well, of course. This makes sense.* More heads will nod in agreement as Donalyn takes us further into transforming students into lifelong readers, especially readers in the wild—those who read not because they must for some assignment but those who elect to share in this community of readers. Wild readers become part of the community of readers because reading is as important to them as eating and sleeping and breathing. Reading simply becomes one other activity in which they engage. They do so not only willingly, but enthusiastically.

How does Donalyn do this? How does she make it seem a foregone conclusion that reading in the wild should be the purpose of every classroom? She does this with a three-pronged approach. First, Donalyn *is* a wild reader. Ask anyone who knows her, who counts her as a colleague and friend. When you sit down to chat with her, the topic of books, reading, authors, and kids always comes into play. If you have followed her (along with Colby Sharp) on the monthly Twitter chat Titletalk, you can witness the depth of her knowledge about books and reading. She is quick to point out titles and authors. And she is just as quick to jot down a book she does *not* know, adding it to her TBR (to be read) shelf or placing an order for the title so that she can add it to her stack. Her reading motivates others—including me—to accept challenges such as book-a-day or the book gap challenge (you can read about these in chapter 4).

It seems almost a no-brainer, but if our friends are wild readers, we tend to be wild readers as well. I have watched Donalyn talk to audiences about building a community of readers. Her talk is always peppered with suggestions about books, authors, series, and the like. The other wild readers in the room show themselves immediately. They are the head nodders who are jotting down titles when they are not nodding in agreement about an author or title Donalyn recommends. This plays out in the classroom as well. Students whose teachers are wild readers are more likely to see this as something to aspire to. They are more likely to model themselves after their teacher. It is not surprising, then, to discover that the students in Donalyn's classes read dozens of books each year and participate fully in their reading community. As Katherine Mansfield observed, "The pleasure of all reading is doubled when one lives with another who shares the same books."

Being a wild reader is not enough for Donalyn. Educators must be able to point to the pedagogical underpinnings of classroom structures and activities. Thus, she takes us further in *Reading in the Wild* by providing the pedagogical base for her approach to developing a passion and love for reading in her students. She coalesces the research, current and historic, that points to the efficacy of what she does in a classroom. That research base is essential. Why is reading aloud important? Donalyn cites the research. How does offering students choice in reading materials work? She provides the research that explains why this is essential. Is it possible to encourage wild reading and still fulfill the demands of the curriculum that must be covered? Donalyn includes that in this book, too. At the very heart of *Reading in the Wild* is the research that underpins the entire focus: Donalyn's survey of hundreds of wild readers, asking them about the practices that helped form them as readers and keep them active as readers.

*Reading in the Wild* is not a program, not a one-size-fits-all approach to instruction. By using broad statements about what wild readers do, Donalyn creates a classroom situation where individual teachers can develop their own forms, schedules, and materials. Although she includes forms and suggestions that educators will welcome, these are easily adjusted to individual needs, other grade levels, and other classes. The research is solid. The implementation is flexible. Have a class of tenth graders? Take the suggestions Donalyn makes about curating classroom libraries, building reading communities, and making reading plans and adjust them for older readers. In a fifth-grade classroom, adapt book sharing and conversations for younger students. Translating the actions of wild readers Donalyn discusses here to a different class or grade or age range is easily done.

Critical to this book are the stories from the trenches. Donalyn is not simply writing about what needs to be done in the classroom. Instead, the voices of students are at the heart of Donalyn's observations. All the wonderful ideas in the world are not worth time and effort without a sense of how this plays out in the classroom. Donalyn takes us into her classroom as kids make plans for vacation reading, set goals for the semester, read and record and reflect on their progress, and build their community of reading that extends past the four walls of the classroom and the school. Her kid-watching skills take us to the very core of wild reading and let us see how wild readers respond. Comments from her students pepper each chapter, providing educators with insight into just how wild readers respond to the activities, strategies, and structure of her classroom. Those voices of readers affirm what Donalyn discusses: given the proper classroom conditions, educators can help students grow from school time to lifetime readers, wild readers.

Ultimately, then, *Reading in the Wild* is about making connections. Think back to the connect-the-dot puzzles we loved as children. As we continued to move our pencils or crayons from dot to dot to dot, a picture emerged. And so it is with *Reading in the Wild*. As we move from chapter to chapter to chapter, the approach to fostering wild readers emerges. The connections we make between book and book, between reader and reader, and between book and reader are perhaps the most important connections we as educators can make. Helping students move from one book to the next and the next, especially helping them become more independent in the process, of knowing where to find more recommendations for books, ensures that their TBR lists and stacks of books grow, that a plan is in place. Assisting students in forging relationships among other readers ensures that students know that a community of readers is another constant in their lives as wild readers. Finally, helping readers connect to the books they are reading, making certain that the books are developmentally appropriate for the students and speak to the very hearts of the wild readers, affirms that the real purposes of reading include personal connections—that books can touch us all deeply and elicit laughter, tears, and other reactions. These connections are part of the very heart of wild reading.

Donalyn reminds readers that books can transform lives. However, in order to do this, books have to be read. An old Buddhist proverb tells us, "If a seed of lettuce will not grow, we do not blame the lettuce. Instead, the fault lies with us for not having nourished the seed properly." Here, then, is the secret to nourishing readers. Donalyn Miller's *Reading in the Wild* is the tool teachers need for the proper nourishment of readers—the tool we need to make sure all our readers are wild readers.

*Teri S. Lesesne*
Professor at
Sam Houston State University
October 2013

# Introduction

*I have long been convinced that the
central and most important goal of
reading instruction is to foster a love
of reading.*

—Linda Gambrell,
"Creating Classroom Cultures
That Foster Reading Motivation"

IN THE FINAL CHAPTER of my first book, *The Book Whisperer: Awakening the Inner Reader in Every Child* (Miller, 2009), I expressed dismay that although I had succeeded in encouraging my students to read a lot during our school year together, many of those students read less or stopped reading altogether when they moved into middle and high school. I blamed upper-level teachers and schools when my former students lost their reading motivation. I knew that given class reading time, the opportunity to choose their own books, and teachers who read and promoted books to them, the children would read. Clearly, it seemed to me, that if they stopped reading, it was because their teachers didn't provide a classroom environment that supported them. I expected teachers to take responsibility for students' reading.

Now I believe that while teachers can provide conditions for their students to develop lifelong reading habits, eventually students need to take responsibility for their reading lives. Reflecting on my own practices, which I outlined in *The Book Whisperer,* I see that our reading workshop classroom built an independent reading culture, but it seemed that some of my students were dependent, rather than independent, readers. When they left my classroom, many had not internalized the lifelong reading habits they needed in order to remain readers without daily support. If my students were truly independent readers, why did they still need a teacher to orchestrate their reading lives?

One student, Ashley, told me, "It is impossible to be a nonreader in your class, Mrs. Miller." A few years ago, I would have taken pride in Ashley's observation, but not now. I want my students to enjoy reading and find it meaningful when they are in my class, but I also want them to understand why reading matters to their lives. A reading workshop classroom provides a temporary scaffold, but eventually students must have self-efficacy and the tools they need to go it alone. The goal of all reading instruction is independence. If students remain dependent on teachers to remove all obstacles that prevent them from reading, they won't become independent readers.

While students' standardized test performance, fluency checks, and use of comprehension strategies indicated whether they mastered basic reading processes, none of the data tell me whether my students are readers beyond a school-based definition. I can prove students' reading levels, I can prove whether they have mastered the reading standards I am required to teach, and I can prove their ability to read strategically. But I cannot prove whether my students will be avid readers in the future. And no one asks me to prove it.

When we teach and assess reading in our classrooms, we cannot overlook the emotional connections avid readers have for books and reading and the lifestyle behaviors that lifelong readers possess. (I shy away from the term *real readers* because it implies that students who read aren't "real" readers.) Call it what you will—lifelong, avid, real, wild (my preference)—readers share an innate love of reading. In order to bridge the gap between a school-based definition of readers and a real-world one, we must consider these affective qualities. The path to lifelong reading habits depends on internalizing a reading lifestyle along with reading skills and strategies. But are we identifying, modeling, and teaching these habits in the classroom? Can we as literacy professionals even agree on what the habits of lifelong readers are? And why is it so important?

Children who love reading and see themselves as readers are the most successful in school and have the greatest opportunities in life. The importance of lifelong reading habits is well documented. The 1996 *NAEP Report* (Allen, Carlson, & Zelenak, 2000), the only national measure we have in the United States that compares children across states (until Common Core State Standards testing kicks in) stresses the importance of lifelong reading habits: "Beyond the research and reform efforts in reading instruction, the development of lifelong literacy habits and abilities that are fostered through family and environmental support are of growing concern. More and more, educators and parents agree that students must not only develop the ability to comprehend what they read, but also develop an orientation to literacy that leads to lifelong reading and learning" (p. 100). In spite of intensive reform efforts to improve the reading skills of American students, the 2010 NAEP scores reveal little growth in this regard (Gewertz, 2010). There is little evidence that we are accomplishing the goal of instilling lifelong reading habits in classrooms.

While I was writing this book, almost every state adopted the Common Core State Standards—sweeping educational reform that promises to improve students' reading achievement and ensure that schools throughout the country prepare every student for advanced education and the workforce. But this work was implemented without a single research study proving the effectiveness of the standards, and it ignores or blatantly dismisses decades of research in child development, educational psychology, and reading instruction. Whether the standards will improve students' reading performance remains to be seen, but we cannot overlook one truth: no matter what standards we implement or reading tests we administer, children who read the most will always outperform children who don't read much.

Our zealous national focus on standardized test performance, often at the expense of meaningful reading instruction and support, has caused us to lose sight of our true obligations regarding children's literacy: fostering their capacity to lead literate lives. We teach the skills that can be measured on multiple-choice tests and secretly hope that our students pick up along the way that reading is a worthwhile endeavor. We are teaching children to be test takers, yet we still aren't markedly improving their test scores. In 2002, the National Academies, a private, nonprofit quartet of institutions chartered by Congress to provide science, technology, and health policy advice, formed a panel composed of national experts in education, law, economics, and the social sciences in order to track the implementation and effectiveness of fifteen test-based incentive programs like merit pay. After ten years, the panel found few learning gains for students as a result of such programs (Sparks, 2011). We are not creating resilient, self-possessed readers who can travel on to the next school year, and the next, and into adulthood with reading behaviors and a love of reading that will serve them throughout their lives.

Readers are also more likely to succeed in the workforce. Researcher Mark Taylor, from the University of Oxford, surveyed 17,200 people born in 1970 about their extracurricular activities at age sixteen and their careers at age thirty-three. He found that "reading books is the only out-of-school activity for 16-year-olds that is linked to getting a managerial or professional job in later life." Reading was linked to a higher chance of attending college, too. No other activity, including sports, attending concerts, visiting museums, or practical activities like cooking and sewing, were found to have the same effect. Reflecting on the survey findings, Taylor said, "According to our results there is something special about reading for pleasure. The positive associations of reading for pleasure aren't replicated in any other extra-curricular activity, regardless of our expectations." When we consider that adults who read have access to better job prospects, fostering wild reading habits in our students appears vital to ensuring their college and career readiness (University of Oxford, 2011).

Failing to graduate a populace that values reading has long-term consequences for everyone. The 2007 National Endowment for the Arts report, "To Read or Not to Read," found that "regular reading not only boosts the likelihood of an individual's academic and economic success—facts that are not especially surprising—but it also seems to awaken a person's social and civic sense" (Iyengar & Ball, 2007). Adults who consider themselves readers vote in elections, volunteer for charities, and support the arts in greater numbers than their peers who read less. Clearly, developing lifelong reading habits matters not only to the individual but to society in general. We all benefit when more people read.

And yet there is debate about whether we can teach students to become lifelong readers at all. According to Alan Jacobs, Distinguished Professor of Humanities at Baylor College, you can't. In his book *The Pleasure of Reading in an Age of Distraction* (2011), Jacobs claims that "the idea that many teachers hold today, that one of the purposes of education is to teach students to love reading—or at least appreciate and enjoy whole books—is largely alien to the history of education. And perhaps alien to the history of reading as well" (p. 113). Some children fall in love with reading, and some don't. Our charge as teachers, some educators claim, is to ensure that our students have at least the minimal literacy skills they need to function in society. This philosophy, however, is a cop-out and reduces opportunities for our students for the rest of their lives.

If readers have the edge academically, professionally, and socially, we limit our students' potential when we decide that lifelong reading habits are not within our abilities to teach or children's abilities to learn. By believing that only some of our students will ever develop a love of books and reading, we ignore those who do not fall into books and reading on their own. We renege on our responsibility to teach students how to become self-actualized readers. We are selling our students short by believing that reading is a talent and that lifelong reading behaviors cannot be taught. I don't subscribe to the belief that avid readers are born and not made or that reading teachers carry no responsibility for creating wild readers. This is, in fact, something I addressed head-on in *The Book Whisperer.*

Even schools and classrooms that embrace independent reading often see it as nothing more than an inroad to improving students' test scores. The value of lifelong reading habits to the individual or society is rarely discussed or considered important. Planned, explicit conversations that model and teach students how to develop reading lives seldom take place. But I believe that they should and that instilling lifelong reading habits in children should be our primary goal as reading teachers.

I asked Susan Kelley to join me in writing this book. Susie has taught reading for over thirty years, and her experiences, thoughtful teaching practices, and continued passion for teaching add an important and necessary voice to this conversation. For every teacher who believes that change is no longer possible, who counts the days until retirement because teaching has radically changed, Susie stands as living proof that veteran teachers continue to evolve in their understanding of children and teaching.

Susie and I want our students to love reading, and we constantly reflect on how our instruction, classroom management, and assessments lead students toward lifelong reading habits and self-efficacy as readers. How do we measure this agency? How do we prove to an administrator, or parent, or even ourselves that we are fostering lifelong reading behaviors in our students? How do we set up a classroom that provides optimal conditions for these habits to develop?

We began with our primary question, "What are the habits of lifelong readers anyway?" Examining our own reading behaviors and the reading behaviors of our students provided some insight. In order to validate our beliefs about the reading habits of lifelong readers, we surveyed over eight hundred adult readers through our online Wild Reader Survey (the survey is in appendix D). In the same way that thoughtful researchers and teachers deconstructed reading comprehension, we sought to unpack readers' lifelong reading habits.

Our Wild Reader Survey respondents provided an operational definition of a reader through their daily habits and thoughts about reading. Through these responses, Susie and I identified five general characteristics that lifelong readers share. This list of habits guided us toward further inquiry, reflective practice, and action research in our classrooms over the next two years. Taking a critical look at our own teaching practices, Susie and I determined what instructional components exist in our classrooms to support students as they develop these qualities and identified how our practices could improve. From lesson design, to classroom management strategies, to formative assessments, we reconsidered every aspect of our instruction with the goal of nurturing these wild reader characteristics in our students. We talked, argued (not much, really), drew big plans on our whiteboards, listened to our students, and tried and retried techniques in our classrooms.

This book offers the results of that work and our journey to reposition our reading instruction around the habits and attitudes of lifelong readers. We include every tool we created, our students' responses, and our reflections about how our discoveries shaped our practices. Each chapter of *Reading in the Wild* focuses on a single characteristic of lifelong readers.

We found that wild readers:

1. *Dedicate time to read.* They spend substantial time reading in spite of their hectic lives. In chapter 1, we share methods for increasing students' reading time both inside and outside school and provide suggestions for working with students who don't spend much time reading.

2. *Self-select reading material.* They are confident when selecting books to read and have the experience and skills to choose books successfully that meet their interests, needs, and reading abilities. In chapter 2, we demonstrate how to build this reading confidence and experience in children and teach students how to choose their own books. Because

access to books is a vital component in providing students choices in appropriate reading material, we include tips for creating, curating, and using a classroom library to foster more reading.

3. *Share books and reading with other readers.* Readers enjoy talking about books almost as much as they like reading. Reading communities provide a peer group of other readers who challenge and support us. In chapter 3, we describe the importance of reading communities to readers and offer suggestions for creating and sustaining a positive reading culture in your classroom.

4. *Have reading plans.* Wild readers plan to read beyond their current book. We anticipate new books by favorite authors or the next installment in a beloved series. We know what we plan to read next and why we want to read it. In chapter 4, we describe how to teach children to make their own reading plans and provide suggestions for increasing your knowledge of children's literature.

5. *Show preferences for genres, authors, and topics.* While we agree that children need to read widely and experience a wide range of texts as part of their literacy educations, we realize that wild readers often express strong preferences in the material they choose to read. In chapter 5, we reveal how to validate students' reading preferences, challenge them to expand their reading horizons, and work with students who seem to be in a reading rut or require additional challenge.

Throughout the book, we share the words of our students and the wild readers we surveyed, which give powerful insight into the experiences and skills that support their reading lives.

We believe that teaching our students to be wild readers is not only possible; it is our ethical responsibility as reading teachers and lifelong readers. Our students deserve it, society demands it, and our teaching hearts know that it matters.

# *How* Reading in the Wild *Is Organized*

Each chapter of *Reading in the Wild* focuses on one of five lifelong reading habits. Although the wild readers we surveyed exhibited a wide range of reading behaviors, Susie and I selected five habits that most readers exhibited that also transferred well to classroom instruction. In each chapter you will find:

- *Community Conversations:* These conversations describe the minilessons we taught our students that focus on aspects of wild reading habits. Each minilesson features a modeling piece, classroom discussion, student practice, and reflection.

- *Conferring Points:* Conferring is the backbone of reading and writing workshop because conferences provide individualized support, relationship building, and assessment opportunities. Each conferring point addresses common concerns observed in workshop classrooms and offers student examples and assessment tools for conferring about wild reading habits.

- *Keeping Track of Your Reading Life:* Students document their reading habits throughout the school year using their readers' notebooks. In this section, we examine components of the reader's notebook that reinforce wild reading habits, describing how each tool holds students accountable for their reading and provides reflection and planning opportunities for both readers and teachers.

In between each chapter are essays on topics of interest that relate to wild reading in the classroom. These essays take a deeper look at some classroom management aspects of reading workshop or explore specific themes in greater detail.

The appendices at the back of the book contain blank copies of all of the forms mentioned in this book and a list of my students' favorite books. I have also included these forms and list at www .slideshare.net/donalynm.

## *Classroom Nonnegotiables*

Susie and I depend on a few classroom nonnegotiables built on a framework of fundamental workshop model components that exist every day throughout the school year. Lesson planning, assessment, resources, classroom management—we check every aspect of our instructional design against these core values. I discussed each one of these foundational elements in *The Book Whisperer: Awakening the Inner Reader in Every Child,* and it is not my intent to revisit these concepts in detail here. Rest assured that these components remain in place as vital elements of our classroom reading (and writing) workshops. Our classroom nonnegotiables are these:

- *Time to read: Students need time to read and write.* Our students spend a significant amount of time reading in class—approximately one-third of every class period. During this daily independent reading time, Susie and I confer with several students about their reading and meet with small groups of students who need additional instruction and support. We encourage students to read at home and remove or reduce homework and busy-work activities in order to provide time for additional reading.

- *Choice: Students need to make their own choices about reading material and writing topics.* Students self-select all books for independent reading. Susie and I expect them to read widely—selecting books from a variety of genres and formats including fiction, nonfiction, poetry, and graphic novels. We support and challenge our students through reading advisory, guiding them toward books that match their interests and reading abilities.

- *Response: Students need the opportunity to respond in natural ways to the books they read and the pieces they write.* Susie and I provide students with daily opportunities to respond to what they read. Students share book recommendations, write response entries, and post book reviews based on their independent reading. They talk about books daily with their peers and us through conferences and classroom discussions.

- *Community: Students need to feel that they are part of a community of readers and writers.* Students develop confidence and self-efficacy as readers through their relationships with other readers in reading communities that include both their peers and teacher. Whether students read below grade level, meet grade-level goals, or surpass grade-level expectations, all of them fully participate in activities and conversations that value individual strengths and viewpoints. Both Susie and I read avidly and share our love for reading every day with our students. We are the lead readers in our classrooms and model a reading life for students.

- *Structure: The workshop rests on a structure of predictable rituals and procedures that support the students and teacher.* Reading workshop follows a consistent routine of lessons; whole class, small group, and independent reading activities; and time for sharing and reflection. Regular conferences, reading response, and reader's notebook records hold students accountable for their reading and provide information about their progress toward personal and academic reading goals.

While these foundational workshop principles provide our students with a scaffold for developing lifelong reading habits, Susie and I realize that our students need more direct instruction in lifelong reading behaviors and deeper reflection about their progress toward developing these habits. Even the best classroom reading communities are temporary homes in our students' lives. In their brief time with us, we must explicitly teach them how to become wild readers.

# Reading
*in* *the* Wild

 # Life, the Universe, and Everything

*A reader lives a thousand lives before he dies, said Jojen. The man who never reads lives only one.*

—George R. R. Martin,
*A Dance with Dragons*

As I BEGAN thinking about wild reading habits, I started at home. I have met many readers over the years, but the reader I know best is my husband, Don. For him, books are an accessory—an essential part of his daily checklist before leaving the house: keys, wallet, lunch, book. I tease him that he would take a book with him to check the mailbox if he could manage it.

I may read more than Don does, but he taught me a lot about being a wild reader. He reads every day—sometimes for ten minutes, sometimes for three hours. He's open-minded about books—willing to give anything a go for at least fifty pages. Don loves bookstores and libraries. He carries three library cards and uses them. He shares random facts from books he reads, starting innumerable conversations with, "Did you know that...?" What Don possesses is a complete acceptance of himself as a reader to the point that reading isn't special or eventful. Reading to him is as ordinary as eating lunch.

Think about the readers you know. How do you know from their behaviors and actions that they are readers? On the surface, reading seems like a passive act, but living a reading life requires some commitment.

Looking across our living room, I know our fourteen-year-old daughter, Sarah, is a reader, although she isn't reading right this minute. She is sitting at the computer with her personal universe spread across the desk and down onto her lap. With ear buds half in and half out of her ears, she's listening to her iPod while she types on the computer. She and her friends write *Hunger Games* fan fiction together—a sprawling epic with its own version of the Games that takes place at their middle school. Sarah stops writing for a moment and pops over to Goodreads, a social networking site for readers, to look up the title of the graphic novel she just finished, *Zita the Spacegirl* by Ben Hatke. Sarah sends a quick text message to her friend, Winter, who wants a book recommendation. Returning to her writing, Sarah thumbs through a copy of Max Brooks's *The Zombie Survival Guide*, which she is using for research.

I marvel at how Sarah flows in and out of all of these activities and still manages it all. Like many other parents these days, I wonder whether she has too many distractions. Looking with my language arts teacher eyes, though, this is what I see:

- She reads for her own purposes during her free time. Nothing she is reading or writing at this moment is for a school assignment.

- She is writing using the books she reads as models and sources of information—in this case, *The Hunger Games* and *The Zombie Survival Guide*.

- She participates in an online reading community (Goodreads, for example).

- She has friends who read (Winter and others).

- She prefers science fiction and reads broadly within this genre: *The Hunger Games, Zita the Spacegirl,* and *The Zombie*

*Survival Guide*—three different types of science fiction at three different reading levels.

- Reading fits into her self-identity. Both her books and electronic devices are tools that advance her personal literacy interests and goals.

I see the same reading behaviors in my students. Reading is nothing remarkable or special for them; it is a regular part of their lives. They are readers, but they are also artists, athletes, writers, gamers, and musicians. For me, this is what wild reading is: readers who incorporate reading into their personal identities to the degree that it weaves into their lives along with everything else that interests them. As teachers and parents, we spend a lot of time gnashing our teeth and complaining that kids don't read. Reading is a big deal to us because we know that reading well unlocks academic, professional, and social opportunities, but for readers themselves, reading is just part of who they are.

I want my students to see reading as something that they do—not something remarkable or rare. I want them to read because they enjoy it and feel comfortable in their reading personalities, but I worry that many of them won't be readers into adulthood. Reading well enough is admired in school, but cultivating reading habits isn't part of the curriculum at most schools. In fact, the practices of many school reading programs diminish and disregard the development of personal reading habits.

I don't believe some teachers consider whether their classroom instruction fosters the development of reading habits in their students. Reflecting on the landslide of crossword puzzles, dioramas, annotations, and reading logs assigned to their students for every book they read, teachers might realize that instead of encouraging students to read, these mindless assignments make kids hate reading. Primarily assigned to generate grades and give teachers a false sense that they are holding students accountable for reading, these counterfeit activities—that no wild reader completes on his or her own—guarantee that their students will avoid reading. If we care about our students' reading lives, we must foster their lifelong reading habits and eliminate or reduce the negative influences of classroom practices that don't align with what wild readers do.

My daughter and her friends complain that they can't read or write what they want during the school year. Without any reading time in class, too much homework, and little choice provided in reading material or writing topics, Sarah keeps her reading life alive in spite of school, not because of it. Our children shouldn't have to wait for adulthood to become wild readers. For many, it will be too late.

# CHAPTER 1

# Wild Readers Dedicate Time to Read

*If you have never said, "Excuse me" to a parking meter or bashed your shins on a fireplug, you are probably wasting too much valuable reading time.*

—Sherri Chasin Calvo

L AST FALL, I went to the ophthalmologist for an eye exam and new glasses. After listening to my difficulties reading small print on menus, labels, and graphic novels (okay, I didn't mention the graphic novels), my doctor suggested it was time for bifocals.

He asked, "Do you read a lot?"

Snorting with laughter, I said, "You could say I read for a living. I'm a reading teacher."

He prescribed the bifocals.

I cannot imagine a day without reading in it. Reading for a living—discovering and sharing books with my students and colleagues, writing about books and reading—is a reader's dream. Without question, I am a better teacher because I read. I pass books into my students' hands and talk with them about what they read. I model what a reading life looks like and show my students how reading enriches my life and can enrich theirs, too.

Professional benefits aside, I read because I love it. I am happiest with my nose in a book, curled up in a chair, with a blanket on my feet. Young adult author John Green said, "Reading forces you to be quiet in a world that no longer makes a place for that" (2011). The noise of my life demands that I find daily solitude within the pages of my books. I can think and grow and dream. I am happier when I make time to read, and I feel stressed and anxious when I don't read for a few days. Reading centers me.

Finding time to read requires commitment, though. I make an effort to carve out reading time because it matters to me. I don't watch much TV, and when I do, I read during the commercials.

Traveling a lot, I read in airports and on planes. I read waiting for Sarah's choir performances and band competitions to begin. Occasionally I bring my book to school and read along with my students during independent reading time. On Friday nights, I spend the entire evening reading, often finishing a book. I read almost half my yearly allotment of books over the summer during my personal book-a-day challenge—reading a book for every day of the break. On rare, luxurious days, I devour books in a single sitting. There are also stretches when I don't read much at all. Many nights, I am too tired to read—falling asleep across an open book before reading one page. If I didn't make reading a priority, it would be easy to skip it. My endless to-do list never shrinks. I always have papers to grade, e-mails to answer, and laundry to fold.

It won't surprise you that daily demands prevent many adults from reading as much as they want. Small children at home, work obligations, and fatigue limit our available reading time. Even when we can steal a few moments, we feel guilty about reading. After all, if we are reading, we aren't cleaning, helping children with their homework, talking with our spouses, or doing any number of seemingly more productive endeavors. Reading becomes a self-indulgent luxury we can't afford. Some of us fall out of the reading habit when we cannot commit to reading on a regular basis. Julie, a respondent to the Wild Reader Survey, admits,

> Parenting has been the biggest obstacle to reading—not enough time and not enough energy. I used to be a big reader. Now I'm out of the habit, and it's actually hard to sit down and let myself read a book. I think it's a skill to simply stop engaging with the world out there and engage with a book instead. There is also so much competing media. If I have twenty minutes, I'll sit down and look at Facebook instead of picking up a real book! Aaagh!

Our students claim they don't have time to read either. The least engaged readers among my students don't spend much time reading at home and wouldn't read at all if I didn't set aside thirty minutes of reading time during class. It seems that children can't find reading time any more than adults can.

## Wild Readers Chime In

"I'd spend all day reading if I could but the laundry needs to get done, I need to go to work, and my kids need to eat."

"Sometimes it's a choice between sleep and reading. I choose sleep."

"I'm often too tired [to read] in the evening. When the book hits me in the face I know it's time for lights out."

"I spend too much time online."

"I have two children so I only have about an hour of reading time each night before collapsing."

"I am very busy with teaching, coaching, grad school, and everything else I have to do, but I make as much time as I can to read."

"When I start reading, I cannot stop . . . I cannot do anything else. I will stay up all night to finish a book—not always practical."

"I feel guilty that I should be doing something else—playing with kids, housework, etc."

## Why Reading Time at School Really Matters

While teachers and teacher-librarians understand the need for students to read a lot, some parents and administrators may not see the long-term value in providing students reading time at school or encouraging children to read every day at home. Research indicates that time spent reading correlates positively with students' performance on standardized reading tests (Cunningham & Stanovich, 1998):

- A student in the twentieth percentile reads books for .7 minutes per day. This adds up to 21,000 words read per year.

- A student in the eightieth percentile reads books for 14.2 minutes per day. This adds up to 1,146,000 words read per year.

- A student in the ninetieth percentile reads for 21.1 minutes per day. This adds up to 1,823,000 words per year.

- A student in the ninety-eighth percentile reads for 65.0 minutes per day. This adds up to 4,358,000 words per year.

No matter what our curriculum requires us to teach or how little class time we have, children must read a lot in order to attain even minimum levels of reading achievement. This requires a daily commitment to reading at school and home. Describing students' academic achievement gains as a result of daily reading often brings on board stakeholders who may not value reading as a worthy individual pursuit.

We cannot blame parents when kids don't read at home and then neglect the need for daily reading time at school. Beyond racking up reading miles, ensuring that our students read every day at school provides students opportunities to fall in love with books and develop stamina for reading. Daily reading practice builds students' capacity for reading outside school in the same way that sports and fine arts practice lead to performance success on the playing field or stage. The more students practice, the more they enjoy and develop confidence in reading and the more likely they are to read in their free time. We cannot tell children they need to read more and refuse to offer any time for them to read during the school day. Imagine schools where band, choir, debate, and athletics participants were not given practice time during the school day yet were still expected to perform. If we expect students to perform well as readers, they need time to practice reading at school, too.

In addition to honing their skills during regular group practice sessions, musicians, actors, and athletes build camaraderie—forming attachments while learning and mastering goals together. This collegiality shapes members' beliefs around core values and offers a sense of belonging. When students read together every day, they forge strong bonds through shared reading experiences that help them define themselves as members of a reading tribe. As legendary musician Charlie Parker said, "If you don't live it, it won't come out of your horn."

During daily reading time, our students practice more than their reading skills; they practice living like readers. Reading together, swapping books, sharing observations and recommendations, and developing reading relationships help students approximate wild reading behaviors. This is why reading time at school really matters. Students need to connect with other readers and participate in a reading culture that values them. Our students must see themselves as readers, or they will never embrace reading beyond school.

When providing reading time at school, we must ensure that all students receive equal access. Administrators, literacy coaches, specialists, and teachers must consider the importance of this reading culture when determining how and when to serve special education and at-risk students. Too often reading intervention specialists pull students who require additional reading support out of class during independent reading time. Disregarding the effect of independent reading time on students' reading achievement undermines our intervention efforts over the long haul. Richard Allington and Anne McGill-Franzen (2013) assert, "There are too many research reports on the relationship between reading volume and reading achievement to continue to ignore the necessity of expanding reading activity for struggling readers" (p. 7). We reduce the effectiveness of reading interventions when we don't provide our lowest-performing students reading time and encouragement. Developing readers need more reading, not less.

Beyond time spent reading, we deny our neediest readers full citizenship in supportive classroom reading communities when we commandeer their independent reading time for reading intervention instead. While more capable readers talk about books, confer with the teacher about reading, or peruse the classroom library together, our at-risk readers don't build reader-to-reader relationships with their classmates and teacher. Our less-capable readers must surely receive defeating messages when they trudge off to another class for drill and skill work while other kids read for enjoyment—for example:

> "Reading is fun for people who can read well, but that's not you."

> "One day, when you get better at this, you can be a reader, but not today."

As Kelly Gallagher writes in *Readicide: How Schools Are Killing Reading and What You Can Do about It* (2009), "We give struggling students a treatment that does not work, and worse, a treatment that turns them off to reading" (p. 23). At-risk students need substantial reading time and access to peer communities that value reading.

## Community Conversations

In spite of the fact that our students spend one-third of every class day independently reading and conferring with us, Susie and I recognize that if our students do not have the ability to find reading time for themselves—and if their future teachers reduce or remove daily reading time at school—many will stop reading. Sharing how wild readers find reading time reveals to our students how they can do it, too.

## Reading on the Edge

> *You will never find time for anything. If you want time you must make it.*
>
> —Charles Buxton (1823–1871),
> English brewer, philanthropist, writer,
> and Member of Parliament

When you ask avid readers how much time they spend reading every day, most can't tell you a concrete number of minutes or hours. They don't know. Wild readers don't keep reading logs. Nevertheless, 78 percent of our Wild Reader Survey respondents reported reading more than four hours a week, and many shared that they read as much as twenty hours a week. During weekends, holiday breaks, and vacations, wild readers read upward of forty hours a week. Wild readers don't have more hours in the day than other people, so how do they find the time? It turns out that they read in the edge times, snatching a few minutes of reading time between appointments, while waiting for their children during dance practice, or before falling asleep at night. Life is full of wasted moments in between our daily commitments.

Sneaking precious minutes here and there for reading is an acquired skill, and children who don't grow up around readers may not understand how wild readers fit in so much reading time (see figure 1.1). During a reading conference, my student Tristen shakes his head when I tell him that I read "constantly," and asks me, "Don't you have a life, Mrs. Miller?" I hear this remark from

FIGURE 1.1: *Sarah reads Laurie Halse Anderson's* Twisted *while waiting for our lunch table at Universal Studios Orlando.*

adults, too, who imply I let my housework go and never talk to my family if I read so much. In fact, I fill every bit of edge time with reading.

I express to parents the importance of reading at home and reinforce to students that they need to read at home as much as possible. Even without a reading log, which can be forged or forgotten, I can determine if students are reading at home by assessing their reading engagement in class and how many books they complete over a set period of time.

If students appear to make slow progress on completing books or the books they primarily complete are short texts like informational books or graphic novels—books they can read in one day at school without ever taking books home—I ask them whether they are reading at home. For the most part, my middle school students admit when they aren't reading at home.

Recognizing that thirty uninterrupted minutes of reading time may be impossible because students lack reading stamina, motivation, or adequate time, I confer with students about their after-school demands.

Tristen confessed that he wasn't reading much at home because of football practice and homework. Taking an all-or-nothing stance, he couldn't carve out thirty continuous minutes for reading, so he didn't read at all. I suggested that he read on the way back and forth to practice. If it was too dark after practice to read in the car, he could grab a few minutes before bed. Tristen was shocked: "You would let me do that? Reading a little bit here and there counts?" I told him, "Tristen, most readers don't have thirty minutes every night to read. We read a little bit here and there, too." I don't think he believed me at first, but over the next few months, he read more outside school.

Reflecting on our conversation later, I realized that many students interpret a teacher's mandates to read for twenty or thirty minutes every night in the same manner Tristen did—all or nothing—never learning that a daily reading habit built on managing time to read matters more than how many minutes they read in one sitting. Years of filling out prescribed minutes on a reading log had crippled Tristen from taking ownership of his reading time or learning to manage it.

It is difficult for many children to become wild readers if they don't read during the edge times. But if they don't have frequent reading time, reading habits never take hold. Teaching specific students to find reading time outside school requires explicit conversations about their individual schedules and how reading fits into it. It takes an awareness of the possibilities. Reading thirty minutes a night presents a challenge for students who are unmotivated to read, overscheduled with after-school activities, helping with siblings, or buried with homework in other classes. Students who avoid reading at home may require individual counseling to identify pockets of time when they can read.

## Reading Emergencies

It's Monday morning and I begin my minilesson by taking my purse out of my desk. Standing at the front of our classroom, I describe my weekend: "We spent Saturday running errands. We needed groceries, Sarah needed reeds for her clarinet, and my car tires needed to be checked. My husband and I had to wait for a mechanic to rotate the tires, so I dug my book out of my purse." Reaching into my purse, I pull out Deborah Blum's *The Poisoner's Handbook*, an adult nonfiction book about the creation of New York City's medical examiner's office during Prohibition. Although it's not the sort of book I would pass to my sixth graders to read, showing them the book helps make my point:

> My husband forgot his book, but we had a few in the back seat of the car, so he grabbed one to read. Looking around the waiting area, I noticed that we were the only people reading. Everyone else was staring into space or fiddling with their cell phones. One man asked me what I was reading, so I chatted with him about my book for a moment. He sighed and said, "I wish I had brought something to read."
>
> It occurred to me that my family and I carry books with us everywhere we go. It's a habit. My husband jokes that you never know when you might have a reading emergency—those unexpected moments when you are stuck somewhere longer than you planned. On those rare occasions I don't have a book with me, I regret it. Taking a book with me when I leave the house is one of the ways I can sneak in some reading time when I have nothing else to do but sit and wait. Talk with your table groups about your weekend. Were there any moments when you were waiting and bored?

After a few minutes of discussion my students share this list of places or moments when they were stuck waiting over the weekend:

Orthodontist's office

Little sister's soccer game

Sofa shopping with Mom

Brother misplaced his backpack

Movie hadn't started

Dog got out

Dad on the phone

Computer downloading a game

Car trouble

Hair salon

Leading my students back through their list, we determine how much potential time they could have spent reading during these moments—anywhere from five to thirty minutes. Anthony admitted, "When we were sitting at my sister's dance practice, I wished I had brought a book with me, but it was too late." Other kids expressed the same regret. I suggest to my students that they take a book with them everywhere they can for the next few days and observe their reading emergencies. I remind them, "If you don't have a book with you, you can't read even when the time presents itself. If you carry a book with you everywhere you go, you can rack up a lot of reading time during these reading emergencies."

During our class conversations and reading conferences all week, we talked about our reading emergencies and how much reading time we found. Sloane was amazed by how much she read when she began throwing a book into her bag before leaving the house: "I think it's easy to find time to read now because if I'm bored, I can pull out my book and get sucked into another world."

My students bring at least one book to class every day. They can take advantage of class reading time because they have access to a book. Students who forget their book or need a new one can get another book from our class library or the school library. When students are away from school, do they carry books with them in case of emergency? Teaching children the simple habit of carrying

## Wild Readers Chime In

"I take a book EVERYWHERE—in the car, to sporting events, even to the grocery store! You never know when you're going to get a free minute to read!"

"I take a book everywhere with me. I tell my daughter that I will never be lonely because I love to read."

"I carry something to read almost all the time. I hate to be left waiting in line or in a car or bus or train or anywhere and I don't have something to read!!"

"I always carry a book with me so whenever I have a free moment I can dive into it. I started a journal and have a goal of how many books I want to read a year. We have a time set aside each day where everyone in the family sits and reads—no distractions, just all reading together."

a book with them for reading emergencies helps them capitalize on the edge time in their days.

## Binge Reading

In spite of favorable book reviews and friends' resounding recommendations, I slogged through the first eighty pages of Melina Marchetta's dark fantasy *Finnikin of the Rock.* Trying to read the book a few minutes each evening, I found myself reading less and less each night. I was unwilling to abandon it, but I couldn't fall into it. On the first night of summer break, I dutifully settled in to read another chapter. When a new character arrived on the scene, the book took a turn and caught me. Swept away by Finnikin, Evanjilan, and their fight to save Lumatere, I stayed up until 3:00 a.m. to finish it—devouring all 336 pages. Exhausted, I paid for my binge reading the next day, but I didn't care: Marchetta's brave characters, exquisite world building, and the delicious thrill of staying up all night reading it cemented *Finnikin of the Rock* as one of my favorite books. When recommending it to friends, though, I warn them about the first eighty pages.

Reading a book in one sitting is a rare indulgence, but many wild readers take advantage of the random Saturday or vacation and read books cover to cover. When you are swept up in a wonderful story, there is something satisfying about falling into a book and walking with the characters until the journey ends. Binge reading depends on reader engagement, though. No reader powers through a four-hundred-page book she or he isn't enjoying—unless a book report is due. Even wild readers read less when they feel disengaged or obligated to finish. When we have the time, do we have something worth reading?

Talking with my students about binge reading, I ask them if they have ever devoured a book in one sitting or spent several days invested in one long book. My students reveal their personal motivations for burning through a book, staying up late to finish one, or spending every possible moment reading it:

> "I wanted to finish *The Enemy* before Jason did because I was afraid he would spoil it on accident."

> "I fell into *Lock and Key*, and I couldn't get out. Ruby was like a friend, and I needed to know what happened to her."

> "*Mockingjay* comes out next week, and I wanted to reread *Catching Fire* before then."

> "Alyssa read *Chains*, and I wanted to hurry and read it so we can talk about it."

> "I kept hoping for a happy ending [reading *Monsters of Men*]. I couldn't stop until I found it."

Readers are more likely to experience intense engagement with a text, known as "optimal experience" or "flow," when reading texts they enjoy and find personally interesting (McQuillan & Conde, 1996). My students' comments reinforce that their engagement and personal motivation drive their binge reading or their commitment to longer books. "When I have a good book, I read about two hours a day," admits Pablo. Brandon agrees, "I read more with good books." Captivated, invested readers make time to read.

Many students admit they never read an entire book in one sitting or chew through a long book in a few days. Encouraging students to read a book so quickly or devote so much time to reading at the expense of other activities is not my goal. Our conversations about binge reading provide additional insight into the conditions that encourage students' motivation and enthusiasm for reading—discovering books that engage them and meet their individual needs and goals. I don't expect or pressure students to plow through books, but I acknowledge and value circumstances when students fall into occasional reading binges. I accept that our reading lives ebb and flow. For every day wild readers spend devouring a book in one sitting, we experience days when we don't read anything.

## Reading Itinerary

> *We do not learn from experience . . . we learn from reflecting on experience.*
>
> —John Dewey,
> *How We Think*

Walking into my classroom, you see kids sprawled on the floor, wedged in corners, or sitting at their desks—all reading (figure 1.2). I quietly move around the room, conferring with students, making book recommendations, and assisting students looking for books. While our students benefit from quiet classrooms and dedicated reading time, Susie and I realize that orchestrating when and where our students read doesn't show our students how to find reading time on their own or determine what reading conditions they prefer.

As the school year wound down, Susie and I asked students to keep a Reading Itinerary (figure 1.3) for one calendar week, recording every place they were when they read and how much time they spent reading in each location. (A blank Reading Itinerary form is in appendix A.)

Documenting when and where they read helped students reflect on their reading habits and determine patterns they might not recognize day-to-day.

Many students do not realize how much time they spend reading, where they prefer to read, or what obstacles prevent them from reading as much as they want. Focusing on reading

FIGURE 1.2: *Jon wedges himself into the corner between two bookcases.*

habits for one week increases their awareness of their own reading behaviors and opens dialogue between readers using their observations as a launching point.

The Reading Itinerary is a reflection piece, not a new version of the reading log or accountability tool. We would never expect students to keep such detailed records over the long term or assign a grade to a self-report. We don't ask students to add up the total amount of time they spent reading during the week or chastise them when we learn from their itineraries that they aren't reading at home, either. The true value in this activity lies in students' discussions, reflection, and increased self-awareness.

We found that this activity works best in the spring after students develop a daily reading habit at school. Using a Reading Itinerary helps students take more ownership of their reading habits away

**My Reading Itinerary**

Reader _Nico_ _____    _Q-17_ _____

Beginning
Date _3·25·10_ _____    Ending
Date _4·1·10_ _____

**Keep a list of your reading travels this week. Record every place you read and how much time you spend reading.**

| | |
|---|---|
| **Day/ Date** | Thursday March 25, 2010 |
| **Place** | My desk in Mrs. Miller's classroom |
| 26 min. | Exact Time = 26 min. |
| **Amount of Time** | 1-15 min. (16-30 min.) 31-45 min. 46- 60 min.    other |

| | |
|---|---|
| **Day/ Date** | Thursday March 25, 2010 |
| **Place** | The hallway in front of Mrs. Millers classroom    Exact time = 4 min. |
| 4 min. | |
| **Amount of Time** | (1-15 min.) 16-30 min. 31-45 min. 46- 60 min.    other |

| | |
|---|---|
| **Day/ Date** | Thursday March 25, 2010 |
| **Place** | My bed in my room |
| 51 min. | exact time = 51 min. |
| **Amount of Time** | 1-15 min. 16-30 min. 31-45 min. (46- 60 min.)    other |

| | |
|---|---|
| **Day/ Date** | Friday March 26, 2010 |
| **Place** | My desk in Mrs. Miller's room |
| 57 min. | exact time = 57 min. |
| **Amount of Time** | 1-15 min. 16-30 min. 31-45 min. (46- 60 min.)    other |

| | |
|---|---|
| **Day/ Date** | Friday March 26, 2010 |
| **Place** | My desk in Mrs. Allison's classroom |
| 21 min. | exact time = 21 min. |
| **Amount of Time** | 1-15 min. (16-30 min.) 31-45 min. 46- 60 min.    other |

FIGURE 1.3: *Nico's Reading Itinerary.*

| Day/ Date | Saturday March 27, 2010 |
| Place | my bed in my room |
| 11 min. | exact time = 11 min |
| Amount of Time | (1-15 min.) 16-30 min. 31-45 min. 46- 60 min. other |

| Day/ Date | sunday March 28, 2010 |
| Place | my bed in my room |
| 28 min. | exact time= 2 8 min. |
| Amount of Time | 1-15 min. (16-30 min.) 31-45 min. 46- 60 min. other |

| Day/ Date | Monday March 29, 2010 |
| Place | My desk in Mrs. Miller's room |
| 53 min. | exact time = 53 min. |
| Amount of Time | 1-15 min. 16-30 min. 31-45 min. (46- 60 min.) other |

| Day/ Date | Monday March 29, 2010 |
| Place | my bed in my room |
| 36 min. | exact time= 36 min. |
| Amount of Time | 1-15 min. 16-30 min. (31-45 min.) 46- 60 min. other |

| Day/ Date | Tuesday March 30, 2010 |
| Place | My desk in Mrs. Millers room |
| 37 min. | exact time=37 min. |
| Amount of Time | 1-15 min. 16-30 min. (31-45 min.) 46- 60 min. other |

| Day/ Date | Tuesday March 30, 2010 |
| Place | My couch in the family room |
| 37 min. | exact time =37 min. |
| Amount of Time | 1-15 min. 16-30 min. (31-45 min) 46- 60 min. other |

FIGURE 1.3 *(Continued)*

from school and transition to reading after they leave your classroom. When evaluating reading itineraries, Susie and I guide our students through several reflection questions that probe students' opinions of their reading itinerary entries.

## Students' Reading Itinerary Responses

### *Where Do You Spend the Most Time Reading?*

At the minimum, Susie and I expect students to read thirty minutes a day during language arts class. Ideally, they read an additional twenty to thirty minutes a night outside school. Students who read outside language arts class make a greater investment as independent readers and are more likely to retain the reading habit without school reading time. Most students indicated that they read more at school than at home, although many read for hours outside language arts class—stealing time after finishing their work in other classes, during lunch, and riding the bus home. Many readers said they read before falling asleep at night, too. Here are some of their comments:

> "I like reading in school because it makes me feel more comfortable. I like being around my class."—Jesah, sixth grader

> "Reading at school is more appealing because you have so much going on, it's good to take a break."—Braylen, sixth grader

> "In Mrs. Miller's class it's such a great reading environment and it's easy to just pull out a book and start reading. My perfect reading place is on the couch or the beanbag chairs in Mrs. Miller's classroom."—Blake, sixth grader

> "I read more during school because at home it is harder to find time, peace, and silence."—Nico, sixth grader

> "I don't really mind where I'm reading as long as the book I'm reading is good."—Christina, sixth grader

> "I like reading in Mrs. Kelley's room because it gets really quiet when everybody is reading."—Hoyeon, fifth grader

### What Do You Like about Reading in This Place?

Although some wild readers develop the ability to block out distractions while reading in public, most prefer a relaxing, quiet environment. A surprising number of our students mentioned that they enjoyed reading in our classrooms because they were surrounded by other readers.

### Do You Read More During or Outside School? Why?

While we know that our students read for long periods at school, they must read outside school in order to internalize wild reading behaviors. If they prefer reading at home over reading at school or vice versa, we want them to reflect on these preferences and determine what conditions they need to continue their reading habits. Our students expressed equal preferences between reading at home or school, but all of them mentioned a need for solitude away from distractions.

### Do You Think That Finding Time to Read Is Easy or Hard for You? Why?

Recognizing personal obstacles that prevent readers from reading as much as they want helps them formulate strategies to overcome these obstacles. Our students reported homework demands, younger siblings, and busy schedules as major obstacles that stopped them from reading at home. Our most enthusiastic readers indicated strong home support for reading or a willingness to read as much as possible—for example:

> "I think it is pretty easy for me to find time to read because you can read about anywhere."—Nam, fifth grader

> "I read more during school because at school it's quiet and I can really understand my book. [At home], finding time to read is a little bit of a challenge to me because between soccer practice, basketball, soccer games, and my sister's practices and games, I don't have much time to read."—Allison, fifth grader

"During school I read more than at home some days. They dedicate some time for reading there."—Emily, sixth grader

"Finding time to read is hard because I have two brothers who won't leave me alone."—Nick, sixth grader

"It's a little hard because I also have chores and homework and guitar practice, but I will always find time to read."—Clarissa, sixth grader

"I think finding time to read is difficult for me because I have other activities after school. In school it is easy because you have big amounts of time to read."—Anthony D, sixth grader

## Describe in Detail Your Perfect Reading Place

Susie and I came up with this, primarily a visualization exercise, because we wanted students to imagine reading in ideal locations as another inroad to identifying their preferred reading environment. Although our students provided some imaginative locations, including desert islands and asteroids, their ideal reading places shared common characteristics—peace, beauty, and quiet.

## What Did You Learn about Your Reading Habits This Week?

We wanted our students to evaluate the information they collected about their reading behaviors to inform their understanding of themselves as readers, recognizing their reading habits and individual preferences. Our students reported reading more than they thought they did or spending more time reading at home than they realized:

"I read on my couch more than I realized. I also read in small chunks more than I realized."—Anthony D, sixth grader

"Almost every night I set a lot of time aside just for reading." —A.J., sixth grader

"It is easy to find time to read because it is so important to me."
—Avery, sixth grader

"Sometimes I don't even realize I read thirty minutes when I thought I had only read five."—Maddie, fifth grader

"I read too much."—Woo Hyun, fifth grader

# Conferring Points

While Susie and I facilitate whole class discussions about wild reading habits with our students, those experiencing specific challenges require individualized support through reading conferences—one-on-one meetings with students to identify needs, brainstorm solutions, celebrate successes, and set reasonable goals that keep students moving forward on their paths to wild reading.

## Fake Reading and Reading Avoidance

Although wild readers embrace any reading opportunity, some students avoid reading or pretend to read during independent reading time. Obsessed with the few students in our classes who spend more time preparing to read than actually reading, chat with friends under the guise of seeking book recommendations, or sit staring at the same page, teachers worry that setting aside reading time for students doesn't benefit them as much as we hoped and question the value of reading time at the expense of other activities.

After a few weeks of school, I recognize students who exhibit blatant fake reading behaviors, but I don't always know what to do about it. Yelling across my classroom, "You aren't reading! Sit down! You may not go to restroom during reading time today," erodes my relationship-building efforts, disrupts students who are reading, and fails to correct the underlying reasons fake reading happens.

Fake reading and reading avoidance commonly occur when students lack independent reading habits, confidence, or adequate reading skills. These disengaged readers may wander, fidget, or talk during reading time; take frequent breaks; or ask to visit the library daily. Some students exhibit obvious signs they aren't reading because they're disruptive during reading time, while others appear compliant—remaining quiet as they pretend to read.

Through frequent conferences, high expectations for students' reading, and reading response activities, savvy teachers eventually ferret out students who fake-read, but we need to do more than catch students who aren't reading and call them on it. We need to intervene and provide individual support. For many non-reading students, especially in upper grades, their fake reading behaviors have worked. They have managed to muddle along in language arts class—perhaps every class—without reading much. Adolescent literacy expert Cris Tovani (2013) observes, "Too many adolescent readers have learned how to fake-read. They have become so good at playing the game of school. They have figured out how to get the grade without getting the comprehension."

Fake reading stems from several factors. In situations when the entire class reads a common text, such as whole class novels and anthology selections, students often glean what they need to know from class discussions, study guides, and teacher lectures without reading the assigned text. Using their listening and note-taking skills, high-achieving, successful students may be the most adept fake readers in our classrooms. For developing readers who may not understand these texts because of poor comprehension, limited English proficiency, or reading difficulties, struggling through difficult text offers little opportunity for reading improvement. They fake-read because they can't access the material.

Disengaged with reading, some students who avoid reading or are faking it aren't motivated to change their behaviors if they can maintain reasonable academic success. In fact, more than a few fake readers successfully navigate school without reading much. Although fake reading catches up with some students over time, it may take years for the increased text demands of secondary school to reveal their reading deficits. By then, many students have faked reading for so long that their poor reading behaviors have become deeply ingrained. It can be difficult to turn around fake reading and reading avoidance unless teachers focus on comprehension and engagement when working with students.

Recognizing why students fake-read is an important step toward providing them with tools to overcome these challenges. First, we must identify students who fake-read and determine the coping behaviors that allow them to hide that they aren't reading. Learn these warning signs that a student is not really reading:

- *Finishes few books or finishes books too quickly.* Students who avoid reading or fake-read spend as little time as possible engaged with reading. Recognizing that reading teachers expect them to read, they avoid finishing books because they know their teacher will expect them to begin another one. Carrying the same book around for weeks while making little progress indicates that a child isn't investing much time in reading. Conversely, students who learn that you value book completion as one marker of reading success may claim to finish books at an unreasonable pace that doesn't match your assessment of their reading abilities.

- *Abandons books often.* All readers experience false starts when selecting books to read. While it is better to abandon a book than pretend to read it, students who abandon book after book aren't reading much. Habitual book abandoners need assistance selecting books and goal setting that celebrates their continued commitment to reading a book.

- *Conducts personal errands during reading time.* Students who avoid reading often express urgent reasons for leaving your classroom during independent reading time. When students regularly ask to visit the nurse, retrieve materials from their lockers, go to the restroom, or turn papers in to other teachers or the office, they waste a lot of reading time.

- *Fidgets or talks a lot.* Students who keep changing reading locations or positions, rearrange their desks or belongings before reading, or draw their classmates into conversations have mastered the art of looking productive without spending much time reading.

- *Rarely has a book to read.* Students who forget to bring a book to class, lose books you provide, or leave books behind in your classroom may buckle down and read during class, but they aren't invested in the books they've chosen and express little interest in reading when you don't demand it.
- *Acts like a wild reader.* It can be challenging to identify students who aren't reading because accomplished reading avoiders often walk and talk like readers but don't actually read much. They preview and select books, discuss books with other readers, and visit the library. They appear knowledgeable and invested but spend more time talking about reading than doing it.

While teachers attempt to limit or reduce fake reading behaviors by restricting trips out of the classroom and isolating restless students, children who pretend to read or avoid reading often possess several fake reading behaviors. When you extinguish or limit one, they employ a different strategy. If I suspect students avoid reading or fake-read, I watch them for several days and record what I notice. Focused observations provide clarity and insight when considering an individual student's fake reading and reading-avoidance behaviors. During class reading time, I sit in a discreet area of the room where I can see, but it is not obvious that I am watching. Accustomed to my daily note taking during reading conferences, my students don't question what I am scribbling on my clipboard while sitting with a group of students or walking around the room.

## Independent Reading Observation

For ten minutes at a time, I record a student's reading engagement. Is the student reading? If not, what is the student doing instead? As long as the student is not disrupting others, I don't redirect this behavior or walk nearby. Acting as an observer, I don't want my proximity or admonishments to influence their behavior during these sessions.

I watch the same student for three days at different times of our independent reading block—during the first ten minutes of reading time on day 1, the second ten minutes of reading time on day 2, and the final ten minutes of reading time on day 3. Any reader can have an off-day because of a rough morning, a headache, or a sluggish spot in their book, so one day's observation isn't enough. I am looking for a pattern of nonreading behavior. After a few days' observation, I may determine that students I suspect are not reading may take excessive time to settle into reading, but in fact spend most of the reading time engaged with text. With students who seem uninterested in reading day after day, I evaluate my notes to determine why the student isn't reading. What trends in nonreading behavior do I notice? Is the student continually out of his or her seat? Does he or she ask to leave the classroom or change books every day? After reflecting, I initiate a conference with the student and share my observations.

Confronting students about their fake reading behaviors requires delicacy and caring. Some students deny they are fake reading or say that they don't care. Forced to hide their inability or unwillingness to read day after day undermines students' confidence and their feelings of self-worth. Trapped in a cycle of reading failure, they lose confidence in their teachers, who seem unable to help them improve. I try to determine if students' nonreading behavior is habitual or book related. If their current self-selected book is uninteresting or difficult, we explore strategies for selecting a new book or working through challenging parts. If children admit that reading is a constant struggle, we talk about why. In some cases, environmental factors play a role. Chatty tablemates or high-traffic areas around a student's desk distract some students from reading. Simply moving students to new seats may fix the problem. For some students, switching seats offers an excuse that protects their self-esteem. I usually agree to it if students don't ask to move next to their friends. Some unmotivated students will read after I move them because they know I have discovered they aren't reading. Changing seats allows them to save face and blame an outside factor.

Students frequently tell me that reading is boring when I ask them why they aren't reading. Such students often lack positive reading experiences, including completing or connecting to the books they read. If a student declares disinterest with reading, I work to help him or her find accessible and engaging books and set reasonable goals for reading progress and eventual book completion.

I knew Nathan was pretending to read some of the books he claimed to finish, but he thought I didn't know. Well behaved and charming, Nathan offered to shelve books in the class library, sat quietly with a book open during reading time, and faithfully documented books on his reading list. From a distance, Nathan looked like an engaged reader. As my student teacher, Malorie, and I were discussing Nathan's reading behaviors, we noticed that Nathan went to the library every day and rarely returned before reading time ended. At the end of the day, I often found Nathan's book inside his desk or beside the couch. If Nathan missed independent reading time in class and left his books at school, when was he reading? Malorie and I decided to take turns observing Nathan for the next few days to determine if he was reading or faking it and used our Independent Reading Time Observation form (figure 1.4) to jot down what we saw (a blank form is in appendix C). Watching Nathan for three days confirmed our suspicions. He spent less than ten minutes reading during ninety potential minutes of independent reading time.

Based on our observations, Malorie and I believed that Nathan struggled to select books he enjoyed and didn't invest time reading. Flipping through several pages at a time during one observation session indicated he wasn't following the story. Visiting the library the next day, he returned with *Magyk*, the first book in Angie Sage's Septimus Heap fantasy series. This book is six hundred pages, crammed with characters, and written from multiple points of view. I feared Nathan would be lost in such a daunting book. *Magyk* in fact was a prop for Nathan—evidence that his extended trip to the library had been productive. The last day we observed him, Nathan read a few pages of *Magyk* but spent most of reading time with his head on his desk.

**Independent Reading Time Observation**          Reader  Nathan G.

| Date 11/1/11 | Start Time 10:45 | End Time 10:55 |
|---|---|---|

| Minute | Reading | | Other Observed Behaviors |
|---|---|---|---|
| 1 | Yes | (No) | talking to tablemate |
| 2 | Yes | (No) | " |
| 3 | (Yes) | No | |
| 4 | (Yes) | No | |
| 5 | Yes | (No) | not turning pages |
| 6 | Yes | (No) | " |
| 7 | Yes | (No) | " |
| 8 | Yes | (No) | turned a group of pages |
| 9 | (Yes) | No | |
| 10 | (Yes) | No | |

| Date 11/2/11 | Start Time 10:45 | End Time 11:15 |
|---|---|---|

| Minute | Reading | | Other Observed Behaviors |
|---|---|---|---|
| 1 | Yes | (No) | Spent reading time in the library — 25 minutes — |
| 2 | Yes | No | |
| 3 | Yes | No | |
| 4 | Yes | No | |
| 5 | Yes | No | |
| 6 | Yes | No | |
| 7 | Yes | No | |
| 8 | Yes | No | |
| 9 | Yes | No | |
| 10 | Yes | (No) | |

| Date 11/3/11 | Start Time 11:00 | End Time 11:10 |
|---|---|---|

| Minute | Reading | | Other Observed Behaviors |
|---|---|---|---|
| 1 | Yes | (No) | head on desk |
| 2 | Yes | (No) | " |
| 3 | Yes | (No) | book open to 1st page |
| 4 | Yes | (No) | " |
| 5 | (Yes) | No | |
| 6 | (Yes) | No | |
| 7 | (Yes) | No | |
| 8 | Yes | (No) | staring out the window |
| 9 | (Yes) | No | |
| 10 | (Yes) | No | |

**My Reflection**
Nathan is not reading, but hides it well by pretending to read.
Goals — discuss book choices, set small goals and check in daily

**Reader's Reflection**
Nathan reports that his last 2 books were boring. Found the small print hard to track and read.

**Our Plan**
① Preview stack — Hatchet, Swindle, Boy at War, Storm Runners, Love That Dog, Amulet, Shelter Dogs
② 20 pages per day

FIGURE 1.4: *Our independent reading time observations reveal Nathan's reading avoidance behaviors.*

The next class day, I invited Nathan to confer with me. Showing him my notes, I said, "Nathan, you are not reading much during reading time these days. I am concerned that you are struggling to find good books for you. Let's work together on this and figure out what's wrong."

At first, Nathan denied that he wasn't reading: "I had a headache yesterday, but I finished that book last night at home."

Skeptical that he read all six hundred pages in one evening, I asked Nathan what he thought of *Magyk*'s climatic ending and asked if he planned to read the next book in the series.

Mumbling something about how boring the book was, Nathan said, "No. I am looking for a new book today."

Nathan accepted my offer to help him select a new book, and we looked through the class library together. I pulled several engaging books that other readers enjoyed, including adventure and mystery titles that start a series or include companion books like Gary Paulsen's *Hatchet, Swindle* by Gordon Korman, Harry Mazer's *A Boy at War: A Novel of Pearl Harbor,* and *Storm Runners* by Roland Smith. Mindful that Nathan needed to feel reading success and accomplishment in a short time, I recommended Sharon Creech's *Love That Dog* and the first book in Kazu Kibuishi's Amulet graphic novel series, *The Stonekeeper.* Nathan could finish these last two books during one or two days of class reading time if he would commit to reading them.

After Nathan selected *A Boy at War,* I encouraged him to record the other books on his books to read list for later reading. (See appendix A for a blank form for this list.) Working together, Nathan and I decided that reading twenty pages a day was a reasonable goal for him. He recorded his page number goals in twenty-page increments in his weekly planner and starred the day he would finish—six days from the day he began. With students who struggle to complete books or set attainable reading goals, writing page goals into their planners or reader's notebook holds them accountable and helps them see that they will finish a book if they read a little bit each day.

Nathan began reading *A Boy at War* on Friday during class. After school, I wandered over to his locker and reminded him to take it home. I hid my disappointment on Monday when he admitted that he hadn't read much over the weekend, but I praised him for bringing the book back to class and sticking with it. Nathan didn't make a big deal out of it when he finished *A Boy at War* on Wednesday. He slid the book on my desk and asked for the sequel, *A Boy No More.* I found the second book and added the third book, *Heroes Don't Run: A Novel of the Pacific War,* on top.

Entrenched in his reading avoidance and fake reading behaviors, Nathan struggled to finish books all year, frequently falling back into days of nonreading. I fed Nathan a continuous diet of books and held him accountable for reading every day in class. For his part, Nathan never lied to me about reading again and tried to stick with a book once he started one. We celebrated these small victories together. I hope that Nathan remembers the books he loved more often than the books he pretended to read.

# *Keeping Track of Your Reading Life*

Encouraging our students to self-monitor their independent reading lives and reflect on their progress toward internalizing wild reading habits, Susie and I require students to keep records throughout the year. We access these documents, stored in reader's notebooks or reading folders, each time we confer with students and refer to them often during classroom conversations. When we began teaching in workshop classrooms, Susie and I used Fountas and Pinnell's reader's notebook setup—described in *Guiding Readers and Writers (3–6): Teaching Comprehension, Genre, and Content Literacy* (2001). As we grew more confident facilitating reading and writing workshop, we tweaked and modified our reader's notebooks to meet our specific classroom needs. Examples of student notebook sections found throughout *Reading in the Wild* reflect this mash-up—combining the original notebooks and our changes.

I admit that when I began teaching in a workshop setting, I implemented reader's notebooks in my classroom without a clear understanding of their purpose or value. All I knew was that students in reading and writing workshop kept notebooks. Now every year, I consider our reader's notebook design, examine how my students and I use our notebooks, and determine what needs to change. Regular reflection reinforces the importance of keeping notebooks, but increased technology integration, larger class sizes, and my commitment to fostering wild reading behaviors have changed our notebook use. The tools we use must support our work as readers and writers, not define or limit our work. Every year, I ask:

- What do my students and I need to know about our reading and writing this year?

- What learning and thinking do we want to record?

- How can notebooks support our academic and personal literacy goals?

Each chapter of this book refers to the charts, forms, and lists our students keep in their reader's notebooks to track their reading lives and provide common information for assessment, reflection, and goal-setting purposes. Consider each document a tool that you may copy, modify, or combine with your existing notebooks. Blank versions of all reader's notebook forms appear in the appendix.

## Response Letters 2.0

In *The Book Whisperer*, I shared several response letters between my students and me that highlighted our conversations about reading and my students' understanding of the books they read. These days, my sixth graders post all of their reading response entries, final drafts of literary essays, and book reviews online through our class Edmodo page. This online platform provides my students with a larger audience for their writing, inviting comments from other students in all three of my classes. Struggling with responding weekly to a hundred or more students in recent years, I have found it easier and more efficient to provide feedback through Edmodo. I no longer drag home a crate of response letters every weekend and now type my responses to students instead of hand-writing each one, creating a permanent record of our exchanges that I can reference weeks or months later. During reading conferences, my students and I can access these conversations through iPads or classroom Netbooks if we want.

Students still use the response sections of their reader's notebooks to draft responses before publishing on Edmodo, record quotes and thoughts about their books while reading, and write responses to literature about the shared texts we read together during minilessons and guided practice.

## Status of the Class

From the beginning, our students must understand that Susie and I take independent reading seriously and set high expectations for their reading. Although implementing meaningful reading conferences, book commercials, and reading response activities takes time, we want students to talk about books and reading as soon as possible. It takes a week or two to get into the school groove.

## Status of the Class

| Date | Title | Page Number | I am at the part where... |
|------|-------|-------------|---------------------------|
| 9/8 | The Divide | 159 | Tansy is searching for Betony |
| 9/9 | The Divide | 178 | Felix and Betony are traveling to Andria. |
| 9/10 | The Divide | 254 | Everyone is reading a newspaper |
| 9/11 | Drums, Girls & Dangerous pie | 196 | Steven is writing a journal entry on Annette's arm. |
| 9/14 | Epic | 94 | Erik is getting ready for the Championships |
| 9/15 | Epic | 179 | Erik is talking to a dark elf |
| 9/16 | Epic | 227 | Erik is sailing on the white Falcon |
| 9/18 | Epic | 366 | Erik talks about Cindella |
| 9/21 | The Ghost in Tokaido Inn | 101 | Seikei is trying to find Tomomi |
| 9/22 | The Ghost in Tokaido Inn | 142 | Seikei is looking at a sword |
| 9/23 | Tangerine | 224 | Paul is trying to save the Golden Dawns |
| 9/24 | Tangerine | 274 | Paul is reading a newspaper |
| 9/25 | Zen and the Art of Faking It | 119 | San is eating Cap'n Crunch |
| 9/30 | Zen and the Art of faking It | 263 | San is washing the dishes |
| 10/1 | Blood Red Horse | 10 | Will and Ellie are going to dinner |
| 10/2 | Blood Red Horse | 29 | Will is getting a horse |
| 10/5 | Blood Red Horse | 90 | Will & Ellie have just been to the monastery |
| 10/6 | Blood Red Horse | 117 | Gavin is getting a doctor for Will |

FIGURE 1.5: *Emma's Status of the Class record.*

Students who don't read much or have lost their reading habit over the summer may not read much at first if we don't hold them accountable for their reading immediately.

On the first day of school, we choose books. On the second day, we build our notebooks and set up Edmodo accounts. On the third day, we start each class with a Status of the Class roll call, taken from

Nancie Atwell's *The Reading Zone* (2007). Using a Status of the Class log kept in their reader's notebooks, students record the title of the book they are reading, the page number where they will begin reading, and a one-sentence, spoiler-free summary of what is happening in the book. A few minutes into class, I call on each student to share his or her Status of the Class entry out loud. (A blank version of the Status of the Class form is in appendix A.)

Emma's Status of the Class record (figure 1.5) reveals her wide reading preferences, selecting books from a range of genres and reading levels depending on her interests. Large gaps between the daily page number she records and the number of titles listed indicate Emma reads a lot at home—finishing books rapidly and beginning new ones away from class.

The Status of the Class form provides multiple benefits. Students practice discussing books in concise, low-risk ways. I reinforce the message that everyone should be reading and every reader has something to share. Students hear about lots of books they might potentially read. And students who may be slow to get started realize quickly that they must share their reading progress, or lack thereof, every day in class or get on board.

Students recorded entries on their Status of the Class form every day for the first four weeks of school, but we stopped using it when they began writing well-developed reading response entries. A Status of the Class roll call requires class time, and I didn't feel we needed it as an accountability tool or sharing activity after we moved into other routines. A Status of the Class form provides a quick check to determine what your students are reading and their progress toward reading goals. When we return from long school breaks, I reinstitute Status of the Class roll calls in order to kick-start students' reading, which often slows during vacations.

• • •

All wild reading habits hinge on how much time readers invest in reading. Showing students how to incorporate daily reading into their lives sets them on the path to wild reading and gives them the practice they need to internalize the other habits.

# Creating a Workshop Schedule That Works for You

B Y THE END of the first day of school, I am three days behind on my lesson plans. And on the final day of school, I am still trying to teach. There isn't enough time to teach everything I must cover or everything my students need to learn. Some factors that influence how we manage our class time are within our control and others aren't. When hammering out our workshop schedule every year, I consider these questions:

• *How much class time do I have?* Our campus schedule takes into account many variables, such as lunch times, extracurricular classes like band, the increased time spent on language arts and math due to testing demands, and our specialists' needs to work with at-risk kids. This year, with all these variables factored in, I have eighty-seven minutes a day for each of my three language arts classes, so our workshop schedule must fit this time frame.

• *Which instructional components am I required to include?* Our school district has adopted a program for our vocabulary and spelling instruction. I must find a place for this program in our weekly schedule. Teachers are also expected to meet with at-risk students in small groups as part of our district's Response to Intervention plan, so I need to build in time for flexible group instruction. Whatever your campus or district has decided is a must-do, you will need to find time for it in your workshop schedule.

• *Which components would I like to include?* The wish list of activities I would like to accomplish with my students seems endless. Every year I look back on our school year and think, *I wish we had spent more time on . . .* I know that opportunities to talk about books, share our writing, and go to the library are important to my students' literacy development. By including these activities in our workshop schedule, I hold myself accountable for ensuring that they happen. It keeps my core beliefs in front of me. If I believe that children should share their reading and writing, when are they doing it? If I think read-alouds are important, when am I doing it? Consider your dream list of things you would like to do in your classroom and look for ways to dedicate time in your schedule for them.

• *What can I change to carve out time for independent reading?* I never sacrifice independent reading time for the sake of other instructional activities. Never. It would be easy to ditch independent reading time and play catch-up. Recognizing the vital role that independent reading plays in fostering my students' reading achievement and their development as wild readers, I must find time for daily independent reading even if it means that I cut something else. I return to my core belief: that students should be reading every single day. If I have too many things on my schedule to give my students reading time, I critically examine everything on that list and compare it against the value of letting my students read. Is it better than reading time? Does it have more impact on my students? Do the short-term benefits of a particular activity help my students as readers and writers over the long term? Quite often the answer is no.

• *Remember the rule of thirds.* Not everyone has eighty-seven minutes for a class block. Many middle school and high school teachers have less than an hour per class. I recommend dividing your class into thirds and planning your time around these basic segments: one-third independent reading, conferring, and small groups; one-third direct instruction and guided practice with your whole class; and one-third independent practice where students spend additional time reading or writing.

I design and teach genre units—alternating my minilessons from a writing focus to a reading focus as needed to align with my district's curriculum scope and sequence. Students read independently and confer with me every day. They write every day, too. During our reading focus units, my students write responses to literature instead of other compositions. One minilesson and writing block every two weeks takes place in the library. Students are free to visit the library during independent reading time, too.

After reflecting on my schedule limitations and opportunities, I put together the weekly workshop schedule I developed for this year, shown in the following two tables. The schedule aligns with my core beliefs about literacy instruction. It incorporates the requirements of my district and campus. It includes many of the dream activities I struggle including on a regular basis, and it allows my students and me some flexibility in what work we decide to accomplish.

*Weekly Schedule: Reading Focus*

| | 15 Minutes | 15 Minutes | 15 Minutes | 15 Minutes | 15 Minutes | 15 Minutes |
|---|---|---|---|---|---|---|
| Monday | Readers' workshop (small groups, conferences, independent reading) | Vocabulary and spelling minilesson and guided practice | | | | Read aloud |
| Tuesday | Readers' workshop (small groups, conferences, independent reading) | Reading minilesson and guided practice | Response to literature | | | Read aloud |
| Wednesday | Readers' workshop (small groups, conferences, independent reading) | Reading minilesson and guided practice | Response to literature | | | Read aloud |
| Thursday | Readers' workshop (small groups, conferences, independent reading) | Reading minilesson and guided practice | Response to literature | | | Read aloud |
| Friday | Vocabulary test | Readers' or writers' workshop (students' choice) | | | Book commercials or read-around[a] | Read aloud |

[a] Book commercials and read-arounds provide students with opportunities to informally share their reading and writing with each other.

*Weekly Schedule: Writing Focus*

| | 15 Minutes | 15 Minutes | 15 Minutes | 15 Minutes | 15 Minutes | 15 Minutes |
|---|---|---|---|---|---|---|
| Monday | Readers' workshop (small groups, conferences, independent reading) | Vocabulary and spelling minilesson and guided practice | | | | Read aloud |
| Tuesday | Readers' workshop (small groups, conferences, independent reading) | Writing minilesson and guided practice | Writers' workshop (conferences, independent writing) | | | Read aloud |
| Wednesday | Readers' workshop (small groups, conferences, independent reading) | Writing minilesson and guided practice | Writers' workshop (conferences, independent writing) | | | Read aloud |
| Thursday | Readers' workshop (small groups, conferences, independent reading) | Writing minilesson and guided practice | Writers' workshop (conferences, independent writing) | | | Read aloud |
| Friday | Vocabulary test | Readers' or writers' workshop (students' choice) | | Book commercials or read-around[a] | | Read aloud |

[a]Book commercials and read-arounds provide students with opportunities to informally share their reading and writing with each other.

Your schedule and instructional activities might differ from mine because our classroom and teaching situations, of course, differ. What matters is that our daily work in the classroom values best practices and doesn't become bogged down with a lot of must-dos and tired activities that crowd out authentic learning opportunities for our students. In order to develop strong literacy skills, our students need reading, writing, and discussion—and lots of it.

Too often we attempt to implement reading and writing workshops or other instructional methodologies because someone told us we should. We try to take it whole cloth and run it in our classrooms, usually with less-than-optimal outcomes. We struggle to channel workshop gurus like Nancie Atwell and Lucy Calkins, and then throw up our hands and declare the pedagogy unsound. We claim we cannot do it this way, this year, with these kids.

We reject what we know is right for what is easier. It isn't the pedagogy. It is our implementation and management of it. Are we creating a place where reading a lot, writing a lot, and thinking a lot happen in *our* classrooms?

Beginning with core beliefs, grounded in best practices, we can individualize our instruction so that we meet the needs of our specific students, school and district mandates, teaching personalities, and community culture. Reflective practice loses its power when it becomes a once-a-month written reflection you turn in to your principal. As teachers, we need to reclaim reflective practice for ourselves and use it as a tool to continuously recalibrate our teaching to our core beliefs, determine what is and isn't working, and focus our teaching so we can continue to offer quality instruction that we can reasonably manage and maintain throughout the school year.

# CHAPTER 2

# Wild Readers Self-Select Reading Material

*Read. Read anything. Read the things
they say are good for you, and the things
they claim are junk. You'll find what you
need to find. Just read.*

—Neil Gaiman

CAUGHT UP IN New Year's self-improvement zeal, Don and I admit that we have too many books. Bookshelves line every room of our tiny house, including the hallway. Almost every shelf groans under double rows of books. Sarah makes it clear that her bookcases are off limits when we begin weeding shelves, but hers are full, too. Overwhelmed by the prospect of getting rid of books, Don and I start with one bookcase in our living room overflowing with hundreds of books we've acquired but haven't read. Don and I spend hours evaluating and sorting the books and together develop a key for determining which books stay and which ones go based on prior knowledge and information we find looking up reviews online. It's a keeper if we answer yes to any of these questions:

- Did the book win a major book award?

- Did the book earn a starred review from a professional reviewer?

- Did our bookish friends recommend it?

- Is the book a sequel to another book we loved?

- Do we like the author's past work?

- Do we still want to read the book even if it doesn't meet any of the other criteria?

Several days into the process, Don and I have identified about twenty books that can go—primarily duplicate titles or books we have read that migrated to the wrong shelf. Scanning our freshly organized but still full bookcase renews our interest in reading these books, but it doesn't do much to reduce our book hoard. Laughing at the futility of it all, we realize that our criteria to decide whether we kept books were the same reasons we bought the books in the first place. When selecting books, Don and I access a lifetime of reading experiences, our pool of trusted reading friends, or the advice of respected reviewers. It works. We rarely read a book that we don't enjoy or at least appreciate.

Like Don and me, the Wild Reader Survey respondents use multiple sources to find out about books they might like to read. Readers get most of their book recommendations from the other readers they know. Not only do our reading friends, family, colleagues, and students know about books, they know us and offer suggestions tailored to their impressions of what we like and would enjoy. Beyond personal testimonials, wild readers name the following sources for discovering books:

- *Professional colleagues.* Readers in the education and publishing fields rely on a network of other teachers, librarians, authors, editors, and readers to provide book recommendations. We trust their book savvy and value suggestions from knowledgeable, experienced reading professionals.

- *Book lists.* From the American Library Association's annual and archived award lists to end-of-year roundups from bestseller lists, readers love book lists and peruse them to find new or notable books.

- *Bookstore and library displays.* Roaming the shelves at favorite bookstores and libraries, readers enjoy immediate access to new, recommended, or featured books. Specialized displays entice many readers, who admit to choosing books based on thematic displays, new title shelves, or hot picks from bookstore employees and librarians.

- *Book review blogs and websites.* Professional and amateur bloggers who review books provide readers with readers' opinions about new books. I suggest many of these websites throughout this book.

- *Authors' blogs and websites.* If you want to find out about new books, the most accurate and updated information usually comes from the authors themselves. Readers enjoy sneak previews of upcoming works, learn about book signing events or release parties, or get the scoop on authors' current works in progress long before books are published.

- *Social networking sites.* Increased use of social networking sites like Facebook and Twitter, as well as sites designed specifically for readers like Goodreads and Shelfari, give readers access to hundreds of book recommendations, reviews, and lists and allow readers to instantaneously share their thoughts about the books they read with a global audience.

- *Periodicals.* Whether it's *O Magazine, Entertainment Weekly*, or the *New Yorker*, mainstream magazines and newspapers often include detailed book reviews and lists.

- *Professional book review publications.* Specialty magazines from professional book review organizations like *Booklist, Publishers Weekly, Horn Book*, and the *School Library Journal* showcase noteworthy titles and provide informed insight into the latest books.

- *Book vendor websites.* Book sellers like IndieBound, Barnes & Noble, and Titlewave offer a mix of professional reviews, amateur ratings, and publishers' product descriptions about books, as well as the ability to tag or purchase books.

- *Publishers' catalogues and websites.* Publishers promote their latest releases and featured backlist titles in their seasonal catalogues. Readers can preview the entire catalogue online on publishers' websites, view book trailers—video teasers about books—or learn more about authors.

- *Book clubs.* Mentioned by many respondents as one of the primary outlets for their reading lives, book clubs lead wild readers to books they might not discover on their own.

- *Chosen randomly.* In spite of the cliché "You can't judge a book by its cover," wild readers admit they select books from the library, bookstore, or online sites because the cover, author's name, or jacket blurb catches their attention. Confident in their own abilities, wild readers are willing to take chances when selecting books. For many readers, it seems that the books choose them.

Susie and I don't expect our students to browse *Publishers Weekly* looking for books. However, we recognize that students must learn how to choose books for themselves. In the classroom, allowing students to choose their own texts fosters engagement and increases their reading motivation and interest (Gambrell, Palmer, Codling, & Mazzoni, 1996; Worthy & McKool, 1996; Guthrie & Wigfield, 2000). When students select their own books to read and enjoy, they develop confidence in their abilities to make reading choices and build their capacity for choosing books in the future. If a book choice doesn't work out, students can fine-tune their book-selecting skills and reflect on what they will do differently next time. Analyzing the body of research about self-selected reading, Johnson and Blair (2003) identify several ways that self-selected reading builds children's self-efficacy as readers. Self-selecting reading material:

- Allows students to value their decision-making ability

- Fosters their capacity to choose appropriate literature

- Gives them confidence and a feeling of ownership

- Improves reading achievement

- Encourages them in becoming lifelong readers

Susie and I see many students who struggle choosing books to read because they lack background knowledge about books and

## Wild Readers Chime In

"I love Goodreads for sharing info about books and receiving info. I wish I could find a book club that 'fits' me. The ones I find are often geared toward socializing rather than talking books, or way too serious."

"I was never told that I 'couldn't' read something. I never had to worry about reading that was too hard or too easy—my interests dictated my choices."

"Since I began reading book review, children's and young adult literature blogs, my TBR (to-be-read) pile has exploded."

"I was given special permission to read selected books from the Adult section of the Public Library because I had 'read out' the Children's section. This was in the 1950s."

"The single most important factor in my learning to be a reader was being read to. My parents read me picture books, but also chapter books and novels. We read Nancy Drew mysteries and books like *Kidnapped* and *Treasure Island* before I started kindergarten."

authors and don't know how to find out about books they might like to read. In the short term, we can support our students by providing book recommendations; increasing their access to interesting, engaging books; and promoting books during reading conferences and book commercials. But our students cannot depend on us to be their personal book shoppers forever. They must build confidence and competence in choosing their own books to read. Students who cannot successfully choose texts that meet their personal and academic reading goals fail to develop a vital skill that all wild readers possess.

## *Community Conversations*

Improving students' ability to choose their own books begins with lots of positive reading experiences and frequent opportunities to preview, share, and discuss books. Reflecting on our classroom practices and rituals, Susie and I identified several activities we already employed that help build students' title and author awareness, understanding of formats and genres, and their overall reading enjoyment and appreciation. Through these shared reading experiences and conversations, we build students' capacity for self-selecting books on their own.

## Read-Alouds

> *Reading aloud with children is known to be the single most important activity for building the knowledge and skills they will eventually require for learning to read.*
>
> —Marilyn Jager Adams,
> *Beginning to Read: Thinking and Learning about Print*

During the last ten minutes of class, my students listen while I read Sharon Draper's *Out of My Mind*, and they are hanging on every word. The book's protagonist, Melody, speaks honestly about her life in a wheelchair and her struggle for acceptance. Reading about Melody's life with cerebral palsy fascinates and inspires us. The book sparks rich discussions, and my students' personal investment in Melody's story pleases me. Every day, Sam accuses me of torturing him, marveling at my ability to stop at a pivotal moment, close the book, and dismiss the class. He asks, "Did you learn how to do that at teacher school, Mrs. Miller? How do you always know when to stop at the most dramatic part?" I love that Sam and my other students enjoy our read-aloud time so much that they groan when it is time to leave. I should probably reveal that I stop at the end of a chapter most of the time. Sharon Draper wrote cliffhanger moments into *Out of My Mind*. I just capitalize on them.

Every school year, I regret not reading aloud more to my students. Committing to daily read-alouds, I set aside ten to fifteen minutes at the end of class every day. I write read-alouds into my lesson plans, considering how each read-aloud choice fits my classroom instruction or community-building goals. On rare occasions, I skip our read-aloud because we run out of class time, or my students need another activity, like more writing time or presenting book commercials, but we don't miss our read-aloud for more than a day. My students and I enjoy these shared reading experiences, and I see how much my students profit.

## Benefits of Read-Alouds

Reading aloud books, poems, articles, and short stories with students gives teachers endless opportunities to highlight great writing and model reading strategies. It also provides additional benefits to young readers:

- *They build community.* Shared experiences create memories that connect us to each other. Reading aloud books with children offers these unifying moments. While reading together, we laugh and cry together—comrades on the same journey. My students and I form a reading community, bonded to each other through the books and reading experiences we share. These connections last long after the book ends. I include a list of books that foster reading communities in chapter 3.

- *They expose children to books, authors, or genres they might not discover on their own.* When choosing books to read aloud, I often pick titles that lead my students to more books they can read independently. Perennial favorites include Gary Paulsen, Gordon Korman, Kallie Dakos, Sharon Creech, Seymour Simon, and Tom Angleberger. When visiting the library or combing through our classroom bookshelves, students often look for authors I have introduced during read-alouds. When students lack reading experiences and author awareness, self-selecting books intimidates them. Recognizing a few names or titles eases their anxiety about choosing books and increases their confidence in finding something they will enjoy.

- *They provide prime opportunities to introduce students to genres they often avoid, like poetry, biographies, and nonfiction.* After discovering books through read-alouds, children are more receptive to reading more books from these genres. You don't have to read the entire book to entice readers either. Frequently I read the first chapter, article, or poem from a book and place it on the whiteboard rail. The book rarely lasts until the end of the day before an eager reader claims it.

- *They support developing readers.* I contend that the more developing readers you have in a class, the more often you should read aloud to them. Reading aloud removes roadblocks to comprehension like unfamiliar vocabulary and contextualizes words that developing readers do not know (Cunningham, 2005). Listening to fluent reading provides students with a reading role model and supports their oral reading development. Teachers can expand students' reading experiences by reading books that are a higher reading level than students can read alone. Reading aloud creates natural opportunities for modeling and practicing comprehension strategies and reading response.

- *They reinforce that reading is enjoyable.* Emile Buchwald said, "Children are made readers on the laps of their parents." Many children trace their earliest reading memories back to these shared reading experiences with parents or caregivers. Children who did not have these early reading experiences often arrive at school with little appreciation for the joy of reading. Reading aloud reminds them that reading is pleasurable, an activity they enjoyed before it turned into an academic chore. For students who lack positive reading experiences, read-alouds are a marvelous way to introduce them to reading for pleasure.

## Selecting Read-Alouds

Because read-alouds serve overlapping purposes in our classrooms, many quality books are good read-aloud candidates. When making read-aloud decisions in your classroom, consider the following suggestions:

- *Choose books from authors who will lead your students to more books.* No matter what grade you teach, there are touchstone authors who appeal to your students, write many books, and provide children with the stories and information they need for their life stage. Talk with your school librarian and grade-level colleagues to identify at least five authors—including poets, playwrights, and nonfiction writers—your students should know. When selecting read-alouds, read at least one book from each author during the school year. If you are new to a grade level or want to improve your knowledge of books for your students, creating a list of five authors provides a great starting point. Share this list with parents and student teachers.

• *Share a variety of texts, including nonfiction, poetry, and online articles.* Children gravitate toward the books we bless in the class-room, and read-alouds are the ultimate endorsement. In the past, I relied heavily on fiction, poetry, and traditional literature like Greek mythology for read-aloud selections. Recognizing that my sixth graders avoid nonfiction texts like informational books and biographies, I now incorporate more nonfiction texts into my read-aloud repertoire.

Students also need more opportunities to read and explore online reading material. Every day my students and I visit Wonder-opolis (www.wonderopolis.org), which offers video, nonfiction text, discussion questions, and vocabulary words relating to one engaging question every day like, "Why do chameleons change their color?" or "Who is Uncle Sam?" Students need explicit modeling and instruction in reading online, which requires us to include online reading in our read-aloud repertoire.

• *Consider time constraints and book length.* For two years, I chose Rick Riordan's *The Lightning Thief* as a class read-aloud because my students loved the series, the book is a rousing read-aloud, and it linked to our class unit on Greek mythology. One drawback is that *The Lightning Thief* is over three hundred pages. Plodding through the book for over a month wore out most of my students. Strong readers grew frustrated at the slow progress we made each day, checked out the book from the library, and finished it. Taking so long to finish the book bogged down the developing readers, too, and they lost interest.

Preferring to read a wide variety of texts to students instead of four or five long novels a year, I critically consider book length and our school calendar when beginning new read-alouds. Picture books, poetry anthologies, nonfiction articles, and informational books take less time to read and provide the text diversity students need. This doesn't mean I never read a longer novel, but I strive for more balance between shorter and longer texts.

• *Decide how students will view illustrations.* When considering picture books, graphic novels, or informational books, determine how you will show illustrations and text features like maps and photographs. Gathering students in a circle around you may solve this problem, but with middle schoolers or in classrooms with limited space, sitting on the floor may be uncomfortable or impossible. If you have a document camera, use it to show detailed illustrations during the read-aloud, or offer students the opportunity to examine the book in more detail later.

• *Read books that you enjoy.* I teach three classes and read the same read-aloud three times a day. Some books I read for several years because students enjoy them and I find the texts meaningful and engaging. Librarians and reading specialists may read a book ten or twenty times in order to share it with every class. Select books that you will still love the third or thirteenth time you read it. If you aren't excited about a book, your students won't be.

• *Ditch the read-aloud if it doesn't work.* Some great books just don't make good read-alouds. Sometimes the narrative pace is too slow. In other cases, students require substantial background knowledge to comprehend or appreciate the book, or the dialect and language make it difficult to read out loud. If a read-aloud isn't working, abandon it. Discuss with students why you are moving on, offer the book as an independent reading selection to students who enjoyed it, and choose a different title to share. Unpacking our reading mistakes reveals to students that all readers, even you, make book selection errors.

## *Reading Community Suggestions*

My students have strong opinions about our read-aloud rituals and texts. Talking with them provides insight into the activities they appreciate most and those that fall short. My students identified the following read-aloud activities as their favorites:

• *Invite students to share their favorite read-alouds.* At the beginning of the year, I ask students to share their favorite read-aloud memories and titles. Even students who don't read much can usually identify books that their parents, teachers, or librarians have read aloud to them. Invite students to bring in picture books and texts they enjoyed from such read-alouds. If students do not have these books at home, I make a list of their favorites and check our school and public libraries for copies or e-mail colleagues to request them. Someone always owns children's classics like Marcus Pfister's *Rainbow Fish*, E. B. White's *Charlotte's Web*, and Dr. Seuss's *The Cat in the Hat*. I make sure that every student has at least one book to read and share.

When everyone has a book, students gather in groups and reread their beloved favorites with classmates. For students who lack any meaningful early literacy experiences or don't read fluently, starting with these easier books provides a community-building opportunity that levels the playing field. Every teacher and librarian should see middle schoolers reading P. D. Eastman's *Go, Dog, Go!* and Margaret Wise Brown's *Goodnight Moon* with their friends at least once! Discussing this activity later, many students comment that it made them realize that they do know some books and have enjoyed a few reading experiences in the past. It's a place to start. When we finish sharing

**READ-ALOUD RESOURCES**

Hahn, M. L. (2002). *Reconsidering read aloud.* Portland, ME: Stenhouse.

Laminack, L.L. (2009). *Unwrapping the read aloud: Making every read aloud intentional and instructional.* New York: Scholastic.

Laminack, L. L., & Wadsworth, R. (2006). *Reading aloud across the curriculum: How to build bridges in language arts, math, science, and social studies.* Portsmouth, NH: Heinemann.

Trelease, J. (2013). *The read-aloud handbook.* (7the ed.). New York: Penguin Books.

our read-aloud memories and books, students write reflections about how these books and memories influenced their reading lives.

• *When you have a guest teacher, leave a read-aloud different from the one you are already reading to the class.* When you are absent, do not ask your guest teacher to read aloud from your class novel. My students express fierce ownership for the books we share together and don't want someone unaware of the story to continue our read-aloud. Leave a short standalone piece for your guest teacher to read, such as a poem, picture book, or nonfiction article. I like to set aside books of random facts for my guest teachers to read, like *Don't Touch That Toad and Other Strange Things Adults Tell You* by Catherine Rondina. These books interest students and don't require following a storyline.

• *Participate in World Read Aloud Day.* Sponsored by Lit World, an international nonprofit organization dedicated to promoting awareness of global literacy issues and working with vulnerable populations to improve literacy rates, World Read Aloud Day (found at http://litworld.org/worldreadaloudday) highlights the importance of literacy to all people and provides opportunities for children to reflect on their literacy and celebrate reading. This day is always the first Wednesday in March. In 2012, hundreds of thousands of readers in over sixty-five countries participated in World Read Aloud Day by sharing books together. (See figure 2.1.)

Lit World offers a free classroom kit of lesson plans, certificates, read-aloud suggestions, and reflection activities for kindergarten through high school students. Invite guest readers to share books with your class, arrange for your students to read with younger children, or arrange a Skype visit between your students and an author or another class.

• *Invite students to select your next read-aloud.* While there are certain books I like to read with students because I know these texts have kid appeal, lead to more reading, or link to instructional points, I do not plan every read-aloud for the year. Presenting book commercials—brief previews about the books I think students

FIGURE 2.1: *Daniel, Michelle, and Ariel share books during World Read Aloud Day.*

will enjoy—on three or four book choices, I ask each class to vote on the book they would like me to read aloud.

Because I teach three classes a day, my students do not always select the same books for read-alouds. That means I get to enjoy reading different books instead of the same one three times a day. Students feel special because they hear a book that the other classes don't. One drawback is that if the books vary widely in length, you may not be able to read as many books with classes that select longer books. When choosing books for read-aloud consideration, look for titles similar in length when possible.

• *Post a list of the texts you have shared.* On the wall near our classroom library, I display a running list of every poem, article, picture book, novel, and informational text we share. My students enjoy watching this list grow throughout the year and I refer to our Texts We've Shared list often when pointing out connections between new reading and texts we've read in the past. The list serves as an anchor chart, too, reminding students how to accurately punctuate and capitalize titles.

• *Ask students to sign their favorite read-aloud selections from the year.* At the end of the year, I ask my students to vote for their favorite read-aloud books of the year. Last year, students chose *Fourteen Cows for America* by Carmen Agra Deedy, *The Strange Case of Origami Yoda* by Tom Angleberger, and *I Want My Hat Back* by Jon Klassen. Designating one book for each class period, I invited students to autograph the book's end papers like a yearbook. Students enjoyed leaving their mark on these books as a legacy of the school year, and I have a unique keepsake from every class.

Read-alouds provide students with support in choosing their own books by increasing their title and author awareness, improving their background knowledge and experience, and fostering increased motivation and engagement with reading through positive reading experiences. No matter how old your students are, they benefit from frequent read-alouds.

## Creating Book Buzz

Susie and I plan other specific activities to highlight books, celebrate reading experiences, and allow readers time to share and promote the books they enjoy. Readers develop confidence in self-selecting books when they recognize books and authors and experience a wide range of material that informs their future book choices.

Whether it's the next book in a popular series, a student request, or a newly published title I discover, adding books to our classroom library excites my students. Since I buy books with my own money, I cannot purchase more than one or two copies of new books, though. Bringing fresh titles into the classroom, I used to display them on the whiteboard rail for students to preview and select. Unfortunately, my first-period students always snagged the most promising books before my other classes got a chance to see them. My second and third classes of the day often went weeks before getting their hands on our new books. Only my adventurous readers, not those unwilling to take a chance on unknown authors or unfamiliar books, selected these new books without a blessing or recommendation from me. When a clear favorite like the latest release from a hot author or series appeared, students bickered over who would get the book first or asked me to keep a reserve list, which I refused to do. I needed a better system for promoting and managing new books.

I needed to find a way to introduce new books to students, increase interest in books the children might not read without my endorsement, and manage demands from a large group of kids who wanted to read our new books. I began holding book drawings whenever I brought in new books. First, I present a book commercial about each new addition, sharing a brief preview of the book's content, my personal impressions if I have read it, connections to other books, and what I have learned from other teachers, librarians, and reviewers about the title, like starred reviews and positive critiques. Then I invite any interested students to record the book's title on their Books to Read List and enter a drawing to read it. (See appendix A for a blank form for this list.) Students record their names and the book title on index cards cut into fourths that I keep for this purpose. I repeat this process with all three classes and draw the name of the first reader at the end of the day.

My students' enthusiasm for book drawings surprised me. It's not reading pedagogy; it's economics. What happens to demand when supply is low? Demand increases. Students flock to enter our drawings, clamoring to enter even before I finish my book commercial. Even students who are unmotivated to read enter drawings because of the status that comes with winning first reading rights. Students beg me to draw another name the instant they see someone return a book drawing title. Concerned about fair allocation of our high-demand books, my students developed a set of guidelines for our book drawings:

- *You must be present to win.* If you are absent or leave early and I draw your name, your slip goes back into the drawing and I pick someone else.

- *You may not have more than one book from a drawing at a time.* Many students enter drawings for every book possible. If you already have a book from a drawing, you may not win another one until you return the first book.

- *You have one week to finish the book.* With a long list of students waiting for Patrick Ness's *A Monster Calls* or *Dead End in Norvelt* by Jack Gantos, you cannot keep a new book for weeks. My students police who has our high-demand titles and nag each other to finish. For lengthy books like Christopher Paolini's Inheritance Cycle series, I reserve the right to bend this rule.

- *You must return books offered in drawings to Mrs. Miller when you finish.* Students return our drawing books to me so that I can draw the next recipient. This helps me keep track of our new books and ensure that I distribute books fairly.

When interest in a new book wanes, I slip the book in our classroom library. These titles remain popular all year, and students who read the title during our book drawing excitement continue to promote it to their friends, increasing interest and engagement long after the initial hoopla fades.

Book drawings are an engaging and fun way to introduce new books to students and encourage risk taking. Students are more willing to try unfamiliar books when I endorse them and classmates express enthusiasm for reading them. Even students who don't enter drawings build title and author awareness.

## Abandoning Books

> *I will abandon a book if it is boring, poorly written, confusing, too weird, or I don't agree with the author. I usually give a book 150 pages before I abandon it, though.*
>
> —Adam,
> sixth grader

Addressing my class one morning, I asked, "Have you ever disliked a book that other readers like?" Hands flew into the air, and students eagerly volunteered the titles of the books they disliked that were beloved by other readers. Bringing the group back together, I held up *Wildwood* by Carson Meloy and said,

> This is exactly what happened to me with *Wildwood*. The book received great reviews. Other readers I trust like the book. It sounds like a book I would enjoy, too. It's about a girl who travels into the wilderness to rescue her baby brother, who is kidnapped by an evil queen. Recommendations from other readers, an interesting storyline, and cool features like maps and illustrations—everything I learned about *Wildwood* led me to believe this would be a great book for you and me to read.
>
> But when I began reading *Wildwood*, I was disappointed. I couldn't connect to the protagonist or her problems. I thought the book rambled. By page 78, I couldn't take it anymore. I have decided to abandon *Wildwood* for now. Since the book is written for readers your age, I would be interested in what you think of it. I may dive back into it again after talking with you about it. Who would like to enter the drawing for *Wildwood* and be the first person to read it?"

Students scrambled to sign up for *Wildwood*. In a classroom where students are encouraged to read widely and experiment with all sorts of books, my students are willing to take on reading challenges—even if they don't work out. After talking with all three of my classes about *Wildwood*, forty readers—roughly half of my students—submitted their names for a chance to read the book.

Over the next few days, several students began and abandoned *Wildwood*. As I talked with each child about the book, they blamed the length and the slow pace of the narrative as challenges to completing it. These conversations about what didn't work for us as readers were just as interesting as if we had all enjoyed *Wildwood*. We explored what we liked about the books we read and how *Wildwood* lacked these elements. I continuously asked, "Who is the right reader for this book? What do knowledgeable readers see in it that we don't? Are we giving *Wildwood* enough of a chance?"

When Shelby won the *Wildwood* drawing, she announced bravely that she was going to be the first person to finish it. Day after day, Shelby trudged through *Wildwood*. I checked in with her daily to see how it was going. She admitted that she wasn't enjoying the book but that she was committed to finishing it. She took on *Wildwood* as a personal challenge. When she finally finished the book, I congratulated her and asked what she thought of it. She told me, "One star, Mrs. Miller. I give it one star because any author who writes a book deserves one star."

When the other students on our team learned that Shelby was the first reader to reach the end of *Wildwood*, she became a celebrity. Students from other classes approached her with admiration and asked her to describe her experiences reading the lengthy, boring book. I think Shelby felt that her efforts paid off in notoriety!

Shelby proved it could be done. I continued to draw names for the chance to read *Wildwood* next. Some readers abandoned it within a few chapters, and others made it halfway. Jack and Clayton both finished it and liked it. The boys' appreciation for *Wildwood*, a book few readers seemed able to complete or appreciate, surprised me. One student compared *Wildwood* to black licorice, claiming, "You either love it or hate it. No one is neutral."

The *Wildwood* challenge opened up another line of classroom conversation: abandoning books. I asked the class, "Who has no problem abandoning books if they aren't working for you?" and we discussed why we abandon books and how long we will read a book before we ditch it. More than a few students admitted that they rarely abandon books and feel committed to a book once they begin reading it, even if the book isn't interesting or proves too hard to read.

I told students that I give a book fifty pages before abandoning it unless the writing is so poor that I cannot endure it. Other readers shared that they have their own guidelines. Maddie admitted that if she is bored with a book, she will read the ending before deciding to keep reading. Her comment elicited gasps from other students: some were shocked that Maddie peeked at the end. Others were surprised because they skip to the endings, too, but didn't realize others did. Some students admitted that a book has very little time to engage their interest—as few as five pages or one chapter.

During this conversation, some students revealed that whether they abandoned a book or gave it more than a few pages depended on how motivated they were to read it in the first place. Brian said that he was less likely to abandon a book I recommended to him because "You are usually right about the books I will like, Mrs. Miller, if I just give the book a chance." Ashley agreed that if other trusted readers suggested a book to her, she would stick with a book longer before abandoning it.

The children rarely abandoned books that were in a series or widely read by other students in the class, either. Enrique labored to read *Alfred Kropp: The Thirteenth Skull*, the third book in Rick Yancey's thrilling trilogy, claiming that the storyline was confusing, but he wouldn't abandon it because he couldn't imagine leaving the series unfinished. Completists will commit to reading an entire series and will not drop this goal even when they find some of the books in the run not as engaging as others.

We talked about *Wildwood* and what was happening with it every week for six months that year. Winning the drawing was a dubious honor at best, but not a single student passed on the opportunity to read *Wildwood* when his or her name was drawn. In a classroom where there's a book for every reader and a reader for every book, *Wildwood* found its place.

Most wild readers abandon a book now and then. When you work with students, it's important to probe why they stop reading a book after starting it. If you are concerned that particular students frequently abandon books, confer with them to determine why they can't finish books they self-select. Perhaps they need more guidance about choosing books. As with most other reading habits, abandoning books presents a problem only when it becomes a trend that prevents students from reading much.

I have noticed that many habitual book abandoners lack reading experience. They don't recognize narrative arcs. The beginning of a book carries lots of engaging content for readers—introducing characters, setting the stage for conflicts, and world building. The action slows naturally during the middle of the story as the author develops characters and creates tension. When children don't read much, they bog down when the story loses momentum. One of my students, Chris, calls this part of a book "the draggy spot." Inexperienced readers don't know that if they keep reading, the story picks up as the author builds to the climax.

High school literacy expert Carol Jago told me, "Books teach you how to read them," and our students build stamina for the draggy spots only when they understand how narratives work. Provide students with minilessons about plot development, pointing out moments when pacing typically slows. Encourage students who don't finish many books to stick with them longer and suggest accessible books that help developing readers build confidence and lots of reading experience. When students self-select books, we must value their choices as much as possible. This means accepting failed attempts when readers choose books that don't work out or select books that span a range of reading levels.

## Guess My Lexile

What do Jeff Kinney's popular *Diary of a Wimpy Kid* and Ray Bradbury's classic *Fahrenheit 451* have in common? What about *Gossip Girl: A Novel*, Cicely von Ziegesar's catty romance, and *The Great Gilly Hopkins*, Katherine Paterson's 1979 Newbery Honor book? While clear distinctions exist between each book's literary merit, age appropriateness, and reader appeal, these titles possess one similarity: they sit within the same Lexile text complexity band (Lexile scores: *The Diary of a Wimpy Kid*, 950; *Fahrenheit 451*, 890; *Gossip Girls*, 820; *The Great Gilly Hopkins*, 800).

The Lexile Framework for Reading by MetaMetrics provides quantitative assessment of students' reading levels and the complexity. Students receive a Lexile measure from certain reading tests. Books and other texts receive a Lexile measure from a software tool, the Lexile Analyzer, which evaluates word frequency and sentence length. Many schools use Lexile measures to assess students' reading levels and match students with appropriately rigorous reading material.

Well-meaning educators, concerned about increasing text complexity and reading rigor, engage in this game of "guess my Lexile" when denouncing the low reading level of children's and young adult literature, elevating certain titles over others, or dictating book purchases and recommended reading lists. But looking at just a few examples reveals problems when narrowly evaluating texts by readability number alone.

I have no issue with assessing students' reading levels and identifying text complexity. As a teacher, I find such information helpful when determining my students' reading ability and what books might fit them. What concerns me is that in many situations, Lexile measures become the sole factor in book selection and recommendation.

While identifying readability can be useful when evaluating textbooks, guided reading texts, or other teaching materials, selecting books for classroom instruction and recommending books for independent reading are two different processes. Avid readers do not always read at the edge of their competence, traveling through increasingly more difficult texts as leveling systems prescribe (Carter, 2000). Given free choice, readers select reading material according to their interests, preferences, background knowledge, purposes for reading, and personal motivation.

I hear horrifying stories about teachers and librarians who rigidly enforce Lexile bands, preventing children from reading books that aren't at their Lexile level; for example, they won't let students read an entire series because every book isn't at their Lexile, or students can't use sections of school and classroom libraries because the books are too easy or too hard according to Lexile measures. Parents even receive Lexile reading lists for their children with strict instructions to use these lists exclusively when purchasing books. In cynical moments, I picture a Lexile store selling tattoo kits, so overly zealous educators can brand students with their Lexiles. Wouldn't this make trips to the library easier for everyone?

According to MetaMetric's website, "Many other factors affect the relationship between a reader and a book, including its content, the age and interests of the reader, and the design of the actual book. The Lexile text measure is a good starting point in the book-selection process, with these other factors then being considered." With Lexile measures touted as one key indicator of text complexity as defined by Common Core State Standards, we must critically consider what Lexile bands offer teachers and students and what they don't. Overreliance on reading level systems hinders children from learning how to self-select books. Bookstores, libraries, and Grandma's bookshelf aren't leveled. Beyond students' and books' reading levels, we must consider content and interests when selecting materials and recommending books for independent reading. Slavish devotion to numbers doesn't benefit readers. We can't shortcut or disregard knowing books and knowing readers, and then building connections between them.

Reading leveling systems like Lexile provide teachers and librarians with one measure for making book recommendations and supporting students as they self-select books, but children shouldn't wear their reading levels like a badge and become defined by them. We create dependent readers when our students need a complex matchmaking system to help them choose books. Students must practice picking books on their own. Recognizing our students' diverse reading experiences, reading levels, and emotional maturity presents challenges when offering reading material. The more we know about books and our individual students, the better support we can provide.

## The Mature Shelf

Students who read above grade level deserve books that challenge and engage them. Matching advanced middle school readers with books presents some challenges. Young adult literature encompasses a wide span of reading and interest levels, and the edgier content in many young adult books isn't appropriate for my eleven-year-old students. Looking at my students' reading experiences and preferences, however, I must consider that most students who read the Twilight saga *before* sixth grade aren't interested in reading a tamer vampire series like Cirque du Freak.

By my desk, away from the twelve bookcases housing our core classroom library, one bookshelf offers reading material for students with above-grade-level abilities and interests. Named the "mature" shelf by students a few years ago, this bookcase contains young adult books (figure 2.2). During the first few weeks of school,

FIGURE 2.2: *Our mature shelf with series stacked on top.*

I do not promote or recommend mature shelf books to my students, although I don't prevent them from checking out any books they might like to read. Based on conversations during reading conferences, results from reading assessments, and discussions with parents, I suggest young adult books to those students who are emotionally and academically ready.

Due to content and reading level (or both), offering above-grade-level books to my students demands more mediation and book knowledge on my part than at- or below-grade-level texts. I might suggest Suzanne Collins's *The Hunger Games* or Jordan Sonnenblick's *Drums, Girls, and Dangerous Pie* to a mature sixth-grade reader, but I don't keep titles written for high school readers like

Laurie Halse Anderson's *Speak* or John Green's *Looking for Alaska* on our shelves because the content is too emotionally mature.

While I haven't read every book in our classroom library, reading every young adult book before I bring these titles to school becomes critical. Because publishers and book vendors don't make distinctions between middle school and high school young adult books, determining which young adult books wind up in our middle school classroom library and which titles I pass to high school colleagues requires me to read them all.

When many students read the same titles, they belong to an organic book club that provides natural opportunities for discussing the books they share. Students who read more difficult books than their peers still need other readers who can address misconceptions, think about issues and topics that edgier books explore, and respond to their personal reactions and questions. Since I have read every young adult book in the library, I can fulfill this role if a student needs another reader with whom to discuss the book. Through reading, I evaluate a young adult book's content, literary value, and reader appeal and convey this information to others from a personal reading stance. If a parent or administrator questions a particular book, I can justify why the book sits on our shelves.

Decide how you will address parent concerns about books in your classroom and reinforce that students self-select their books. If parents disapprove of a book their children bring home, encourage students to choose something else.

## Selection Reflections

Encouraging students to reflect on their reading choices reveals students' methods for discovering books to read. If students cannot choose books without substantial guidance from teachers and librarians, they have not developed the skills and confidence they need to select books for themselves. Do students know other readers who can recommend books? Do they access online or print review sources? Can students preview, evaluate, and pick books from a library or bookstore? Do students enjoy the books they self-select or struggle to finish the books they choose?

Susie and I asked our students to look back through their reading lists and examine the last five books they chose to read. They identified how they selected each book, offering their basic impressions of each title. Digging deeper into their book selection methods, students considered their self-selection methods and abilities (figure 2.3).

The My Selection Reflection form (a blank form is in appendix B) asks these five questions:

- *How do you find out about books that you would like to read?* Parents, siblings, and classmates—personal connections to other readers—provide our students with a consistent source of book recommendations. Wild readers depend on their reading networks for most of their book suggestions, and it's important for students to develop these relationships with readers at home and school. Many students access Goodreads, Amazon, and authors' websites looking for book suggestions, too. For example:

    "If the book gets recommended to me, it's written by my favorite author, or if the book is part of a series that I read, I will read it."—Blake, sixth grader

- *When you see a book or hear about it, how do you decide that it is a book you would or would not like to read?* Students rely on their reading experiences when selecting books—accessing what they know about the author, genre, or series to inform their choices when looking at new books. When students don't know much about the book or its author, they rely on other readers' opinions. For example:

    "If a book has a lot of good reviews from trusted readers, then I will read it. If a lot (of my reading friends) don't enjoy the book, I won't read it."—Reed, sixth grader

- *Do you ever abandon a book? Why or why not?* A student's willingness to abandon a book now and then reveals confidence and self-awareness as a reader. Wild readers know

**My Selection Reflection**

Reader _John_

List the last five books you have chosen to read. Include the book you are currently reading or any books that you have abandoned. Describe how you chose each book.

| | |
|---|---|
| **Title** | The Sea of Monsters |
| **Author** | Rick Riordan |
| **How did you choose this book?** | 2nd Book in the series |
| **Rate this book** | It was amazing.　It was good.　It was boring.　(I am still reading it.)　Abandoned |

| | |
|---|---|
| **Title** | Crocodile Tears |
| **Author** | Anthony Horrowitz |
| **How did you choose this book?** | 8th book in the series |
| **Rate this book** | (It was amazing.)　It was good.　It was boring.　I am still reading it.　Abandoned |

| | |
|---|---|
| **Title** | Hate That Cat |
| **Author** | Sharon Creech |
| **How did you choose this book?** | 2nd book in the series |
| **Rate this book** | It was amazing.　(It was good.)　It was boring.　I am still reading it.　Abandoned |

| | |
|---|---|
| **Title** | Alfred Kropp #1 |
| **Author** | Rick Yancy |
| **How did you choose this book?** | Reccomendation from Nico |
| **Rate this book** | (It was amazing.)　It was good.　It was boring.　I am still reading it.　Abandoned |

FIGURE 2.3: *John's reflections on his selections.*

| Title | *LEVIATHAN* | | | | |
|---|---|---|---|---|---|
| Author | *Scott Westerfeld* | | | | |
| How did you choose this book? | *Recomendended by Joee (Mrs. Miller)* | | | | |
| Rate this book | It was amazing. | It was good. | It was boring. | I am still reading it. | Abandoned |

Answer the following questions about your book choices.

How do you find out about books that you would like to read?

*Interesting covers, cool 1st book, Author, (series) etc.*

When you see a book or hear about it, how do you decide that it is a book you would or would not like to read?

*Interesting title or cover.*

Do you ever abandon a book? Why or why not?

*No because you have already put time into it. why waste time?*

Are you successful in choosing your own books to read? Why or why not?

*Yes because I have the "Good Book Sense"*

FIGURE 2.3  *(Continued)*

that there is always another book waiting for them if a book they choose to read doesn't work for them. Students who frequently abandon books lack this confidence and experience. For example:

> "No, I don't [abandon books]. I always like to think there's a great ending."—Jonah, sixth grader

> "Yes, I do abandon books. Sometimes, they hit a slow point or just don't hook me."—Sarah, fifth grader

- *Are you successful in choosing your own books to read? Why or why not?* Students who expressed confidence when self-selecting books identified varied methods for determining what books to read. Critically examining their processes helps students explore how they choose books and reevaluate why their books choices do or don't work. For example:

> "I'm pretty successful choosing books because my friends give good recommendations and because most of the books I read are very popular or have won awards." —Anthony, sixth grader

> "No, I am not successful because I choose books by the cover, and they're right, you can't judge a book by its cover." —Braylen, sixth grader

Asking students to reflect on their book selection processes reveals their capacity and confidence in choosing reading material. While our classroom conditions provide temporary support for students who lack reading experience, they must learn to self-select books and determine why a book worked for them or didn't. Students who regularly choose books that they can't read or don't enjoy are unlikely to read much or find reading personally gratifying. Exposing students to lots of books and positive reading experiences while building a network of other readers who support each other provides students with tools that last beyond the classroom setting.

# *Conferring Points*

At the 2013 Michigan Reading Conference, keynote speaker Kelly Gallagher said, "There are only two things [that teachers do] that move writers forward—modeling and conferring." Although Kelly was talking about writing instruction, I believe his thoughts transfer to reading instruction. When conferring with students, I never lose sight of my primary aim: fostering their independence. Pressured to confer with many students each day, teachers might find it faster to simply hand a student a book and urge him or her to read it, but this practice does not show young readers how to find a book on their own. Providing students with scaffolded opportunities to preview, evaluate, and choose texts gives them the practice they need in self-selecting books.

Unpack your thinking when evaluating a book and share it with students. What do you consider when deciding whether you want to read a book? How do genre, preferences, and need influence your reading choices? Encourage students to develop their own criteria for determining whether a book meets their personal goals.

## Preview Stacks

Students regularly ask me for book recommendations. They trust me because I know them as readers and I know about books. When making reading suggestions, though, I am careful not to influence students' opinions of the books too much or take away their ability to choose freely what they want to read. I want my students to trust themselves and develop the ability to make their own book choices. Creating preview stacks for my students meets students halfway. I use my expertise as a guide to select several books a particular student might like and offer the child a stack of choices. Students are free to choose any books that interest them or reject them all. Even if they do not select books from the preview stack I make for them, they practice previewing and evaluating books and build up their book knowledge.

Another way I help students select books is at the class library. I ask students questions like what genre they would like to read. This helps me guide them toward a section of the library and allows me to focus on particular types of books. I question students a bit about what they are looking for in a book: a new series, something like another book they enjoyed, or a particular author, for example. As I listen to them, I am pulling from my knowledge about their reading levels, personal interests, and what types of books they have read in the past. I never tell students they cannot read a book they pick up, but I do guide them toward books that I think would be a good fit for them. I think of myself as a reading mentor—a reader who can help them find books they might like. I pull five or ten books out of the bins, describing each one to students as I pass the books to them to preview. Everyone around us laughs when they see me piling books into a student's arms, but they all know that I have placed wondrous books into that preview stack (figure 2.4).

FIGURE 2.4: *Taylor peers over her preview stack.*

Asking students to tell me when they have enough books to examine, I direct them to take a look at every book in the stack, select one or two to read, and write the titles of any books they would like to read in the future on their Books to Read List. Although I enjoy digging through the library to help students find books, my aim is to help them develop self-confidence in choosing books for themselves. With preview stacks, students look at many books and learn more about the types of books available for them to read. Writing a few titles on their to-read lists ensures that they will have a few titles to look for when they investigate the school or classroom libraries on their own.

When students are sitting at their desks with a pile of books in front of them, I have noticed that other readers at their tables will point out books from the stack that they have read and offer recommendations and reviews about books they know. Always mindful that I should not be my students' sole source of book recommendations, I encourage these conversations and often ask other students to comment when I suggest a book.

## Building Preview Stacks

Making preview stacks requires you to reinforce and support readers' self-selection efforts while tapping into your knowledge of their reading interests, ability, and expressed needs when offering books. Ask students:

- *What genre do you want to read?* Class requirements, personal preferences, and popular class titles inform students' genre choices.

- *What have you already looked at today?* Walk students to the class library if they aren't already standing near the shelves. Reinforce to students that they can and should look for books on their own.

- *What was the last book you finished that you really liked?* Through conferring and other assessments, you probably know what books this student prefers already, but if you don't, ask.

- *What sort of book are you thinking about?* Is the child looking for a new series? A book similar in style or topic to one just read? A particular author?

As you look through books, consider your personal goals for and your experiences with that student. Think about the child's reading level and previous reading when selecting books, and use your informed opinions about each reader to select books that you think are a good fit.

Offer brief testimonials about each book as you place it into the child's hands, and ask other students you know who have read the book to give their opinions. This reinforces to students that you value their thoughts about books just as much as your own and reminds students that their peers can be knowledgeable sources for book recommendations, too.

Always offer several books at once. Suggesting one book takes away students' ability to choose, dismisses them when they may need more options, and doesn't allow them the opportunity to learn more about the many books available for them to read. Encourage students to jot down any books that look interesting on their Books to Read List and select one or two for immediate reading. Over time, press students to review this list when they need another book instead of immediately asking you for help.

Creating preview stacks for students should scaffold students toward independence by providing sheltered opportunities to look at books that you determine meet their interests and needs. As students develop experience and confidence, they will be able to choose their own books with less guidance from you.

## Keeping Track of Your Reading Life

In their reader's notebook, students keep a reading list documenting every book they read. (A blank Reading List form is in appendix A and an example in figure 2.5.) At the beginning of the year, the reading list serves primarily as an accountability tool. Susie and I check reading lists when conferring with students,

| Title | Author | Genre | Date Started | Date Finished |
|---|---|---|---|---|
| 8 Rebel Angel | Libba Bray | F | 9-17-10 | 9-19-10 |
| **Star Rating** | **How did you choose this book?** | | | |
| ★ ★ ★ ★ ☆ | 2nd book in a triology | | | |
| 9 Unwind | Neal Shusterman | SF | 9-20-10 | 9-21-10 |
| **Star Rating** | **How did you choose this book?** | | | |
| ★ ★ ★ ★ ★ | Mrs. Miller gave it to me. | | | |
| 10 Graceling | Kristin Cashore | F | 9-21-10 | 9-23-10 |
| **Star Rating** | **How did you choose this book?** | | | |
| ★ ★ ★ ★ ☆ | Mrs. Miller said it was a good book | | | |
| 11 Memoirs of a teenage | Gabrielle Zevin | RF | 9-24-10 | 9-24-10 |
| **Star Rating** | **How did you choose this book?** | | | |
| ★ ★ ★ ★ ☆ | Mrs. Miller recommended it. | | | |
| 12 Sea | Heidi R. Kling | RF | 9-24-10 | 9-27-10 |
| **Star Rating** | **How did you choose this book?** | | | |
| ★ ★ ★ ★ ☆ | Mrs. Miller recommended it. | | | |
| 13 Chains | Laurie Halse Anderson | HF | 9-27-10 | 9-29-10 |
| **Star Rating** | **How did you choose this book?** | | | |
| ★ ★ ★ ☆ ☆ | I needed a Historical Fiction so Mrs. Miller recommended it. | | | |
| 14 Stormbreaker | Anthony Horowitz | SF | 9-29-10 | 10-1-10 |
| **Star Rating** | **How did you choose this book?** | | | |
| ★ ★ ★ ★ ☆ | I read the Crocodile Tears so I read the last one. | | | |
| 15 Shiver | Maggie Stiefvater | F | 10-1-10 | 10-1-10 |
| **Star Rating** | **How did you choose this book?** | | | |
| ★ ★ ★ ★ ★ | Mrs. Miller recommended it. | | | |

FIGURE 2.5: *Hoyeon's reading list.*

discussing their book choices and their experiences reading each book. Examining reading lists during conferences, we look for trends in students' reading behaviors and identify strengths and areas for growth:

- What do we notice about students' reading choices?

- What suggestions can we make that encourage students to read widely and take risks?

- How can we support students who don't finish books or don't enjoy or appreciate what they read?

Reading list entries provide significant information about students' reading lives.

Reading list entries ask for this information:

• *Title and author name:* Students list the title and author of each book when they begin reading it. The titles and authors reveal the variety of books students read and helps you determine whether they prefer certain types of books. Students who stick to one genre, author, or series have strong preferences, but may need encouragement to expand their reading diet. I also compare the reading levels of students' book choices against their reading levels from formal assessment instruments and my knowledge of their reading abilities. Wild readers select books from a range of reading levels and based on need, motivation, and interest. Given free rein to choose their books, students may choose titles at, above, and below their independent reading levels. If students consistently pick books they cannot read or don't find much of a challenge, they need advice and support for making better choices.

• *Genre:* Students record the genre of each title using the genre categories from our class genre requirements. Their notations indicate their preferences and how narrow or wide their book choices are. In addition, I examine if students correctly identify the genres of what they read and understand the characteristics of different genres within the context of independent reading events. If students struggle to determine a book's genre, we discuss their misconceptions, referring back to genre notes and anchor charts from minilessons.

• *Date started and date finished:* Students note the date they start reading a book and the date they complete it. Assessing these dates, I see how long it takes them to finish books. I don't want them to rush through books, but if they spend several weeks reading the same book, I question whether they read much at home, understand the book, or connect to it. Conversely, if students blaze through books in a day, I consider the types of books they choose to read. Are the books primarily short books like graphic novels and informational texts? Are the books several steps below their reading levels?

If students abandon a book, they record "abandoned" in the Date Finished box of their reading lists. The books students begin but don't finish reveal as much about their reading habits as the books they complete. How did they select that book? Why did they abandon it? Do they plan to finish it at some point? A false start now and then doesn't concern me, but if students abandon book after book, they need reading advisory and monitoring.

• *Star rating:* Using a scale of one to five stars, students rate each book they read. Star ratings are ubiquitous in online reviews, and students enjoy using the same system to rate their books. Assessing students' ratings shows me their impressions of what they read and whether they consistently enjoy or appreciate their book choices. If students indicate low ratings for several books in a row, I work with them to find books that better match their interests and tastes. Star ratings provide insight into students' reading comprehension, too. If they don't understand a book, they often identify it as boring instead of hard to read.

Students' star ratings guide me when I am weeding our class library or adding titles. If a book receives low ratings from several students, I reread the book and ask students why the book lacks kid appeal. If I don't have another instructional purpose for low-rated books, I get rid of them. If an author, topic, or series appeals to my students, I look for additional titles that match these interests.

• *How did you choose this book?* Students document how they choose each title they read. As I review these comments, I am mindful that they need a variety of methods for finding books to read. If I am the sole source of their book recommendations at the beginning of the year, that's okay from a scaffolding standpoint. If I am still their sole source of book recommendations in April, it's a problem. Students must develop relationships with reading peers and use online, print, and other resources to inform their book choices, or they will not develop the confidence and capacity they need to self-select books successfully.

When students frequently select books that don't work for them, I consider the methods they employ for selecting books. Recommendations from friends don't always work out if there is a mismatch between what your friend and you like to read or wide differences in your reading levels. Students who use less critical methods for selecting books, like popularity or cover art, may need guidance and instruction on how to preview, skim, and evaluate books for a better fit.

• • •

As the school year progresses, students' reading choices show their growth as independent readers. Their book selections evolve based on influences from our classroom community and lots of positive reading experiences throughout the year. Given plenty of choice, high expectations for reading widely, and access to books, students' reading selections naturally increase in rigor under our guidance (Miller, 2009; Lesesne, 2010). They also take more risks, dipping into complex texts and sampling genres and authors they haven't read in the past.

Empowered and knowledgeable, wild readers know they can walk into any library or bookstore and find something to read. Our students must develop this confidence and capacity to become wild readers themselves.

# Curating a Classroom Library

*A good library will never be too neat, or too dusty, because somebody will always be in it, taking books off the shelves and staying up late reading them.*

—Lemony Snicket,

*Horseradish: Bitter Truths You Can't Avoid*

EVERY YEAR, I must pack and store our classroom library books, so our custodians can shampoo the classroom carpet. Sorting, evaluating, and cleaning over three thousand books is a massive undertaking. While I could begin this task over the last few weeks of school, enlisting my students' help, I don't want to imply to my students that we are finished reading

## Ranganathan's Five Laws of Library Science

1. Books are for use.
2. Every reader his book.
3. Every book its reader.
4. Save the time of the reader.
5. A library is a growing organism.

*Source:* Ranganathan (1963).

by limiting their book access or choices. Stalling until the last possible moment, I typically spend a few days after school ends going through our books—and as I do, I wonder if we have too many books. Recognizing the importance of a well-tended classroom library to my students and me, I shrug off my misgivings and start cleaning.

Why do we need classroom libraries? After all, most school campuses contain a school library. Doesn't it provide students with the reading material they need? No. I believe that children need both school and classroom libraries. According to the 2005 National Assessment of Education Progress Report (Kelley & Clausen-Grace, 2010), students in classrooms with well-designed classroom libraries interact more with books, spend more time reading, demonstrate more positive attitudes toward reading, and exhibit higher levels of reading achievement. Study after study confirm the report findings that access to books in the classroom results in increased motivation and reading achievement (Guthrie, 2008; Kelley & Clausen-Grace, 2010; Worthy & Roser, 2010). As Richard Allington and Anne McGill-Franzen (2013) remind us, "Children must have easy—literally fingertip—access to books that provide engaging, successful reading experiences throughout the calendar year if we want them to read in volume" (p. 13). Over the years, students discover their reading lives in our classroom library. This book access matters.

Offering students an engaging, diverse classroom library requires more than buying books and putting them on bookshelves. The heart of a reading and writing workshop is the classroom library. More than just a source of books for independent reading, the classroom library provides authentic material to support the reading and writing work we do. We use our books to examine elements of genre and craft, discover titles and authors, and research topics that expand our knowledge. Managing a classroom library requires curation—selecting the best, most current materials for both curriculum needs and students' interests.

## Factors to Consider When Building a Classroom Library

Building an effective classroom library is an ongoing process. As you select books for your classroom library, think about your students and what books you want to offer them to read. A robust classroom library includes a range of reading levels, genres, and topics so as many students as possible can find books to read that match their interests and reading abilities. Begin with books that have wide appeal to many readers, such as popular titles like Suzanne Collins's *The Hunger Games, Holes* by Louis Sachar, and Lois Lowry's *Number the Stars.* When considering series, make sure you include at least the first three or four books in your collections. Students who discover a series are frustrated when a book in the series run is missing. Research award lists and book review websites to locate exemplary texts for students, but don't load up your bookshelves with award-winning titles if they lack kid appeal. It's a waste of money and space. Include a mix of engaging, easy-to-access titles as well as more challenging texts that stretch students' worldview and deepen their reading experiences. Full bookshelves don't matter much if your students won't (or can't) read the books.

## *Introducing Students to the Classroom Library*

From the first day of school and for every day after that, I want my students to read. This means selecting books from our class library immediately. As I describe in *The Book Whisperer,* we begin our first class with a book frenzy—inviting my students to go into our class library and choose a book they might like to read. I help students who need guidance finding a book, while students who are more confident in selecting books feel free to browse. I learn a lot about my students' reading experiences and preferences during the book frenzy. In turn, they learn that I am serious about reading and invested in giving them choices about what they read.

Turning children loose to rummage through your carefully ordered bookshelves before discussing with them how to use the library and care for the books may fill you with anxiety, but it helps me to remember that the books don't belong solely to me once the children arrive. It is *our* classroom library—ours to learn from and share and enjoy for the entire year. Building a reading community begins by getting books into my students' hands.

*Blake looks for a book in our classroom library.*

After the children have selected books, we discuss the finer points of using the library. Over the next few days, we work as a class to determine classroom library procedures and explore how our books are organized. Consider the following discussion points when introducing your students to your class library.

## How to Check Out and Return Books

Unhappy with every paper and computerized checkout system I have ever used, I was thrilled to discover Booksource's Classroom Organizer (http://classroom.booksource.com), an online library organizer and free app. Using the barcode scanner feature, my class librarians (students who volunteer for this classroom job) and I scanned every book in our classroom library. Booksource's website searches the cloud using each book's unique International Standard Book Number (ISBN), autofilling the author's name, title, reading level, and copy blurb. After adding my class lists into my private Classroom Organizer account, my students and I use a Netbook or iPod to check out and return books. Readers can record a book's condition, assign a star rating, or write a quick review, helpful information that survives from one school year to the next. Using the computer motivates many students who refuse or forget to update their reading lists. I can also print out overdue book reminders for students who have kept a popular book for too long. I know that I can keep better track of our classroom library inventory, too.

## How to Take Care of Books

As a class, I ask students to develop rules for taking care of our books. Working in table groups, students brainstorm a list of guidelines for protecting our books, and we use their ideas to create an anchor chart displayed in our classroom. I keep a few damaged books from past years as examples and show these to students, so they can see what happens to books when we don't take care of them. I reinforce to students that readers will not have access to all of our books if we destroy the ones we have. Last year my students developed these rules:

**Our Classroom Library Rules**

- Use a bookmark.

- Keep your book away from liquids, small siblings, and pets.

- Keep your book away from markers and pens.

- Carefully slide your book into your backpack or locker.

- Shelve your books in the correct bins.

- Do not pick off the plastic or stickers.

- Return books in a timely manner.

- Report any damaged or lost books to Mrs. Miller.

My sixth graders already knew how to care for books, but creating our rules together helped build our classroom community and publicly commit to taking care of our classroom library.

## How the Library Is Organized

I organize our classroom library by genre. For two weeks, I read a different picture book, short story, poem, or article to my students and ask them to determine what the genre of the text is. We create a class set of notes on the characteristics of each genre and determine what types of characters, plot lines, and settings we commonly find in each fiction genre. For poetry and nonfiction texts, we look at the text structure and text features, too. After students have been exposed to every genre and discussed genre characteristics, I give them several book tubs from our library and ask them to determine the genre of their tubs using their notes and their reading experiences. Previewing the selections in the tubs, students identify the genre of each book. I give each group a genre label for their tubs, and students stick the label on the front of the tub. This activity helps students locate books by their individual interests and reading goals and reinforces how books are categorized by their commonalities.

During these activities, students have examined and discussed scores of book titles and familiarized themselves with the types of books available to read. Our ultimate goal for building and maintaining our classroom library is to promote and encourage reading by providing students with access to lots of books. Teaching our students how to select and care for our classroom library books fosters ownership and confidence and reinforces that these books are an important resource for our reading community.

## *Is Your Classroom Library MUSTIE?*

Inhabiting the same classroom and teaching the same grade level, I have been lax about removing books from our classroom library collection in recent years. Packing for my recent move offered a clear opportunity to handle and consider every book and determine its future use with my students. I should regularly remove any worn-out books from our classroom library and critically evaluate each book for reading appeal.

My teacher-librarian friend John Schumacher directed me to the acronym MUSTIE for the six negative factors librarians consider when weeding and evaluating library books (J. Larson, 2012):

**M = Misleading.** Remove any nonfiction books that contain factually inaccurate or outdated information. Consider scientific advances, geographical changes, revisions in thought or new information. Goodbye, Pluto: our solar system books classifying you as a planet are obsolete.

> ## MUSTIE in Short
>
> **M** = Misleading
> **U** = Ugly
> **S** = Superseded
> **T** = Trivial
> **I** = Irrelevant
> **E** = Elsewhere

**U = Ugly.** Books with stains, torn pages, split bindings, or funny smells turn off readers. Heavily circulated books eventually wear out, too. If a book is yellow with age or depends on tape to remain in one piece, throw it away. Regularly dust books, shelves, and book bins, and repair minor damage like small page tears. The physical condition of the library says a lot about its currency and how much we value readers. Unless you can work a Reparo spell, that copy of *Harry Potter and the Goblet of Fire* (swathed in packing tape) has to go.

**S = Superseded.** Replace books continually updated like *The Guinness Book of World Records*, almanacs, sports records, and Best of . . . lists when new editions appear. Be mindful of nonfiction books that suggest outdated websites or technology. When examining several copies of the same fiction title, remove books with dated, unappealing covers in favor of more inviting editions. Mass market paperbacks, while inexpensive to purchase, often contain print that is too small for children to read comfortably. When reducing how many copies of the same title you keep, eliminate books with tiny print over copies with more accessible text size.

**T = Trivial.** In my never-ending quest to entice kids to read, I occasionally purchase books that tap into particular students' niche interests. While these books may engage one or two readers for a single school year, titles that lack wide appeal, literary merit, or research value don't warrant long-term residency in a classroom library. Similarly, I don't keep more than the first three to five books in extensive, ongoing series like Warriors, Midnight Library, Star

Wars, or Goosebumps. If a student really loves these series after reading the first few books, I can scrounge up subsequent titles for them. The same goes for trendy books like television show and movie tie-ins. Anticipating that novelizations of movies like Pixar's *Brave* will appeal to my new fourth graders, I bought a few copies, but I know that I will weed these out in a year or so when interest declines.

**I = Irrelevant.** Readers' tastes change. Hot books in my classroom six years ago, like Cornelia Funke's *Inkheart* and Edward Bloor's *Tangerine*, don't interest as many readers now. While you shouldn't eliminate quality books in good condition from your library, reduce the number of copies you have on hand to accommodate newer, more relevant titles. Continuously trying new lessons and discovering books, I often purchase texts for use during a specific author's study, genre unit, or research project. Reflecting on curriculum changes or students' responses to these books, such texts sets should evolve and change.

**E = Elsewhere.** With the exception of rare editions, books personally inscribed to your class and you, or students' published writing, every book in your classroom library exists somewhere else. As a new teacher, I scanned every yard sale, eBay listing, and used bookstore for Newbery and Caldecott Award winners. I didn't know much about children's literature, and these exemplary titles seemed like a good foundation for a classroom library. A decade later, I can count on one hand how many students have read *Rifles for Watie* by Harold Keith or Katherine Paterson's *Jacob Have I Loved*. Knowing that our school and local public library carry these older titles, I don't have to keep them.

Because throwing away or donating books we purchased with our own money is always difficult, remember why we build classroom libraries in the first place: so our students will fall in love with reading and find the right book at the right time. We cannot offer our students meaningful book access with damaged, outdated, or uninteresting materials.

# CHAPTER 3

# Wild Readers Share Books and Reading with Other Readers

*Where we love is home,*
*Home that the feet may leave,*
*but not our hearts.*

—Oliver Wendell Holmes Sr.

AT FIRST GLANCE, there is surprisingly little reading going on in my classroom at this moment, but if you looked more closely, you would see how much reading drives everything we do. Camrynne and Sabrinna perch on beanbag chairs in the corner, editing each other's book reviews before publishing them to our class blog. Michel digs through the classroom library, looking for *Eagle Strike,* the fourth book in the Alex Rider series. At the rate he is going, he will finish the series soon, and I consider which books he might like to read next. Hayden, Simba, and Cameron sit around a laptop, researching historical information about the Hitler Youth organization in Germany during the 1930s and 1940s. Reading and passing back and forth Susan Campbell Bartoletti's *Hitler Youth* and *The Boy Who Dared* intrigued them. Sloane and Jesah work on the storyboards and script for their *Hunger Games* book trailer. They hope to persuade other students to read the book, too. You might not see me at first, but I am sitting at a desk next to Armann while he shows me how he infers what happens between the panels in *Maximum Ride,* a graphic novel by James Patterson. I record his observations in my conference notebook. Engaged in different tasks, our shared purpose—to enrich our lives through reading and writing—unites us.

I jokingly tell my sixth graders, "You are my People," but I believe it. By the end of the year, they believe it, too—*People* with a capital P like Native Americans, for we are one tribe. Swapping books back and forth, sharing favorite lines from our writing, or searching for my keys (*again*), we build a classroom family united in our common need to learn more about the world and ourselves. My interactions with students reinforce that I respect them and expect great things for them. I worry about my students long after they leave me, and my life becomes entwined with theirs for one school year at least, and often longer. As much as I hope to change children's lives, my relationships with students transform me. I want my students to remember our classroom as a home that they may leave, but it will never leave them. They are forever mine, and I am forever their teacher.

I envision our classroom as a supportive place where my students and I take risks and learn. I see caring people who embrace our differences and discover what we have in common. We laugh and cry together. What my students need to learn is important, but the conditions that allow learning to happen concern me more. Successful learning communities require cultivation, and I spend a lot of time forging relationships with my students and helping them connect to each other. While standards and learning targets dictate the content I must teach, I am the one who—with the help of my students—constructs the classroom environment. How my students and I interact creates a climate that both supports learning and provides social and emotional safety.

At a recent conference, renowned author and teacher Jeff Wilhelm asked his keynote audience, "What's your bottom line? What do you really want to happen for your students? Now, how does what you do every day serve that bottom line?" I want my students to see themselves as readers and writers. I want

## Student Readers Chime In

"It's important to have other readers to talk to because if you were the only reader, and no one else talked—the book, the emotions, the characters, would remain secret."—Abby, sixth grader

"Almost all the people in my class have recommended a book to me."—Carson, fifth grader

"I have a lot of friends who like to read the same types of books I do. And if I really love a book, it doesn't seem fair not to tell them."—Zoe, sixth grader

"I talk to my mom all the time about books."—Anna, sixth grader

"My brother used to not read that much but I brought home books from school and now he reads a lot. Right now he is reading *The Red Pyramid.*"
—Cody, sixth grader

them to know how much I believe in them. I want my students to feel they have something to contribute to the world. Working each day of the school year to build a classroom community that values and supports every member serves my bottom-line goals. It's easy to get lost in the mindless drudgery that comes with teaching— grading, meetings, testing. Focusing on our goals provides clarity of purpose and reduces our willingness to compromise the real work of our classrooms: helping children develop their capacity to have meaningful lives filled with purpose and joy.

## Embarrassed to Read

Unfortunately, participating in an engaging reading environment for one year isn't enough to make wild readers out of many kids. Being surrounded by cultural forces that fail to support reading or diminish reading outright erodes students' interest in reading and prevents them from sustaining any reading motivation. Children must receive constant encouragement for reading. It takes more than one classroom with one teacher for one year.

A recent National Literacy Trust report found that 17 percent of children surveyed would be embarrassed if their friends saw them reading (Clark, 2012). Embarrassment is tied to our need for social acceptance. If you have ever chased a naked toddler, you know that children aren't born with an understanding of socially acceptable behaviors and must learn cultural norms from people who model and teach them.

Children's future success depends on their acquisition of literacy skills. Children must learn to read and write in order to achieve an education and perform job and life functions that require accessing and communicating information. Possession of fundamental literacy falls within our social norms: we expect everyone to learn how to read and write. There seems to be a line between reading well enough and reading as a leisure pursuit, however. It's okay for children to read when asked to perform academic tasks, but if they would rather read than watch TV or play outside, readers sometimes become social outliers (except to other readers).

Negative stereotypes connected to reading bombard kids: readers are intellectual snobs, socially inept nerds, and bookworms. So where do children learn that wild reading is socially unacceptable and embarrassing?

Children also receive the message that avid reading isn't cool from some adults. When parents don't model reading, teachers grade and control everything kids read, and communities and schools close or defund libraries, we communicate to children that reading isn't something that our culture values as a life activity. If we want children to read more, we must provide them with classrooms, libraries, and homes where reading is the norm. If cultural acceptance includes wild reading, then children will read. If reading isn't held in high regard, they won't. Why would anyone read if they receive overt and implied messages that reading is weird? Reading shouldn't be an extraordinary act performed by a bookish few who stand outside of mainstream culture.

When we promote books to children and share our reading lives with them, we offer more than another great book recommendation or reading cheerleader: we invite them into a society that reveres reading and readers. Society benefits when more people read, but we have to show that our culture values it. Schools must consider how cultural factors affect students' views toward reading and evaluate how implicit and explicit messages from adults influence students' reading lives. How do parents view reading? What role does reading play in our school culture? How does reading weave through every class? How do we make reading ordinary and expected in children's lives?

## Fostering School and Home Reading Communities

Schools provide literacy hubs for families that need reading support and resources. Educating parents about the importance of daily reading, increasing book access through libraries and book ownership, and promoting the value of reading aloud must take prominence in parent outreach programs. Sending home book orders and celebrating Dr. Seuss's birthday aren't enough. According to Baker and Moss (1993), "Reading needs a broader social context that offers endless opportunities for shared learning among and between students, parents, and teachers" (p. 24). Building reading communities that support children begins by addressing the experiences and perspectives of community stakeholders. Many parents lack strong, positive reading experiences in their own lives and don't see the urgency or understand how to support their children's literacy in meaningful ways. When flooding students with pro-reading messages, we must flood their parents, too.

Here are some ways that our school gets the message out to students and parents:

• Include reading recommendations and home reading tips when communicating with parents in newsletters and class websites.

• Along with many colleagues, I add a weekly student book recommendation to my e-mail signature.

• Teachers share book recommendations and reinforce the importance of reading role models through regularly updated "I am currently reading . . . " signs outside their classroom doors. Students announce their book recommendations with "I am currently reading . . . " cards on their lockers, too.

• Our principal regularly invites students, staff members, and visitors to share book recommendations during morning announcements.

• The school librarian, students, and I create quarterly book lists to share with parents looking for gift ideas, vacation reading, and library guides. Consult your state library association and local public library websites or ask your school or public librarian for reading lists. Work with colleagues to create lists that match your students' needs and interests.

• Support students and parents who don't have books at home. Hold library card sign-up events and ask your public library to share information about summer reading and enrichment programs.

• Loan classroom library books to parents and siblings. Keep stacks of books in the office and other public areas for parents to borrow and read with their children. Pass out books during parent conferences and PTA/PTO meetings. Hold a book swap or book drive, and redistribute book donations to families.

• Increase children's access to books. When schools close for the summer, many children, particularly children from low-income homes, don't have access to books. Consider initiatives that increase book access during the summer months. We open our school library two days a week all summer. The library opens for two hours Tuesday mornings and two hours Wednesday afternoons, with parents and faculty members volunteering for one or two slots. At our fifth- and sixth-grade intermediate campus, we invite rising fifth graders and sixth graders, as well as our departing sixth graders, to visit the library and check out books. Many teachers loan books from their classroom libraries over the summer, too. Providing greater book access to students who may not read much over the summer far outweighs the cost of replacing any lost books.

• Teach parents simple ways to incorporate more reading into family routines. Discuss with parents the need for daily reading time, and show them how to squeeze more reading into boring activities like waiting at the doctor's office and traveling to and from errands and appointments. Both Scholastic (http://www.scholastic.com /parents) and Reading Is Fundamental (http://www.rif.org/us /literacy-resources.htm) offer useful resources about home reading that you can share with parents. Every parent conference, communication, and school event should reinforce a reading culture at school and the extension of this culture at home.

At the campus level, scrutinize every component of the school day to determine if your procedures, policies, and systems support or hinder students' reading. I hear from teachers all over the country who fight their school cultures in order to implement independent reading components into their classes. Instilling the habits of lifelong readers requires intentional, systemwide support for teachers, librarians, and students.

Carving out meaningful blocks of time for independent reading isn't an optional frill. Administrators shouldn't assume that students read every day, especially if the school schedule doesn't allow time for it. When designing your campus schedule, discuss when, where, and how long students will read every day. While we cannot control whether students read at home, we must consider school demands that affect students' available reading time, too.

Many middle school and high school students report that they have so much homework they don't have time to read for pleasure. Numerous studies found no academic benefit to assigning homework to elementary students and minimal benefit for secondary students (Kralovec & Buell, 2000; Bennett & Kalish, 2006; Kohn, 2006a, 2006b). Well-regarded researcher and educational reformer Alfie Kohn (2012) believes, "If we're making 12-year-olds, much less five-year-olds, do homework, it's either because we're misinformed about what the evidence says or because we think kids ought to have to do homework despite what the evidence says." In spite of research evidence, many parents, teachers, and administrators believe that kids should complete hours of homework after school.

As a parent, I question the value of most homework assignments. When Sarah brings home an S. E. Hinton crossword puzzle to complete for her seventh-grade gifted and talented English class as part of a unit on *The Outsiders,* I know her time would be better spent reading. I believe that individual schools must consider their cultural beliefs about homework and reflect on school homework policies. We must engage in deep conversations about the types of homework we ask students to do, how it benefits them academically (not just how we think it does), and our expectations for families regarding homework assistance and completion. Homework assignments should not penalize kids who lack home support, technology access, or other resources.

Examine how much total time we ask students to spend on homework each night, too. Teachers underestimate the amount of time it takes students to complete their homework assignments by as much as 50 percent (Dolin, 2010). Teachers must talk with grade-level colleagues across subject areas to determine the total home-work load for their students and consider when students will read at home. Research proves that students' ability to read well affects their performance in every class (Krashen, 2004); therefore, all teachers, not just those in the English department, must commit to schoolwide literacy initiatives and support students' reading devel-opment. If we assign so much homework that our students don't read much, we may be harming them more than helping them.

In addition to school schedules and homework policies, stake-holders must consider the role school funding plays when develop-ing schoolwide reading initiatives. Most teachers who possess classroom libraries invest their own funds to purchase books. Schools that have classroom libraries with large supplies of books have students who read more frequently and students who read success-fully (Allington, 2006). Librarians spend substantial time fundraising to supplement meager library funds in order to provide students and school staff with necessary materials and services. Although school libraries and degreed librarians have a positive effect on students' achievement and engagement at school (Francis, Lance, & Lietzau, 2010; New York Comprehensive Center, 2011), too many schools have eliminated professional librarians and slashed library budgets. There always seems to be money for test preparation materials, assemblies, and curriculum kits, yet we run out of money when it comes to purchasing books and funding professional development.

What we spend our money on reflects our true values. If schools want kids reading more (which they should if they want them to be successful in all subjects), there are a number of things they can do, including these:

- Buy a wide variety of books for classroom and school libraries instead of one hundred copies of the same book for a unit on one novel.

- Hire a degreed librarian.

- Send teachers to literacy conferences and subsidize membership in professional literacy organizations like the International Reading Association, National Council of Teachers of English, and the American Library Association. Professional development is not an expense. It is an investment.

- Subscribe to educational journals like *Reading Teacher* and the *Journal of Adolescent Literacy*.

Building successful schoolwide reading communities requires parent education, investment from school stakeholders, and systems that support teachers and students.

## Benefits of Reading Communities

> *To live factionless is not just to live in poverty and discomfort; it is to live divorced from society, separated from the most important thing in life: community.*
>
> —Veronica Roth,
> *Divergent*

Susie and I were surprised that so many of the Wild Reader Survey respondents revealed that they didn't read as much as they wanted because they lacked social relationships with other readers. One participant admitted, "My husband is not a reader—to spend time with him, I have to change my reading habits." Many readers crave connections with other readers who enjoy discussing and sharing books and believe that these relationships enrich their lives and their reading experiences. Your reading community might be one friend who discusses books with you over lunch or your book club group. My reading tribe includes my husband and daughters, my students and school colleagues, the members of my monthly book club, and countless reading friends. Relationships with other readers support my reading life and connect me to other people interested in reading. Who would you include in your reading community?

## Wild Readers Chime In

"I love how reading and discussing what I'm reading connects me to students on a special level. One of my favorite parts of teaching is sharing a common experience through a story with students."

"I enjoy reading books with my 13-year-old son and have treasured every moment that I have been able to inspire and follow his reading interests since he developed his early love of books."

"My aunt developed my love of reading by giving me favorite books of hers that she treasured—she passed it on to me and I have passed it on to my children as well as my husband. He was a nonreader when we were married almost 30 years ago. Last year he read over 75 books!"

"I love sharing books with children! Whether I am reading aloud or recommending books to them, nothing gives me greater pleasure than turning someone on to a book."

"Most of the books I read are recommendations from friends."

One survey respondent expressed her need for these connections and her dismay when interacting with nonreaders:

> When you come across other book lovers, it's like the quality of the oxygen in the room increases! But even as an adult, many are dismissive of us avid readers & talk about how incredibly busy *they* are, as if to shame readers & label us as people with no lives (or why else would we be reading?). I feel sorry for everything those people miss in the reading community.

We are all social beings who seek affiliation with others who share common values and interests. Readers need other readers. Classroom reading communities benefit avid readers and less motivated readers by providing a reading home that supports all readers no matter where they are on the path to wild reading.

Reading communities have these benefits:

- *Foster connections with other readers.* Building relationships with other readers sustains a student's interest in reading because it reinforces that reading is an acceptable and desirable pastime. Readers don't stand out as social outsiders when everyone reads. For students disinterested in reading, a reading community provides positive reinforcement and nonthreatening reading role models by forging relationships with classmates who enjoy reading more. For avid readers, classroom reading communities offer status and acceptance for their reading behaviors.

- *Increase how much readers read.* Reading communities demand lots of reading. Students invest more time in reading so that they can fully participate in book discussions and finish books their peers recommend. Reading alongside a friend adds reading to the list of enjoyable experiences students share and fuels their willingness to read more.

- *Challenge readers to stretch.* Constant exposure to books, authors, genres, and writing styles encourages readers to branch out and try reading experiences they might not discover or attempt on their own. Students develop more confidence in their abilities to read longer books and commit to long-term reading plans like finishing a series because they see their reading peers successfully accomplish these goals. Students enjoy the status that comes with being the first person in a class to read a new book or introduce a new author to their friends.

- *Improve readers' enjoyment and appreciation of what they read.* The only thing readers enjoy almost as much as reading is talking about books with other readers (figure 3.1). Discussions with other readers help students clarify and deepen their understanding of what they read. When a friend likes a book a reader enjoyed, that connection reinforces the reader's appreciation for that book, builds the reader's confidence in his or her choices, and strengthens a connection to the other reader. They have one more thing in common. I have even seen students bond because they hated the same book. When two readers

FIGURE 3.1: *Enrique and Anthony formed a reading community of their own, recommending and swapping books between them.*

disagree about a book, debating the book's merits and deficits often leads both readers to a deeper analysis of the book's themes, structure, or plot than if they both agreed.

• *Suggest titles for additional reading.* The number one way that readers find out about books they would like to read is through recommendations from other readers. Students must build reading relationships with other readers who offer reading suggestions, support their reading choices, and lead them to more books. Many students maintain these reading relationships outside school.

• *Encourage mindfulness about what you read and share.* Our fellow readers help us prioritize what we read. Hearing about a book from several trusted readers heightens students' interest and helps them select certain books to read over others. When suggesting books, readers consider what they know about their friends as readers and how specific books meet their needs and interests. The more that students read and develop bonds with other readers, the more reinforcement they receive for their own reading choices and experiences.

## *How Wild Readers Share Books*

Reading is ultimately a social act. Our Wild Reading Survey respondents share their love of reading and books through both online and face-to-face interactions. Chatting with coworkers at the copier or jotting down suggestions for a stranger in the checkout line, the most frequent way wild readers share books with other readers is swapping recommendations. Offering recommendations requires more than instant recall of recent favorites. Readers consider both their reading experiences and their knowledge of the other reader when making book suggestions. Sifting through potential titles, readers evaluate each book and reflect on what they enjoyed about it and why it might appeal to another reader. When providing recommendations, readers may offer additional information about the author, similar titles that connect to the proffered book, and their personal reactions to the text.

If we know the other reader well, we wild readers suggest books that connect to that person's interests and experiences. When providing recommendations to someone we don't know well, we rely more on literary merit and professional criticism because it lends credibility to our suggestions. This process of reflection, selection, and suggestion defines authentic reading response in its truest sense. Listening to their book recommendations, we learn a lot about other readers even if we never read their suggested books. Reflecting on our book recommendations, we can discover a lot about ourselves and what we value about books. After all, most wild readers don't compose critical reviews or post to a blog. We certainly don't build dioramas or write diary entries from a character's point of view. When we finish a book, we consider our personal reactions to it, and if we appreciate it, we share the book.

The majority of our survey respondents were education professionals and parents, so it was not surprising that many indicated that they share books and reading with children through traditional classroom and home activities like read-alouds and shared reading. Reading and discussing books together benefits children and builds relationships among readers who share these experiences.

Over half of our survey respondents participate in book clubs with reading friends, which provide social outlets for reading and sharing books. Many wild readers identified their fellow book club members as their primary community for receiving and giving book recommendations even when the books shared were not book club selections.

Wild readers share books with other people by loaning, donating, and trading their books, increasing book access in their reading communities in the process. Talking about a book heightens interest, but passing a book directly into the hands of another reader adds a sense of urgency and excitement to a book recommendation that few readers can resist.

Many wild readers offer their impressions about the books they read with a larger audience through personal blogs and amateur reviews posted to book vendor websites like Amazon and Barnes and Noble. The ability to share their opinions about books gives readers an opportunity to influence other readers and publicly announce their reading interests.

> ## Student Readers Chime In
>
> "I text Grace about books a lot." —Adam, sixth grader
>
> "Marina and Adam have told me about books that I have to read, and the books they recommended have become some of my favorite books." —A. J., sixth grader
>
> "I think actually reading is more productive than talking about it." —Michel, sixth grader
>
> "I have changed as a reader because I find myself encouraging other people to read. I even made a process for my sister to read books." —Allison, fifth grader
>
> "Sometimes I have an urge to tell someone when I am on an exciting part." —Winter, fifth grader

## Online Reading Communities

The rise of social networking sites like Facebook and Twitter, as well as reading-themed sites like Goodreads, gives readers opportunities to connect with other readers around the world and offer vibrant reading communities not limited by geographical proximity.

Immediate access to other readers provides a deluge of recommendations and continuous support for our reading obsessions. When my granddaughter, Emma, showed an unusual interest in turtles, I sent a query for books about the reptiles on Twitter and received thirty book recommendations in less than fifteen minutes.

If you're seeking connections with other literacy professionals, want to ramp up your book knowledge, or need compatible readers to support you, consider the following online reading communities:

• *Twitter* (@twitter): I cannot overstate the value of Twitter as an ongoing source of professional development. Twitter offers an endless stream of book recommendations and information about reading and teaching. Connect with like-minded educators, keep track of the latest education policy developments, and follow hundreds of authors, publishers, teachers, librarians, and reviewers who regularly share sneak peeks of upcoming books, links, and resources for using books and sharing them with other readers.

• *Nerdy Book Club* (www.nerdybookclub.com, #nerdybookclub, @nerdybookclub, http://www.facebook.com/nerdybookclub): The Nerdy Book Club is a network of librarians, teachers, authors, reviewers, and parents through a community blog that invites readers to write blog posts and reviews. I began this blog with two friends, Colby Sharp and Cindy Minnich, as a home for readers who want to celebrate children's and young adult literature and share books and reading with the children in our lives. The tenets of the Nerdy Book Club are these:

If you read, you are already a member of the club.

Every reader has value and a voice in the community.

Vote for your favorite children's and young adult books in the annual Nerdy Book Club Awards (the Nerdies). Buy a nifty Nerdy Book Club coffee mug with original logo designed by Tom Angleberger (the merchandise proceeds support literacy organizations), or skim the extensive blog roll for the best reviews and commentary about reading and books.

- *Goodreads* (www.goodreads.com, @goodreads): I consider Goodreads a social networking site for readers, my reading brain. Customize your Goodreads shelves and create unique categories like "books that make you cry" or "books about World War II." Goodreads friends provide an endless source of recommendations and reviews that inform your reading plans, and its free phone app helps users look up books during bookstore and library crawls. You can also follow authors' reviews and blogs, enter giveaways and contests, or create book discussion groups.

- *Facebook Centurions* (http://www.facebook.com/#!/groups /243348159758/): At the end of each month, over seven hundred readers converge on the Centurions page to share the books they have read over the past month. Centurions challenged themselves to read 113 books in 2013, but the page provides an excellent source of book recommendations even if you don't reach this goal. Growing beyond the monthly tallies, Centurions post recommendations, opinions, and questions all month long, and the page offers an excellent starter list of reading friends you can connect with on Facebook.

- *Titletalk* (#titletalk): This is a monthly Twitter chat that takes place on the last Sunday of every month at 8:00 p.m. Eastern Time. Each month, my cohost, Colby Sharp, and I lead a discussion about one reading topic like read-alouds, genre studies, or launching a year of reading. The first half of Titletalk involves a conversation about instructional practices, resources, and ideas for working with young readers. The second half of the chat is a flood of suggested books from participants that relate to the chat topic. Cindy Minnich maintains the Titletalk wiki (http://titletalk.wikis paces.com/), which houses archives of every chat, so you can access the information when you cannot attend or reference it later. For tips on how to participate in a Twitter chat, visit Colby's helpful tutorial on the Sharpread blog (https://sharpread.word press.com/2011/11/26/november-2011-titletalk/).

Through these online reading communities and others, engage with like-minded readers and expand your reading life. Online communities connect wild readers to a global reading group that supports and encourages you to read more and shares your thoughts about books and reading or your work with young readers.

## Becoming the Lead Reader

> *Reading Teacher (RT): a teacher who reads and a reader who teaches.*
>
> —Michelle Commeyras,
> Betty Bisplinghoff, and Jennifer Olson,
> *Teachers as Readers*

Assigned to my class for student teaching, Malorie arrived in January for her twice-a-week observation rotation. Reading and writing workshop were well under way by this time of year. Students had read scores of books and were at ease with the flow of conversations about books and reading that took place in our classroom every day. Chatting with Malorie on her first day, I summarized our daily routines, showed her students' reading and writing notebooks, and probed her knowledge of workshop pedagogy. As I invited her to sit in on reading conferences, it occurred to me that if she didn't know much about children's literature, she wouldn't have much to contribute during these conversations with students.

Reluctant to offend her, I asked Malorie, "Where would you rate your knowledge of children's books? I imagine you haven't been able to read much in your free time because of your course work, but that's something we could work on while you are here."

Malorie admitted, "On a scale of 1 to 10? About a 2. The last children's book I read that I enjoyed was *The Giver*. I read it in fifth grade."

Shocked, but not surprised, I said, "Malorie, we have to fix this. You need to know more about books, so you can talk to the kids and suggest books to them." Dashing over to the bookcases, I began digging through bins. Where did we start? How could Malorie help lead our classroom reading community when she didn't know much about books? Looking through titles and considering my students' reading habits, I decided that Malorie could start with touchstone books that many children enjoy, like *The Lightning Thief* by Rick Riordan and Gary Paulsen's *Hatchet* (figure 3.2). Beginning with well-loved, notable books would give Malorie the ability to talk with children who've read these books, recommend good books to students who hadn't read them, and help her build a foundation of high-quality literature that she could share and promote later with her own students. Remembering her appreciation for Lois Lowry, I slid *Number the Stars* into Malorie's preview stack, suggesting that she would like it, too. Several students sitting near the library laughed when they saw my pile for Malorie.

Enrique said, "Oh, she does that for everyone. You can trust her. She knows a lot about books."

Caught up in our enthusiasm, Malorie asked, "What do the kids like? What do they think I should read?"

Impressed, I knew Malorie was going to be a great teacher. I could teach her about books and lesson planning and the business

FIGURE 3.2: *Malorie reads* The Lightning Thief *during independent reading time.*

of running a classroom, but I couldn't teach her to care about what the kids think. Turning to my students, I said, "Hey, guys, Miss White wants to read some of the books you are reading, so she can talk to you. What should she read?"

Around the room, students shouted, "*The Hunger Games!*"

Anthony took his copy of *The Hunger Games* off his desk and brought it to Malorie, proclaiming, "You will love it!"

Amused by the entire scenario, Malorie laughed and announced her plans to read *The Hunger Games* first. Perched at the horseshoe table one morning, totally absorbed in *The Hunger Games*, Malorie sat softly weeping. Discreetly looking at the side of her book to see where she was, I realized Malorie was deep in the woods with Katniss and Rue.

Watching Malorie talk with two of our students about the book later, I realized that Malorie had crossed over. She wasn't a classroom observer anymore. She was part of our reading community with powerful reading experiences and opinions to contribute. Our students respected Malorie's teaching role in our class, but they embraced her because she read alongside us.

The most effective reading teachers are teachers who read. According to Morrison, Jacobs, and Swinyard (1999), "Perhaps the most influential teacher behavior to influence students' literacy development is personal reading, both in and out of school" (p. 81). Teachers who read for pleasure are more likely to employ best literacy practices in their classrooms than teachers who do not read for pleasure (Morrison, Jacobs, & Swinyard, 1999; McKool & Gespass, 2009). Examining research into the influence teacher readers have on their students' reading behaviors, Dreher (2002) found that "teachers who are engaged readers are motivated to read, are both strategic and knowledgeable readers, and are socially interactive about what they read. These qualities show up in their classroom interactions and help create students who are, in turn, engaged readers" (p. 338). Teachers who read are better equipped to build successful reading communities in their classrooms and connect their students with reading and books.

Applegate and Applegate (2004) assert, "It stands to reason that if reading models affect readers, then teachers will be influenced by their own model of reading or system of beliefs as well" (p. 555). As engaged, enthusiastic readers, we offer students powerful role models and invite them to become engaged readers themselves. Every child deserves full participation in literacy communities where all learners, including teachers, embrace their roles as readers and writers and share their literary lives. We must show our students what a wild reader looks like through our examples.

## Community Conversations

I first noticed the book because it didn't have a dust jacket on it. Because dust jackets tear easily, I store them whenever students check out our hardcover books. It keeps the jackets in one piece and helps me keep track of the more expensive books in our classroom library. Our hardcover books are typically newer books—always in high demand. I wondered if this nondescript book was one of the books on our long list of book hostages—books that seem to be checked out forever. Engrossed in the book, Andrew didn't see me until I appeared at his desk. When I peeked over his shoulder to see what book it was, he hid the cover from me and looked embarrassed.

I asked, "Andrew, what are you reading? Is it one of our hostages?"

He mumbled into his lap, "No, it is a book that I borrowed from Adam." Adam has progressive taste in books and often brought books from home to share with his friends.

"Well, if Adam likes it," I told Andrew, "maybe it is a book that everyone would like to read. What book is it?"

"*Be More Chill*," Andrew admitted. Several boys from various parts of the room began to snicker and avoid looking at me. "I don't think it is a book that you should read, Mrs. Miller," Andrew said.

"Why not?" I asked.

"If you read it, you may try to stop us from reading it!" Adam called out.

Horrified, I asked, "Have I ever tried to prevent you from reading a book? Why would I stop you from reading a book?"

"It's mature! There's boy stuff in it!" Andrew blushed. "I don't think it's appropriate for the class."

"Look, if so many boys in the class are reading this book, and clearly they are," I said, looking around at Braylen, Andrew, Adam, Reed, and the other boys who were avoiding eye contact with me at the moment, "then I should read it so we can talk about it."

It was Andrew's turn to look shocked, "We don't want to talk about it with you! That would be awful. It would be embarrassing!"

*Be More Chill* by Ned Vizzini is a science-fiction coming-of-age story. The book explores the protagonist's experiences with puberty and his growing male sexuality. The book intrigued my middle school boys who are curious about their own changing bodies and emotions. While we often discussed and shared book recommendations and reviews in class, the idea of a female teacher—even me, whom they trust—discussing this book with them was not something these boys wanted to do. They feared I would limit access to *Be More Chill*, tell their parents, or, worst of all, try to talk to them about the content of the book.

While I agree that teachers and parents must be mindful of the content of reading material that children read, we walk a fine line when we decide to limit book access because we are uncomfortable with difficult or provocative topics. One of the reasons wild readers enjoy reading is that books can answer our questions and help us explore our experiences. How old should children be before they can read books about their own lives? Books like *Be More Chill* provide opportunities to discuss uncomfortable topics with children while remaining detached from the reality of these issues. All of us must decide what books to allow in our classroom based on our book knowledge, our experiences with students and parents, and our school culture.

That afternoon, I bought a copy of *Be More Chill* and read it over the weekend. I should have just left the boys alone on this one. As a reader, I didn't think *Be More Chill* was that good. As a teacher, I didn't know how to discuss the book with the boys. Clearly they were sharing the book because of its humorous slant on sexual topics like masturbation. How could I confer with Andrew, Adam, and the rest of the boys without talking about why they liked the book? Because of *Be More Chill*, my boys discovered that books could be subversive contraband, worth passing back and forth among friends. Books hold secrets that you can share with other boys. While my students feared that I would take *Be More Chill* away from them, it bothered them when they discovered that I read it. *Be More Chill* lost its appeal, disappeared from my classroom and my students, and I never really discussed it.

I realized later that I had taken *Be More Chill* away from them.

When I insinuated myself into the reading community that grew organically from my students' shared experiences reading *Be More Chill*, I ruined it. If we really want our students to become wild readers, independent of our support and oversight, sometimes the best thing we can do is get out of the way. My role changed from reading advisor to reading policeman, and the boys didn't like it. While we need to stay informed about what they read and remain connected to our students, we don't need to participate in every discussion or endorse every book. If students depend on our validation for every book they read, they aren't reading for their own purposes and needs. They are playing the teacher-pleaser game. These days, when I see my students passing books between them, like Regan, Sarah, and Winter reading Lauren Myracle's edgy *ttly* during recess (figure 3.3), I just smile and walk away.

FIGURE 3.3: *During recess, Regan, Sarah, and Winter share one copy of Lauren Myracle's* ttyl.

## Books That Build Communities

*If you give people a good book to talk about, you can build a community out of a diverse group. A common language grows out of it.*

—Nancy Pearl,
*Book Lust*

Reading books together creates shared experiences that foster community building and students' literacy development. Consider the following books as beginning-of-the-year read-aloud selections that will forge connections among your students and introduce them to high-quality, engaging texts.

### Communities That Read and Write

*Ask Me* by Antje Damm. From commonplace ("Who is your best friend?") to thought provoking ("Whom do you miss?"), this nifty book of questions invites children to reveal personal information, reflect on their lives, and learn more about each other. Engaging illustrations accompany each question and provide further response opportunities. Designed as a conversation starter between parents and children, *Ask Me* is a unique resource for writing and discussion topics.

*BookSpeak! Poems about Books* by Laura Purdie Salas. This collection offers twenty-one poems on everything bookish, from characters to indexes, to falling asleep while reading. At turns humorous and informative, *BookSpeak!* is the perfect text to start a reading year and reinforce a love of reading.

*Forgive Me, I Meant to Do It: False Apology Poems* by Gail Carson Levine. Modeled after William Carlos Williams's "This Is Just to Say," Levine presents over forty insincere apologies for misdeeds. Children, who are encouraged to apologize by character-building adults, will appreciate Levine's honesty and humor and consider writing false apologies of their own.

## Communities That Value All Members

*Hound Dog True* by Linda Urban. Shy and self-conscious, Mattie Breen dreads starting another school year. Apprenticing herself to the school custodian, her Uncle Potluck, Mattie hopes to avoid her classmates when school begins. Brilliantly written, *Hound Dog True* is a powerful book to share at the beginning of the school year when many students feel apprehensive and worry about finding friends.

*Out of My Mind* by Sharon Draper. Eleven-year-old Melody has cerebral palsy. She lives in a world of silence, unable to talk or write. Although she is extremely intelligent, her classmates and more than a few teachers see her as simple-minded. Sharing this book sparks powerful conversations about embracing all students in our schools and valuing every child's right to learn.

*The Strange Case of Origami Yoda* by Tom Angleberger. Dwight is a loser, so weird that even the other sixth-grade misfits in his class avoid him. For mysterious reasons, Dwight creates an origami Yoda puppet, wears it on his finger, and uses it to dispense advice to his classmates. The other kids usually avoid Dwight, but they are drawn to Yoda's seemingly helpful wisdom. This book sends the message that all kids have something to contribute. Read aloud *The Strange Case of Origami Yoda*; then introduce students to Angleberger's sequels, *Darth Paper Strikes Back* and *The Secret of the Fortune Wookiee.*

*Wonder* by R. J. Palacio. Auggie Pullman is born with Treacher Collins syndrome, a genetic disorder that results in severe facial deformities. He is homeschooled for many years because of his ongoing need for extensive surgery and his parents' fear about how Auggie will be treated. When Auggie begins fifth grade, his parents decide to send him to a public school. *Wonder* is a remarkable book about courage, love, and the difference one person can make in the lives of others.

## Communities That Have Fun

*Interrupting Chicken* by David Ezra Stein. It's time for Little Red Chicken's bedtime story, but she's so enthusiastic about the book that she can't help interrupting Papa. If there is a chicken on the cover, you can predict the book is funny. Children will see themselves in this clever story. Use this book as a springboard for conversations about classroom etiquette, or just enjoy the chickens.

*I Want My Hat Back* by Jon Klassen. Bear has misplaced his pointy red hat. Questioning the other woodland animals, the distracted Bear finally discovers the location of his hat. Amused by the dark and hilarious surprise ending, my sixth graders declare *I Want My Hat Back* one of their favorites. Klassen takes his deadpan visual humor into the ocean in the Caldecott-winning follow-up, *This Is Not My Hat.*

*The Wonder Book* by Amy Krouse Rosenthal. What do you wonder? This random assortment of riddles, word games, and poems offers answers to our wonderings and encourages inquiry. Short selections are perfect for transitions, energizing breaks, and the beginning or end of class.

## Communities That Care about the World

*A Bus Called Heaven* by Bob Graham. One morning, Stella discovers an abandoned bus outside her house. The bus, labeled Heaven, inspires Stella's diverse neighbors, who turn the bus into a community space. This is a sweet book about one community and the dilapidated but still useful bus that brings them together.

*Fourteen Cows for America* by Carmen Agra Deedy. In 2002, Kimeli Naiyomah returned home to his Maasai village from New York City with news of the 9/11 terrorist attacks. Moved by the horrific news, the Maasai respond by donating their most sacred and valuable possessions, fourteen cows, to America. A powerful book about compassion and hope,

*Fourteen Cows for America* shows our connections in a global community.

*Laundry Day* by Maurie J. Manning. When a red cloth floats down from the clotheslines overhead, an honest shoeshine boy climbs from window to window in a New York City tenement building searching for the cloth's owner. The boy's journey up the building celebrates America's rich immigrant heritage and the importance of honesty and caring in every culture.

Books provide opportunities to laugh, cry, learn, and bond through common literacy experiences. Sharing thought-provoking, engaging books with your students facilitates the growth of a reading community in your classroom. As you consider which books to share with your students, think about how each text fosters your reading community.

## Reading Graffiti

Dedicating our classroom walls to student work and anchor charts, I like to put up displays that my students and I add to throughout the year. During a writing lesson on crafting strong leads, taken from Jeff Anderson's work (2005), we read and collected leads from our independent reading books, posting each title's opening lines around the classroom. My students enjoyed reading and comparing leads from their books, and the activity sparked many discussions about writer's craft, what we could predict about the books, and how mentor authors influenced our writing. Reflecting on this activity, I recognized my students' enjoyment and engagement with analyzing and collecting quotes from the books they read, and I saw an opportunity.

I covered one long wall over our classroom library with black butcher paper, bulletin board border, and a "Reading Graffiti" label. Using a gold marker, I scrawled *The Hunger Games'* catchphrase "May the odds be ever in your favor!" across the bottom of the paper, and I invited my students to share any lines from their books that stood out to them. Our Reading Graffiti wall extended

FIGURE 3.4:  *Our Reading Graffiti wall.*

our sentence collection into a reading response activity—selecting and sharing the lines and words from our books that stood out as remarkable or special to us (figure 3.4).

Our Reading Graffiti wall became a classroom focal point—the first thing visitors noticed when they came into our room (besides all of our books). Every line became an endorsement—for the book and for the reader who selected and drew it (figure 3.5). Students often wandered along the wall, reading quotes and inquiring about titles or tracking down the classmates who wrote them. Many readers selected books after reading one line from them off the wall. If I had required my students to annotate every book they read to select meaningful quotes, they would have balked, but more than one reader crammed their books with sticky notes flagging potential "perfect lines to put on the wall."

## Book Commercials

Similar to book talks, book commercials are impromptu testimonials about books that my students and I present. I often use the last five minutes of class time or transitions between activities for book

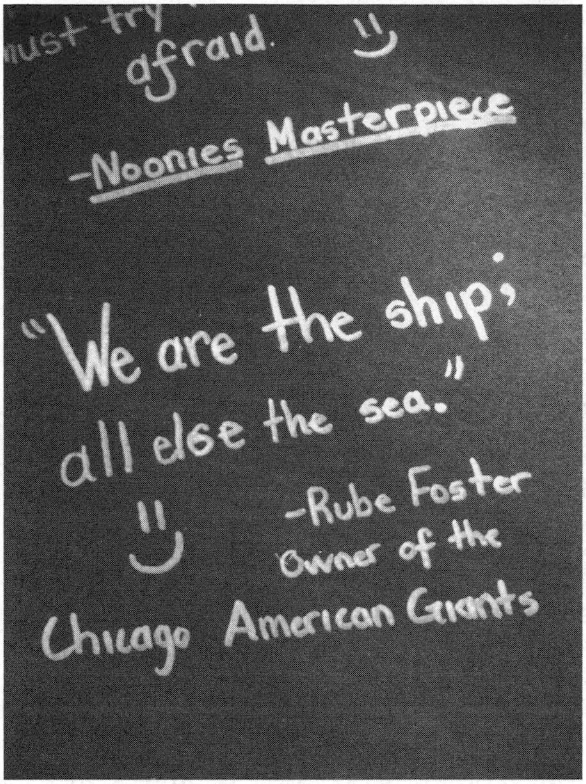

FIGURE 3.5: *Alicia's quote on the graffiti wall came from Kadir Nelson's* We Are the Ship.

commercials. Presenting book commercials requires little preparation on the part of teacher or students and mirrors how readers share books in the wild. Readers scrawl the book's title and author on the whiteboard, sit in my green chair, and share brief information about the book's content, offering suggestions about what kind of reader might enjoy the book next (figure 3.6). After a reader introduces a book, I immediately ask if anyone else in the class has read the same book and invite other readers to share their impressions.

When students finish their book commercials, they write the book title and author on an index card, and I add it to a running list displayed in our classroom. Students record any books that interest them on their Books to Read lists kept in their notebooks for this

FIGURE 3.6: *Travis presents a book commercial on John Boyne's* The Boy in the Striped Pajamas.

purpose. Students refer to this list when visiting the library, previewing books in the classroom, or discussing their reading plans with me during conferences. Book commercials value students' reading choices, tap into their expertise about these books, and provide an opportunity to influence other readers. They develop confidence in their book selections when promoting books to other readers, who increase their title awareness about books they might like to read.

## Reading Doors

Teachers often create classroom bulletin boards and door displays to celebrate the new school year and welcome students into their classrooms. Some personalize these displays with family photos or information about themselves, share what they did over the summer, or give students a sneak peek of upcoming projects or units of study. Our school community taps into these beginning-of-the-school-year displays by creating schoolwide reading doors. Our faculty and staff members, from our principal to counselor to librarian, and every classroom teacher, showcase the books, magazines, web pages, newspapers, or journals they like to read. For a reading door, copy book jackets and screenshots and create a collage of books. Then add photos of your staff members enjoying their favorites. Reading materials can tie back to content areas or personal interests like cooking, sports, and travel. My reading door included books I read during my summer book-a-day challenge, as well as the magazines, journals, and blogs I regularly read (figure 3.7). I added quotes about reading that I felt students would appreciate and enjoy, like Gary Paulsen's advice to young writers, "Read like a wolf eats."

Before we revealed our reading doors on Meet the Teacher Night, our first parent meeting at the beginning of the school year,

FIGURE 3.7: *My reading door.*

our faculty recognized the benefits these displays offered students. Students would see every teacher, not just the reading teacher, as a reader. Our doors highlighted our schoolwide focus on reading and kicked off a year of sharing and discussing texts in every class. Lining our hallways and offices with reading doors bestowed unanticipated benefits on our faculty, too. Conversations about reading sprang up between colleagues who never talked about reading with each other. One science teacher is a fossil hunter who subscribes to several publications that explores this interest. One of our physical education teachers mounted his daily copy of the *Wall Street Journal* to his door because he said, "I doubt some of our kids have seen or held a real newspaper." Our principal, Susan, divided her door into two sections, professional reading and personal reading, and added books to this display all year. At the end of the year, Susan remarked to me, "I have more books in my personal section than my professional section this year." I asked, "How do you feel about that?" She said, "I feel great. I rediscovered reading for pleasure. Before, I read only for work."

A few weeks into the school year, I turned my reading door over to my students. Working in groups of three or four, the kids selected a topic for their display, chose book titles, and pitched their idea to the class. Students voted for their favorite idea, and that design was added to our door for the next two weeks (figure 3.8). I did not assign this activity to all students, but I encouraged and supported any students who had reading door ideas to develop a plan. Often students polled their classmates for book suggestions after picking a topic for their door. In this way, most of my students contributed something to the overall project. This activity taught them about persuasive speaking, designing a plan and implementing it, and teamwork. Students evaluated texts based on self-selected criteria and considered their audience when choosing topics and titles.

If you cannot put paper displays on your classroom doors due to school or district restrictions, consider creating similar recommendation displays using digital picture frames in the library; posters in the halls, gym, or cafeteria; or recommendation sections on your class blog or website. Encourage staff members to share their

FIGURE 3.8:  *Katherine, Avery, and Rose's reading door.*

reading suggestions, too. Announce to students, families, and colleagues that your school community reads and supports each other's reading habits.

## Conferring Points

Susie and I understand that we are the most influential readers for our students at the beginning of the year because many of them lack confidence in selecting books for themselves and don't know much about books, authors, or resources that lead them to more reading material. This temporary dependence helps our inexperienced readers navigate the library or try out books they would otherwise overlook. But we recognize our students must learn how to select books for themselves and that this means forging reading relationships with other readers who support and encourage them.

## Epicenter Readers

The epicenter of an earthquake is the point on the Earth's surface directly above the explosion. Seismic waves radiate out from this central point, decreasing in intensity but transforming the landscape. We refer to epicenters in art and business, too, as a way of acknowledging the influence and innovation we can trace back to common sources, like Silicon Valley, as an epicenter of software design or Seattle as the epicenter of grunge music. Early in the year, I look for students who will be good epicenter readers—the ones who already know a lot about books and appear confident in selecting books to read.

When Katherine walked into my class on Meet the Teacher Night, she strolled immediately to the class library and began flipping through book bins while I talked with her mother. Wandering over to Katherine, I asked, "What sort of books do you like to read?" Smiling, Katherine rattled off an impressive list of books, stopping to ask me if I had read any of them. By identifying herself as a reader right away and questioning my reading experiences, Katherine was covertly determining whether I read much and had anything to offer her as a reading mentor. Leading Katherine to a stack of new books on my desk, I invited her to borrow as many as she wanted. When she walked out of my classroom with books to read before school started, she knew that I valued her as a reader and could recommend books and expand her reading life.

As the school year continued, I looked for ways to challenge Katherine. Getting her to read wasn't a problem, and she was open-minded about the books she chose—reading almost everything I recommended and discovering more books during library visits. But I noticed that Katherine didn't talk much with the other students about books and reading. Shy and quiet, she chatted with me about books every day, but she didn't offer recommendations or discuss books with her friends. When I asked Katherine why

she never volunteered her impressions about books to her classmates or gave recommendations, she confessed that she doubted
the other kids would like the same books she did.

We must identify the epicenter readers in our classrooms, support
their growth, and expand their influence. These wild readers can be
powerful reading peers for other students, serving as resources of
book information and models of wild reader reading habits.

When you think about the readers in your class, who would you
identify as epicenter readers or those who have the potential to
become epicenter readers? It is easy to overlook the needs of
students who already enjoy reading when they enter our classrooms. Relieved that these wild readers require little direction from
us, we are tempted to focus our attention on the students who
struggle with reading. But we must remember that all readers
deserve opportunities to grow. Katherine loved to read, but she
lacked confidence in her reading influence and didn't develop
reading relationships with her classmates. Without connecting to
other readers her own age, she saw herself as an outlier—someone
who needed to keep her reading life to herself or risk scorn from
the other kids. How can we help children like Katherine who
have the potential to become epicenter readers but don't share
what they know with other students?

Acknowledging our epicenter readers, continuing to feed their
development as wild readers, and fostering relationships between
them and other students requires some finesse on our part. You
don't want your students to think you prefer a few students over
others or primarily value the children in your class who already like
reading. Encourage epicenter readers to promote and share book
suggestions with other students through class blogs and book
commercials. Publicly value your epicenter readers by asking their
opinions about the books they read. Flooded with new books I can't
read fast enough, I invite classroom epicenter readers to read and
review books before adding them to the class library. These avid
readers enjoy the opportunity to read new books before anyone
else, and I value their expertise and insight into what knowledgeable readers their age like to read.

## My Personal Epicenter Readers

When I am looking for a specific book recommendation or targeted advice about books for an individual child in my classroom, I may seek out readers who possess expertise in the types of books I need, but there are a few individuals who provide me with wide-ranging recommendations and help me expand and deepen my knowledge about books and resources for my students and me. As I think about my reading life, I recognize my own epicenter readers—people who influence me through their extensive book knowledge, enthusiasm for reading, and willingness to share recommendations and resources. Considering the never-ending list of librarians, teachers, and friends who influence my book choices, I identify two epicenter readers who provide a starting point for teachers who want to stay on the leading edge of book releases, online and print resources, and ongoing conversations about children's literature and reading.

**John Schumacher (aka Mr. Schu)**
**Blog: Watch. Connect. Read. http://mrschureads.blogspot.com /@mrschureads**

John Schumacher is the school library director at Brook Forest Elementary School in Oak Brook, Illinois. Named one of *Library Journal*'s 2011 Movers and Shakers, John is also a member of the 2014 Newbery Award selection committee. In 2011, he set an ambitious goal: to read 2,011 books. He read 2,090. John shares book trailers, author interviews, behind-the-scenes information, website links, tips for engaging students with reading, and thorough book recommendations and book lists through his prolific blog posts, tweets, Goodreads reviews, and Pinterest pins. If John recommends a book, I buy it. If I already own the book, I read it next.

**Dr. Teri Lesesne (aka Professor Nana)**
**Blog: The Goddess of YA Literature: Pearls from the Goddess.**
**http://professornana.livejournal.com/@professornana**

Teri Lesesne is professor in the Department of Library Science at Sam Houston State University, in Huntsville, Texas, where she teaches classes in literature for children and young adults. Teri has served on numerous book award committees, including the 2010 Printz Award Committee, the Odyssey Audiobook Awards, and ALAN's Amelia Elizabeth Walden Committee. An advocate for adolescent readers and young adult literature, Teri writes widely about adolescents' rights to engaging and relevant reading experiences. Through her books, frequent blog posts, professional development presentations, book reviews, and book lists and tweets, Teri stretches my thinking about young readers and challenges me to investigate books and formats I might not discover without her endorsement, including audiobooks, graphic novels, and titles for lesbian gay, bisexual, and transgender teens.

• • •

If I had to start over rebuilding my Twitter friends' list, Goodreads account, or blog feed, Teri and John would lead me back to hundreds of reading colleagues in less than a month. Savvy about books and publishing trends and generous with their resources and time, they feed a vibrant reading community online and influence many children through their teachers, librarians, and parents. You don't need a contact list full of names to find a reading community. All you need is one person who shares your love for books.

## Reading Influences

Understanding the importance of students' relationships with other readers to sustain and support their reading lives, Susie and I asked our students to consider the readers who influence them and provide them support. We also wondered how students

## Students' Reading Influence Responses

"I give book recommendations to my little sister all of the time. I recommended *Firegirl* to her."—Allison, fifth grader

"Matt loaned me his copy of *Killer Pizza* because the class copy was checked out!"—Nico, sixth grader

"Grace and I talked about *The Knife of Never Letting Go*, along with many others who read it, too."—Emma, sixth grader

"Adam and I are always talking about the best books that we've read."—Reed, sixth grader

"I talk to my mom sometimes about my book if I think it is really good."—Brian, sixth grader

"I rate books and post comments sometimes on Goodreads."—Christina, sixth grader

"I gave a book commercial on *Harry Potter and the Order of the Phoenix* to the class."—Winter, fifth grader

saw themselves as influential readers, a role that demands a level of confidence and self-efficacy as readers. Those who feel connected to other readers are more likely to remain invested readers after leaving our classroom reading communities.

Ideally, students name a mix of family members and friends. It is okay if students list teachers and librarians, too, but we shouldn't be the only readers children can turn to for book discussions or recommendations.

Students who influence other readers and develop reading relationships with them feel empowered and knowledgeable. Our students identified various ways they interacted with other readers by recommending, discussing, and promoting books, such as taking and giving book recommendations, loaning and borrowing books, discussing books, presenting book commercials, writing reviews, and posting comments to online sites.

Inviting students to consider the important role other readers play in their reading lives, we asked them to examine how other readers influence them and how they in turn influence other readers. Students recorded these reflections on a Reading Influences form (figure 3.9). You can find a blank copy in appendix B. Christina credits her dad for encouraging her to read from an early age. "My dad read to me when I was little and brought me to the library a lot." Now Christina encourages her dad to read "more fictional books" and recommends books to her cousin. Reed, an epicenter reader in my third-period class, declares that he influences "everyone I meet." It isn't far from the truth.

**My Reading Influences**

Reader ___Reed___

Think about the other readers that you know and how you share books. Answer the following reflection questions about your reading influences.

List readers that you know who talk to you on a regular basis about books and reading.

Adam                              A.J.

Mrs. Miller                       Brandon

Marina                            Blake

Think about how you share books and reading with other readers. Provide an example for each one that applies to you.

**Take book recommendations**

Adam reccomended the City of Bones to me & now I'm hooked.

**Give book recommendations**

I recommended The Kife of Never Letting Go to Brandon & he hooked too.

**Loan your personal books**

I loaned my copy of Monsters of Men to Adam.

**Borrow another reader's personal books**

I borrowed Jesah's personal copy of City of Glass

**Talk to other readers about what you are reading**

Me Adam & I are always talking about the best books that we've read.

FIGURE 3.9: *Reed's reading influences reflection reveals his confidence and wide reading community.*

**Book Commercials**

In book club, I gave a book commercial about The Book Thief.

**Write book reviews**

I wrote a book review on Drums, Girls, + Dangerous Pie.

**Post comments to online sites**

I comment on Goodreads.com about books daily.

**How have the other readers you know influenced your reading?**

Yes. Adam

**How have you influenced other readers?**

Yes. Everyone I meet.

**Is it important for you to have other readers to talk to about books and reading? Explain why or why not.**

Yes because that's the second best thing about reading.

FIGURE 3.9  *(Continued)*

Bryan admits, "My friend, Joseph, made me start reading. Every time he added a book to Goodreads, I read it and talked to him about it." Marina considers her reading friends the best source of book recommendations: "My friends almost always have great taste about books, and if they love the book, I almost always love it too, or at least I am glad I read it."

Our students' responses reveal the power that reading communities have to increase their reading motivation and engagement.

Surrounded by peers who enjoy reading and books, students accept the social expectation that reading is something we do. Reading weaves through our culture. During our reflection conversations, students stressed the importance of their relationships with other readers. "I know that I am not reading the book alone and I have people to talk to," Riley said. "[Talking with other readers] is important to me," Marina proclaimed. "Plus, I enjoy talking about books!" Matt asked, "What's the point of reading if you can't share it?"

## Keeping Track of Your Reading Life

Unlike other wild reading habits explored throughout this book, the reading notebook tools we use don't link directly to our students' participation in reading communities. Instead, the entire notebook feeds students' conversations about books and reading. Susie and I see students refer to their notebooks often when discussing books and reading experiences with their classmates. Reading lists provide students with a common format for sharing and comparing their reading experiences. Students swap reading lists during classroom discussions and activities, exchange book recommendations, and chat about the books they've read or plan to read. Accepting recommendations from reading peers broadens students' knowledge about books and forges relationships between students who read the same titles.

Considering our students' wild reading lives, we understand that few of them will keep detailed records about every book they read after leaving our classrooms. These tools scaffold and support our students, providing information that aids their reflection and planning, but our reader's notebook forms are temporary school-based tools. Moving students from dependent classroom readers to wild independent readers necessitates conversations about why some readers document their reading lives and how they do it. Throughout the school year, I introduce my students to the same online resources I use to keep track of my own reading life such as Goodreads. These online reading communities provide students accessible ways to remain connected whether they wind up in the same school or English class the following year.

• • •

I hope my students continue supporting each other in all the ways they can—as readers and members of a caring community. Reading seems like something we do alone, but it isn't. Every book begins and ends with other people—the readers who suggest the book to us and encourage us to read it, the talented author who crafted each word, the fascinating individuals we meet inside the pages—and the readers we discuss and share the book with when we finish. Children's author C. Alexander London (2011) writes, "It's a fact: people can survive without books. People can even have wonderful, full lives without books. But they can't long endure without community, and a community is built on stories." Our classroom year includes countless stories both on and off the page. Every book we read and share connects us to each other. That's the best part of our story—the part that lasts long after the book ends.

# Conferring: What's the Point?

WHEN I BEGAN implementing reading and writing workshop in my classroom, I knew that I was supposed to confer with my students on a regular basis about their independent reading and writing. Conferences, one-on-one meetings with students to assist them with their individual needs, are an important teaching opportunity and a meaningful way to connect with children about their individual goals.

I didn't understand what I was meant to accomplish during conferences, though. What would my students and I talk about? How would I meet on a regular basis with thirty or more students in every class? While I recognized the value of talking with every student about their reading and writing, I couldn't manage it. So I created elaborate checklists of conference questions and wandered around my classroom talking to my kids: "Hi, Enrique, you're still reading *Chasing Lincoln's Killer*? I hope you are enjoying it." Check a box next to Enrique's name on the checklist. Conference done. Make eye contact with Avery as I walk past her desk. She is happily reading *Uglies*. Check a box next to Avery's name. Conference done. Then Chris asks for help finding a book to read, and I spend the next ten minutes digging in the shelves as we discuss what he is looking for in a book. My conference goal for the day—meet with at least six kids—grinds to a screeching halt. I wasn't conferring with my students; I was a box checker, a slave to my checklist and what someone else told me I should be doing with my kids. It was dreadful.

Every Friday I looked at my scant conference records for the week and the blank spots alongside too many children's names and swore I would do a better job next week. For several years, I ditched conferences altogether and spent my time wandering around helping children here and there with whatever they needed at the time. I considered it progress if I stopped conferring with my students later in the school year than I had stopped the previous year.

Formal conferences were too difficult to manage in my classroom. I had too many kids, not enough time, and didn't know what to do during the conferences anyway other than chat with my students about their books and check to make sure they were reading something.

At times like these, I do what I have always done: step back and look at my goals. What did I really want to know about my students' reading? What did I really hope to accomplish during reading conferences? How could I make conferences meaningful for my students and me?

As I reflected on my beliefs, what stood out for me was the importance of building relationships with my students as readers, writers, and people. In large classes with a block schedule, it is challenging to connect with every student. I have students labeled at-risk. I know who they are, and I meet with my teaching partners and their parents. I work with these students in flexible groups and tutoring. I check in with them daily and provide extra support. I also have students with strong personalities—the kids who raise their hands every time I ask a question and attempt to dominate class work and discussions. I know who these kids are, too. Then there is everyone else: the children who come into my classroom, do their work, and don't need much extra support but rarely raise their hands during class discussions or put themselves into leadership roles. These children disappear in my classroom if I don't make an effort to build relationships with them.

*Conferring with Ashley G.*

Conferring with every student helps me forge relationships with each one. I decided that this was the primary goal of conferring for me: to make sure that I spoke to every child as often as possible and that no one disappeared. Eye contact across the classroom wasn't enough. Once I decided that fostering relationships was the most important outcome for conferring with my students, I found clarity of purpose.

Next, I had to critically consider my teaching style. I am a talker. I love to talk about books and engage with my students about their reading. It occurred to me that discussing Chris's reading plans and working with him to find books to read not only fed our reader-to-reader relationship but also moved Chris along as a reader. Why didn't I consider this a conference? Perhaps I had been conferring with my students in a casual way all along, but I didn't label these conversations as conferring events because they didn't fit into my prescribed notions of what a conference was. Talking one-on-one with children, guiding them as readers, and helping them move forward in their understanding seemed a lot like a conference when I stepped back and thought about it.

Reflecting on what I was already doing and accepting the value of these conversations with my students, I could make these discussions more intentional. While talking to the children, I began to see what was really happening during these conversations: I was guiding them, valuing them, and offering support on a child-by-child basis. These conversations were not a waste of time or a distraction that eroded my conference goals. Accepting what I was already doing that worked, albeit inadvertently, helped me focus my attention where I needed to improve.

## The Golden Gate Bridge Conference Method

My friend Jim who lives in San Francisco told me that maintenance workers continuously paint the Golden Gate Bridge. Workers paint as well as they can as far as they can every day, accepting any conditions that affect their progress such as the fog, which limits the number of hours in a day they can paint. When they are done painting in one area, they start on another. The crew never really finishes the job; they just continue.

Managing reading conferences in my classroom, I embrace the same process. I confer with as many of my students each day as I can, as well as I can, until I have engaged in a meaningful conference with every one of my students; then I start over. Some days I manage to confer with five kids. Such days are rare. Other days, I meet with one child for the entire time. My role during a conference is responding to a child's needs and providing support. Some students require more support than others on any given day. No matter how many students I confer with daily, I accept that every child got what he or she needed from me and I learned more about that child through the conversation. No more box checking.

## Conference Record Keeping

Reflecting on my workshop management practices, I saw that one deficit was the lack of consistent record keeping during conferences and goal setting with my students. Off-the-cuff conversations as I walked around the room provided inconsistent support and didn't give me evidence of students' growth over the long term. I marvel at colleagues who keep organized binders on every class with a labeled section for each child. I know that I would set up these binders and start cramming papers into them by October. I tried to keep conference cards on every child, but after dropping index cards all over my floor every class period for a week, I decided that didn't work for me either. My classroom is clean and organized because I believe in less paper, not more. I prefer to use record-keeping systems that are easy for me to maintain and implement after I design them. I am not spending an hour after school every day filing. I know this about myself.

Accepting my limitations and my need for simple systems that I can maintain, I have cobbled together a record-keeping system that works for me. I keep a file folder for every student in my file cabinet. I store work samples, parent contact notes, copies of progress reports, benchmark testing data, and conference records in these files. When I meet with my teaching partners, administrators, and parents or need to prepare forms for progress monitoring or testing referrals, I have everything I need. I imagine many teachers keep similar files.

As for managing my conference records, I copy my conference forms and keep them on colored clipboards. When I set out to confer with students, I grab a clipboard and record notes while the student and I talk.

I use my phone to record conferences into Evernote or Dragon Dictation. Recording conferences has been invaluable for me as a reflection tool because I can listen to my conversations with my students. I can determine areas for self-improvement and goal setting for each reader and evaluate my actions and language during the conference. My school colleagues prefer a mix of computer-based and paper record keeping. My friend Kim prints off package labels with each student's name printed on each label. She scrawls anecdotal notes on the labels, and then sticks the label inside every student's file folder. The labels give her a complete record of her conversations with her students, and she can quickly tell whom she still needs to meet with because she still has that child's blank label on the roll.

The system of record keeping you use doesn't matter. What matters is that you have a record-keeping system for keeping track of your conversations with students and you maintain it all year. Select one that acknowledges your teaching and management style and stick with it.

I am pleased with a management plan that fits my real-life needs and focused, stripped-down goals: building relationships with my students and moving each one forward as readers. Conferring with my students is finally meaningful and manageable.

# CHAPTER 4

# Wild Readers Have Reading Plans

*I was born with a reading list I will never finish.*

—Maud Casey

PREPARING FOR A conference trip, I begin packing my suitcase. After piling shoes and toiletries onto my bed, I rifle through my bookcase, deciding which books to take with me. I select Eliot Schrefer's *Endangered* for my outgoing flight. Since it was shortlisted for the National Book Award, I have been eager to read it. I add *Flying the Dragon* by Natalie Lorenzi for the return trip. After a few minutes, I have five books set aside. Don laughs when he sees my book pile: "I thought you were only going to be gone for two days! How many books do you think you can read?"

Unable to predict how a trip out of town will unfold, I always take more books than I need. Delayed flights, airport waits, bad hotel TV: traveling offers me abundant reading opportunities, but I must plan ahead. My Kindle broke during a ten-day trip last year, so I don't take it with me anymore. I can't take a chance that I will run out of books to read. I have been stuck reading *American Way* and *Sky Mall* magazines more than once. Besides, a few books keep me company while I am traveling and provide one of the comforts I associate with home—a delicious stack of unread books.

Working to encourage my students to read both in and outside school, I notice that many disengaged readers haven't picked up this lifelong reading habit—planning for future reading. We wild readers talk about the books we are currently reading or just finished, but we also speculate on the books we plan to read next. The anticipation of another great reading experience drives our continued enthusiasm and interest in reading. If the last book we finished was less than stellar, that's okay. There's always the next one. Even if we drop out of our daily reading habit for a period of time—all wild readers experience ebbs and flows in our reading lives—it doesn't occur to us that we will never pick up another book.

The difference between readers and nonreaders is that readers have plans (Kittle, 2012). For children, setting reading goals and reflecting on progress toward these goals increases their self-efficacy as students (Schunk, 2003). Planning for future reading provides students with direction and purpose, reinforcing that they are readers today and will still be readers tomorrow.

## *Another Day, Another Book*

How do our Wild Reader Survey participants plan for future reading? How can their habits inform our work with students? We wild readers look ahead to that next book, accessing various sources to find out about books we might like to read and help us plan what we will read next (I shared sources for finding books in chapter 2), although as one participant said, "I don't always actually read the books I preplan to read!"

While a small number admit that they depend on serendipity to lead them to books, most of our respondents plan ahead. Wild readers:

- *Keep to-read stacks of books.* Piled on nightstands and desks (or the floor), crammed on bookcases, downloaded to e-readers, wild readers keep an endless supply of reading material on hand for future reading. Wild readers who devour book after book crave continuous book access. One reader said, "I have always had a stack of books that I keep all year and devour during my summer break. When I hear of a good book I buy it and put it in my stack."

- *Keep a to-read list.* Wild readers maintain to-read lists using both online and offline methods they access when purchasing books or browsing the library. I keep my to-read list on Goodreads, but other wild readers pin covers on Pinterest, jot titles in a journal, or create wish lists on Amazon.

- *Reserve books at the library.* Wild readers request books from public libraries and access services such as interlibrary loans in order to find the books they want to read. Holding a spot on the reserve list for several books guarantees a steady flow of books.

- *Preorder new releases, books in a series, or books from favorite authors.* In order to stay abreast of the newest books, many wild readers order books in advance of their release dates—reading plans that can stretch a year into the future. Keeping up with an ongoing series or books from a beloved author provides wild readers with tried-and-true reading material based on books they already read and enjoyed.

- *Make use of book award lists.* Announcements of major book award finalists and winners spur sales for a reason. Those award seals and lists influence discriminating readers who seek well-regarded, high-quality reading books. For many wild readers, award lists guide them to worthy books they might otherwise have missed. Reading every title on an award list gives wild readers a focused plan for remaining current on noteworthy books.

The wild reading behaviors we explored in previous chapters help readers build lifelong reading habits, but making short-term and long-term reading plans helps them sustain and expand their reading lives. One reader offers this caution: "Knowing what book to read next would keep me reading, I'm excited every time I do read and especially finish a book of my own choice, it feels good. But if I don't have another one to start, or the next one I start isn't good, then I usually take a long break from reading."

In addition to planning for future reading—intentionally considering when and what they will read next—wild readers also consider their reading experiences and habits—identifying areas they would like to improve or enrich. They set personal goals like reading a certain number of pages each day or declare intentions to read everything written by an author, say, Charles Dickens. While some reading plans include the goals of our reading communities—think of book clubs that agree to read the same book every month—wild readers primarily make reading plans that suit their own tastes and needs. This individual cycle of reflection, goal setting, and action supports each reader's self-determination and ownership for reading. When working with students, we must provide opportunities for them to reflect on their reading experiences, identify personal reading goals, and implement plans for achieving these goals. School-based reading measures often impose external reading goals on students: required reading assignments, fluency targets, reading logs, reaching specific reading levels, and standardized reading tests. How do students develop ownership for reading when they are never given ownership? Who are students reading for?

For students who enjoy reading, maintaining their own reading goals can seem impossible in the face of an onslaught of school reading requirements that drain their available reading time, limit reading choices, and disregard their interests. Students who haven't developed their own goals for reading may ask, "What's the point?" You don't need a reading plan when someone else has one for you. We must consider whether school and classroom reading initiatives and assignments support students' development of wild reading habits or hinder them. Students must learn how to make their own reading plans, reflect on their individual accomplishments, and find personal reasons for reading or they will never become wild readers.

## Community Conversations

This week, my students and I conducted one of our favorite classroom rituals—planning for reading over an upcoming school break. We will be out for two weeks over Christmas, and my students know that I expect them to continue reading. We discussed and made reading plans before the recent Thanksgiving break, so the children dove into the task this time—swapping books, carrying out piles, and recording titles in their reader's notebooks. At this stage of the year, I don't need to reiterate my expectations: students eagerly look forward to the extra reading time available during vacation and prepare for it.

Katherine begged me to lift our classroom library four-book checkout limit because she "needs at least ten books." She didn't have to beg much. Blake promised Kamron he would finish *The Scorch Trials*, the sequel to James Dashner's harrowing dystopian mystery, *The Maze Runner*, so that Kamron could take it over the break. Kamron checked out the final book in the trilogy, *The Death Cure*, just in case. During our weekly library visit, my students swarmed the book carts, eager to grab the hot titles before our librarian reshelved them.

Dashing from child to child—making recommendations, loaning book bags, and digging into closets for extra copies of Michael Buckley's *NERDS*, *The Hunger Games* by Suzanne Collins, and Laurie Halse Anderson's *Chains*—I overheard conversations between my students that made me smile:

> "Ben, you should take all three books in the Boy at War series. You would hate to finish one and not have the next."

> "Can I please borrow your copy of *The Knife of Never Letting Go*?"

> "I asked my mom for books for Christmas. She looked surprised."

> "How many books do you think I'll need? We are driving to Colorado to see my grandmother, and we will be in the car forever."

In the days leading up to school breaks, students' excitement creates a distracting classroom environment. Excited about trips to visit relatives or looking forward to days spent sleeping late and lounging, students find it difficult to concentrate on school work. Recognizing my students' need to share their holiday plans, I set aside a few minutes for discussing our upcoming vacations. While students share, I encourage them to consider when they will read. These conversations offer insight into their reading habits. We chat about who can read in the car and who gets carsick. We describe our experiences reading in airports. Jacob details his plan to stay up all night reading. Maddie sparks a laughing fit among her classmates when she reveals that she uses reading as an "excuse" to escape her "annoying" toddler-age cousins. During reading conferences, I ensure that everyone checks out books for the break.

After considering our holiday schedules and choosing books, my students and I record our reading plans in our notebooks—setting goals and sharing them with each other. Writing down these plans and verbalizing them to each other makes these plans concrete and real for my students. Reading isn't something we *might* do during the holidays; we have reading *plans.*

When students return from the break, we talk and write about our vacations—celebrating the big events and small moments we want to remember. Students also reflect on the reading plans they made before the break and write a reflection about whether they met their reading goals or didn't. These written reflections hold students accountable for following through on their reading plans and provide useful information about students' reading habits and experiences (figure 4.1).

Examining Enrique's Thanksgiving break reading reflection, it's clear he did not enjoy the two books he read. In our conference, he admitted that he chose *Eighth Grade Bites,* the first book in the Chronicles of Vladimir Tod series by Heather Brewer, because a friend recommended the book and the vampire storyline intrigued him. His second reading choice, *Alfred Kropp: The Thirteenth Skull* by Rick Yancey, disappointed him, too. Enrique wrote an additional page about why he didn't like it! Invested in the previous Alfred Kropp books, Enrique expressed satisfaction about completing the trilogy, even though he felt the series ended abruptly. Talking together, Enrique and I celebrated his accomplishments: he read during the holiday break, he branched out and tried something new (vampire books), and he finished a series he started. Enrique noticed that he wrote his longest reading response entry of the year about books he disliked, admitting that it was easier to identify the reasons a book didn't work for him than determine why one did.

Using his written reflection as a planning tool, Enrique and I agreed that he should work to identify what he likes about the books he enjoys. Heightening awareness about his preferences would help

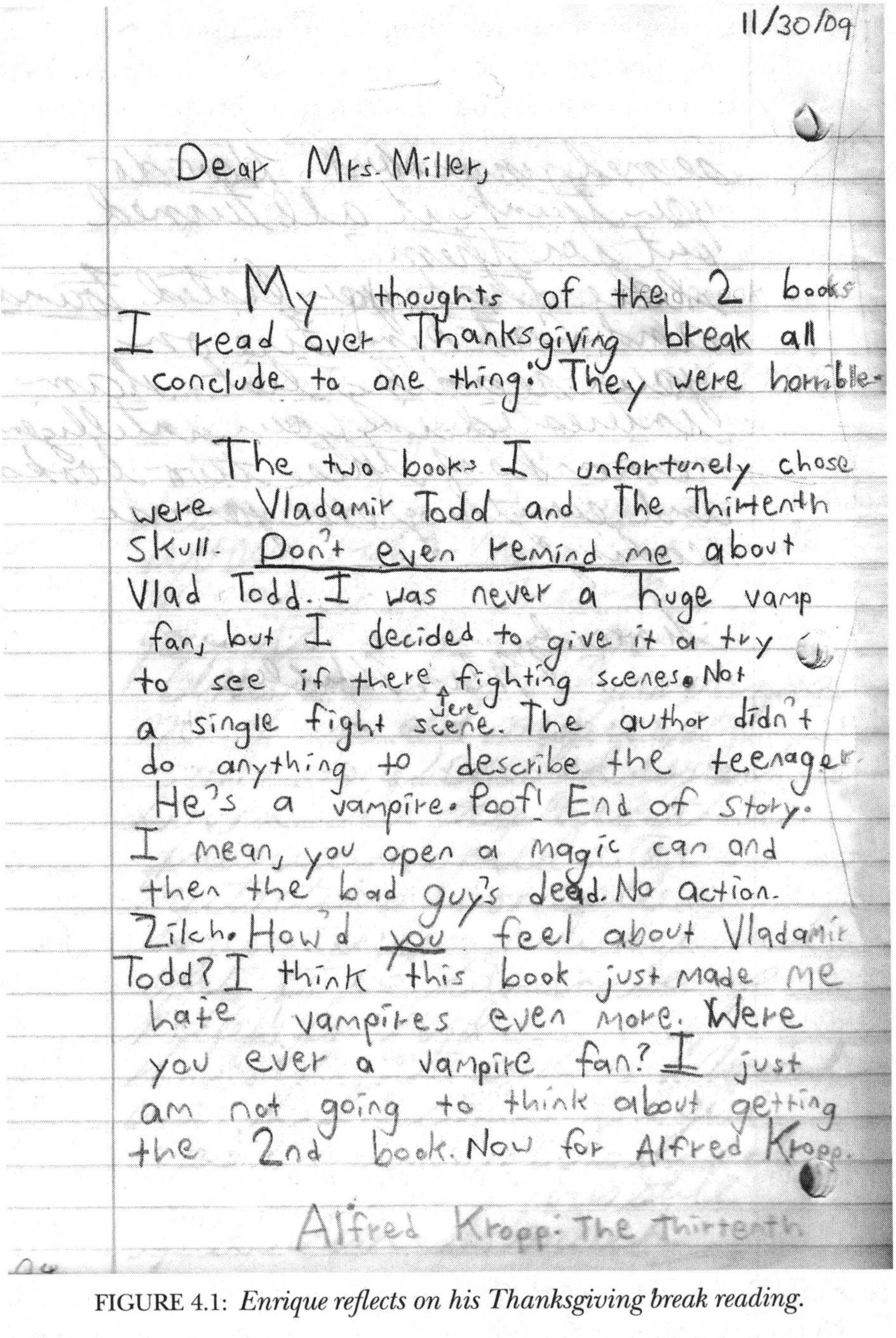

11/30/09

Dear Mrs. Miller,

My thoughts of the 2 books I read over Thanksgiving break all conclude to one thing: They were horrible.

The two books I unfortunely chose were Vladamir Todd and The Thirteenth Skull. Don't even remind me about Vlad Todd. I was never a huge vamp fan, but I decided to give it a try to see if there fighting scenes. Not a single fight scene. The author didn't do anything to describe the teenager. He's a vampire. Poof! End of story. I mean, you open a magic can and then the bad guy's dead. No action. Zilch. How'd you feel about Vladamir Todd? I think this book just made me hate vampires even more. Were you ever a vampire fan? I just am not going to think about getting the 2nd book. Now for Alfred Kropp.

Alfred Kropp: The Thirteenth

FIGURE 4.1: *Enrique reflects on his Thanksgiving break reading.*

Enrique make better book choices and increase his reading engagement.

## Types of Reading Plans

While readers set both long-term and short-term reading goals, we can categorize reading plans into two types: commitment plans that build a strong foundation of reading habits and challenge plans that expand our reading horizons. Wild readers need both to maintain their reading behaviors and continue growing.

### Commitment Plans

Wild reading requires commitment. As John Lennon said, "Life is what happens when you are making other plans." Without conscious effort and planning, wild readers could easily fall out of daily reading habits. Our students must commit to reading and plan actions that address obstacles they might come up against. Without this personal commitment to reading, students remain dependent on outside forces that temporarily drive their reading habits such as classroom expectations for reading. When we remove these drivers, students who lack internal motivation for reading may stop reading.

#### Finding Reading Time Every Day

Students who read on an inconsistent basis never develop an attachment for reading. Those who read only at school remain vulnerable if they don't invest in reading at home. As I mentioned in chapter 1, students must dedicate time for reading and commit to reading as much as possible outside school. Helping students evaluate their schedules, identify opportunities, commit to reading, and reflect on their success of this reading plan provides them with feedback they need to become invested readers.

When students make a commitment to reading every day, they report improved reading ability and engagement with reading. Encourage your students to reflect on how their reading has improved over time, and reinforce to them that all of their other reading goals depend on this regular commitment.

## Increasing Book Completion

For students struggling to finish books or commit to reading, setting small goals helps them achieve success quickly and rack up positive reading experiences, which feed more reading. Recommend high-interest short story collections such as David Lubar's Weenie books or Jon Scieszka's Guys Read series. Reading short stories provides students with the satisfaction of completing a story in less time and builds stamina. Offer shorter books, like Patricia McLachlan's *Sarah, Plain and Tall*, Gary Paulsen's *Lawn Boy*, or Jacqueline Woodson's *Locomotion*, which require less time investment from developing readers while introducing them to prolific authors they can read. When students select longer books, check in often to determine progress and offer positive reinforcement for completing chapters or meeting page goals.

## Looking at Specific Titles, Authors, Genres, and Series

If students are having trouble thinking of what books to read next, give them some questions to ask themselves that might spark ideas (see the Conferring Points section later in this chapter):

- What books have you been reading?

- What books have caught your attention that you might like to read next?

- What are you looking for in your next book? Are you in a reading rut?

- How can you challenge yourself with your next book?

Setting aside titles they want to read, looking back over their reading experiences, and planning to move forward, my students continue to develop their reading lives.

# Challenge Plans

Wild readers need opportunities to expand their knowledge and stretch. Driven by personal desires and the ongoing need to keep reading interesting, wild readers look back on their reading lives, consider their accomplishments, and look for ways to add challenge. When you already read a lot, how do you keep reading engaging and fresh? What do you read? How do wild readers keep growing? Setting ambitious goals offers wild readers individual challenges that value where they've been and where they would like to go. Reading challenges allow them to fantasize about their wildest reading dreams, fill in gaps in their reading repertoire, and push themselves.

Reading challenges are not competitions between readers or groups of readers. While many wild readers may set similar challenges, each reader is unique. Reading challenges must allow wild readers as much autonomy and free will as possible. Already invested in reading, wild readers want opportunities to choose their own goals unencumbered by others' expectations or limits.

When working with students who love reading and possess lifelong reading habits, teachers can find it difficult to provide sufficient rigor. Teaching students how to develop their own reading challenges reinforces the importance of reading for their own purposes and encourages these students to read widely, identify areas for growth, and push themselves toward the edge of their reading capabilities. Giving free rein to read and guidance from a more knowledgeable reader, how far can a wild reader go?

## The Nerdbery Challenge

Bestowed annually by the American Library Association, the Newbery Medal Awards (Newbery Medal and Honor Books located at http://www.ala.org/alsc/awardsgrants/bookmedia/newberymedal /newberyhonors/newberymedal) recognize "the most distinguished contribution to American literature for children." In January 2012, children's literature gurus John Schumacher and Colby Sharp announced their commitment to read every Newbery Medalist in order, beginning with 1922's winner, *The Story of Mankind* by Hendrik Willem van Loon. Dubbed the "Nerdbery Challenge," Colby and John blog weekly about each award-winning book and share their experiences as they work through this ambitious reading plan (John's blog: http://mrschureads.blogspot.com/; Colby's blog:

http://sharpread.wordpress.com/). Always up for a new reading plan, I decided to join Colby and John in the Nerdbery Challenge. I had read many of the Newbery winners over the years—first as a fourth grader looking for good books to read and again as a new teacher—but I knew that I had avoided or missed many of these notable titles. I researched the Newbery Award lists, jotted down the titles I still needed to read (figure 4.2), and downloaded *The Story of Mankind* and 1923's winner, *The Voyages of Doctor Doolittle* by Hugh Lofting, to my Kindle.

After winter break, I gave my students a little background about the Newbery Award, shared my Nerdbery list, and announced my reading plan: "This year, I am going to join my friends Mr. Sharp and Mr. Schu on their reading challenge to read all of the Newbery Medal winners." Christina scrutinized my list: "You've never read *Shiloh*, Mrs. Miller? I read that in fourth grade!"

Jonah laughed, "Haven't you read everything by now?"

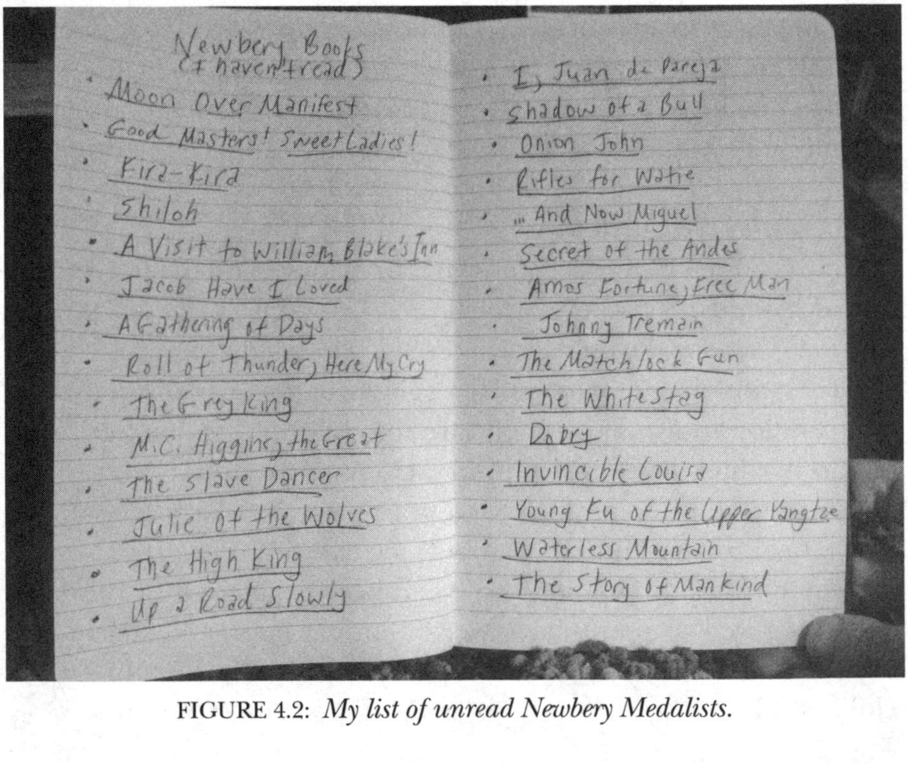

FIGURE 4.2: *My list of unread Newbery Medalists.*

I explained, "No matter how much I read, I still have books I missed or skipped and personal reading plans. Setting personal reading challenges keeps reading interesting and stretches me as a reader. How many of you have skipped books other readers know?"

"I never read *Shiloh*, either!" Nico shouted.

Christina walks over to the class library, grabs two copies of Phyllis Reynolds Naylor's classic dog story, dumps one on Nico's desk, and presents the second copy to me. My students and I talk about personal book challenges. Announcing my reading plans helped my students see that all wild readers continuously seek ways to expand our reading lives. When my students and I make reading plans, we reinforce our ownership and dedication to reading. We grow stronger as readers and continue to keep reading challenging and interesting.

Intrigued by the Nerdbery Challenge, my sixth-grade students admitted they had read few of the Newbery Medal winners. While lauded titles like Louis Sachar's *Holes* and Lois Lowry's *Number the Stars* and *The Giver* remain popular, my students express avoidance or ignorance of outstanding books like Jerry Spinelli's *Maniac Magee*. Recognizing students' fresh enthusiasm, I collected as many Newbery winners as possible and invited my students to participate in their own Newbery Challenges. Every student selected three Newbery winners and set personal time lines for reading and evaluating each book. Students critiqued two of their Newbery Medal choices, posting their reviews to our class blog.

As a culminating activity, students described both their positive and negative experiences during the project. Many admitted to discovering new books they might have missed. Even students who disliked the books they selected gained insight into their reading tastes and broadened their reading experiences.

*The Story of Mankind* dampened my enthusiasm for the Nerdbery Challenge. I can't imagine offering my students history texts that express such narrow, prejudiced perspectives today. After reading several didactic, dry books in a row, I quit the Nerdbery Challenge before I made it to the 1930s. Because of Christina's persistence, I did read *Shiloh*. I confessed my failure to my students, and we discussed why reading plans fail: we aren't personally motivated, we set unreasonable goals, or we need different ones. I encourage students to reflect on their progress toward achieving their reading plans often and consider whether their goals still meet their personal abilities, needs, and interests. We learn as much from the plans that don't work. What matters most is moving forward as readers, determined to improve and grow.

Deconstructing our reading plans for students reveals that all wild readers set personal goals that expand and enrich our reading lives. Through these frank conversations about our own reading successes and shortcomings, we reduce students' stress about their perceived reading deficits and help them design attainable, individualized reading plans.

### Book-a-Day Challenge

Overwhelmed by my staggering pile of unread books and excited about the chance to read over summer vacation, I launched the book-a-day challenge on my *Book Whisperer* blog in 2009. The challenge is simple: read one book for every day of your summer vacation. When I began the challenge, announcing my insane goal online was a way to hold myself accountable. Over the years, a thriving book-a-day community grew and participants post and share book titles all year long on Twitter using the #bookaday hashtag and posting reviews through Goodreads and blogs. Book-a-day is a great way to meet other wild readers, discover books, and stretch yourself to read more.

The guidelines for the book-a-day challenge are simple:

- Read one book per day for each day of vacation. This is an average, so if you read three books in one day (I have done this!) and none the next two, it counts.

- Set your personal start date and end date.

- Any book qualifies: picture books, nonfiction, professional books, poetry anthologies, graphic novels, or fiction—youth and adult titles. A participant last year decided to read one professional journal each day of her break. Whatever reading you want to accomplish fits into your personal book-a-day plan.

- Participants keep a list of the books they read and share them over social networking sites like Goodreads or Shelfari, a blog, Facebook page, or Twitter feed. You do not have to post reviews, but you can if you wish. Titles will suffice.

Sharing my plan to participate in book-a-day with my outgoing students encourages many of them to read over the summer, too. The end of a school year doesn't mean our reading lives go on hold until September. Each fall, I walk into my classroom with bags of new books and a summer of reading moments to share with my new students. For both groups—the students who leave me and the students who arrive—book-a-day sends one more message that I don't ask them to read when I don't, and reminds them that reading is a worthwhile leisure activity.

## Book Gap Challenge

I never finished *Huckleberry Finn* or *Moby-Dick*. I would rather read *Pride and Prejudice* for the fifth time. No one who reads should apologize for their preferences and reading experiences, but we wild readers aspire to stretch ourselves or fill perceived deficits in our reading lives. Chatting with my reading friends, we admit our reading gaps—the books we avoid or titles we haven't read in spite of popularity or acclaim. Even the most avid, open-minded readers confess to skipping award winners, avoiding certain genres, or postponing books for so long they remain unread.

My book gap is clear from my groaning bookshelves: I have series commitment issues. A devout fantasy and science-fiction fan, I can't keep up with the endless tide of sequels. *Bitterblue, Insurgent, Flesh and Bone*, and *The Mark of Athena* glare at me from the closest bookcase. I started *Froi of the Exiles*, the second book in Marlena Marchetta's Lumatere Chronicles, four months ago. It sits in limbo on my nightstand—never finished and never abandoned. Maggie Stiefvater's *Forever* held a similar spot last year. I read her new (thankfully stand-alone) book, *The Scorpio Races*, THREE times, but it took me six months to finish the Mercy Falls trilogy. Instead of finishing series, I endlessly start new ones. I read *The Raven Boys, The Diviners,* and *Shadow and Bone*—all three launch new fantasy series. This year, I resolve to read more sequels and commit to finishing story arcs that I started.

What are your book gaps? Open conversations with your students about the books you avoid, always wanted to read, or didn't finish. Whether you shy away from science fiction, never read Walt Whitman's *Leaves of Grass,* or still haven't read that Abraham Lincoln biography you bought last summer, we all have personal reading challenges. Share why filling your book gap matters to you, and encourage students to consider their own gaps.

In a classroom where everyone reads, talks about books, and shares recommendations, my students admit they feel overwhelmed by the sheer number of books they want to read and often think they miss out on great books other readers know. A few students admit that they avoid popular titles like *The Hunger Games* and Harry Potter because everyone else reads them. After a period of time, they feel the window for reading these books closes.

For our students, some books match developmental stages or interests. If students don't read Andrew Clements's *Frindle, Because of Winn-Dixie* by Kate DiCamillo, or E. B. White's *Charlotte's Web* by the end of elementary school, it is unlikely they will ever read them. Invite your students to share their personal must-reads, and create lists on your class website and blog or display these titles in your classroom. Encourage students to share why they believe these books are must-reads. During conferences, ask students about their book gaps and help them locate these books. Reading plans can take us back as well as forward as we continue our reading journeys.

## Conferring Points

During classroom conversations and reading conferences, my students and I discuss their current books, but I often guide them to consider what they might read next. How can students' reading experiences, interest, and goals lead them to the next book, and then the next? How can unmotivated readers develop reading plans that build momentum and increase engagement? How can students with strong reading habits and preferences continue growing?

## Reading Series

Series books based on the same characters, events, or topics appeal to many readers. If you ask adult readers, most can point to a series they loved as a child. I spent most of my childhood reading series books. I read Beverly Cleary's Henry Huggins books and Encyclopedia Brown. Because of the popular TV shows, I collected and read Nancy Drew, The Hardy Boys, and Laura Ingalls Wilder's Little House books. As a teenager, I stashed V. C. Andrews's creepy Dollanganger series in my closet. My mother didn't worry too much about what I was reading, but I knew she would draw the line at incest and arsenic poisoning.

I read James Herriot's memoirs about his life as a country veterinarian, an early interest of mine. Don read comics, saving his allowance to buy the latest *X-Men*, *Fantastic Four*, and *Spiderman*. We read Neil Gaiman's *Sandman* when we were newlyweds. Our daughters, Celeste and Sarah, read innumerable Magic Tree House books and Judy Blume's Fudge series when they were younger. Sarah reads *Locke and Key* and her favorite dystopian science-fiction series like Veronica Roth's *Divergent* and Allie Condie's *Matched* these days. And she still keeps up with the ongoing series she discovered when she was younger, requesting *Babymouse* and George O'Connor's Olympians when new releases appear.

My students love series, too. Some teachers and parents express concern when students exclusively read series books because they think children aren't reading widely enough, but series books benefit readers and provide paths to lifelong independent reading habits (Krashen, 2004). When half the kids in your class are reading *Diary of a Wimpy Kid* or 39 Clues books, you may wonder if they will ever branch out and read something else, but consider the support that reading a series can provide.

Reading series books provides students with both commitment and challenge plans, depending on readers' needs and interests. It provides a scaffold for students who lack confidence or cannot follow through on their own reading plans. And it provides readers familiarity so students are much less likely to end up floundering with unsuccessful book choices or abandoning books that didn't work. Invested in the same characters or storylines, students develop attachments to series books that cement connections to reading in general. Students who read series walk into each subsequent book with background knowledge from previous installments. As students continue the series, their comprehension improves, which increases their confidence and reading enjoyment.

For students engaged with reading, completing an entire series gives these wild readers a sense of accomplishment and builds expertise. Students who read the complete Percy Jackson series or every Bone graphic novel become epicenter readers for that series and provide support for other students who may show interest in a series or want to know more about it. This expertise helps teachers and librarians who may struggle to read every book in every series in order to keep up with their students' interests. Directing students to these classroom experts forges reading relationships between students and reminds them that you are not the only reading expert in the classroom.

Nico's expertise with Anthony Horowitz's Alex Rider books helped that series spread throughout our classroom. Although I read the first two books, *Stormbreaker* and *Point Blank*, I didn't keep up with the series. I suggested the series to students often, particularly boys looking for adventure or science-fiction titles. After recommending the series to a reader, I always followed up with a suggestion that the student talk to Nico about it. Over the year, Cameron, both Anthonys, Enrique, John, and Blake fell into the Alex Rider books because of this collaboration between me, Nico, and Anthony Horowitz.

When conferring with students who can't consistently self-select books they enjoy, flounder between books, or don't seem engaged with reading, offering series titles has become my fallback strategy. I look for short series that include a lot of action or engaging characters. While it seems that every book published these days is part of another epic series, I don't usually recommend lengthy fantasy series like Eragon to my unmotivated students because the sheer length of these books and the complex world-building frustrate them. Reading series provides a great reading plan that reduces pressure to constantly look for another book. You can find my students' favorite series listed in appendix E. Some of my go-to favorites are listed in the box.

**MY GO-TO SERIES**

Alex Rider series by Anthony Horowitz

Amulet series by Kazu Kibuishi

Boy at War series by Harry Mazer

Cirque du Freak by Darren Shan

Clique series by Lisi Harrison

Diary of a Wimpy Kid series by Jeff Kinney

Guys Read series by Jon Scieszka

Olympians series by George O'Connor

Storm Runners series by Roland Smith

Swindle series by Gordon Korman

Weenies series by David Lubar

## Reading Resolutions

When we return from winter break, students reflect on their reading habits over the past year, celebrate their growth as readers, and set reading goals for the year ahead. Encouraging students to make reasonable plans, we discuss our reading achievements and identify areas we want to improve. Each student records his or her reading resolution on a slip of colored paper and we share our resolutions with each other (figure 4.3). Ethan and Casey commit to reading more at home. Emma and Bryan announce plans to read more poetry—a genre they typically avoid. André resolves to read more with his little brother.

We display our reading resolutions in the classroom and reflect occasionally on our progress toward these plans. Setting reading goals for the upcoming calendar year instead of a semester or school year communicates to my students that their reading lives extend beyond our classroom and continue into the future.

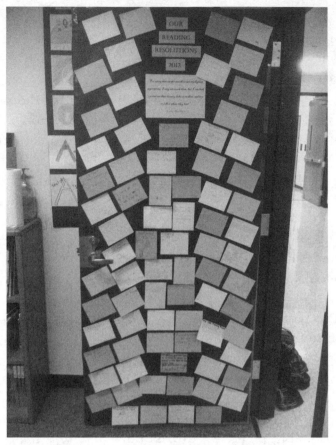

FIGURE 4.3: *Students' reading resolutions.*

## Launching Summer Reading

Reading research indicates that many children's reading abilities decline between the end of one school year and the beginning of the next. My sixth graders can tell you why this happens: they don't read much over the summer. Students can offset this summer reading slump by reading as few as four or five books over the summer (Kim, 2006). Of course, we would love for children to read more than this small number of books, but it's a start. Consider these suggestions for launching a summer reading initiative at your school:

- *Provide lots of opportunities for students to recommend books.* Hang recommendations on the walls in the hallways and in the library. Present book commercials over the announcements and in school newsletters. Provide student-created lists or podcasts on the school website. Discussing books students might read over the summer sends a message that you expect them to read and gives them titles to consider.

- *Encourage children to make lists of at least five books they would like to read.* Setting goals to read at least a few books sends students off for the summer with a reading plan and some specific titles they have self-selected to read. If you can, loan books from the school or classroom libraries. As I mentioned in chapter 3, classroom and school libraries provide primary book access for many of our students. Consider how your students will find books to read over the summer when school closes.

- *Hold a book swap.* Invite students to donate old books in exchange for a ticket. During the book swap, students may select another book for every ticket they hold. We have held a book swap for many years at my school on the last Saturday before school ends. Our teachers and the librarian cull personal and classroom collections, too, and often donate their tickets to kids who don't have books. If you have extra books when the swap ends, find a local charity, hospital, or children's organization that could use the books.

- *Host a library card sign-up event.* Librarians are a wonderful resource for children who need book recommendations. Many public libraries offer summer reading programs, author visits, and other events to entice children to read more over the summer. Invite librarians or volunteers from the local library to attend a PTA meeting or open house and explain the library's summer programs. Encourage families to sign up for library cards.

- *Advise parents to dedicate time for daily reading and encourage children to pack books for trips and errands.* Reading for thirty minutes a day keeps students' vocabulary and reading ability growing during the summer and can be a wonderful activity for rainy days, household errand running, and long waits in the car or the airport during summer travel.

Freed from the mandates of assigned school reading, the summer break gives wild readers time and space to explore their passionate interests. When else can readers devour the entire Harry Potter series from beginning to end or indulge their obsession for mysteries? While it is challenging to require or monitor students' summer reading, we must stress to students and their parents the need to continue reading over the summer or lose the gains students made during the school year. Look for ways to include parents and children in your summer reading initiatives, and you will have more buy-in and motivation to participate.

## Keeping Track of Your Reading Life

Helping students plan for future reading, Susie and I consider how wild readers keep track of the books they might like to read and set goals for future reading. Encouraging students to take responsibility for their reading plans reduces their dependence on teachers and parents for determining when, where, and what students will read. Armed with personal reading plans and goals, students feel empowered and confident.

Inside their reader's notebook, students keep a running list of books they plan to read—using their Books to Read List form. This list collects titles that they discover from book commercials, conversations with friends, reading conferences, preview stacks, and library crawls. Students use their lists as a goal-setting tool and refer to them often when considering what to read next. My students and I take our lists with us during weekly library visits. Bringing those lists with us to the library ensures that library visits are intentional and purposeful. Armed with individualized lists of books that interest them, students spend less time wandering the library or swarming the library computers. Our librarian, Susan, and I can focus our efforts toward assisting students who can't find a particular book or need additional advice. Students take more ownership of the books they select because the books on their Books to Read List represent their choices.

Keeping lists of books to read provides students with a reading plan that promotes independence. When conferring with students who are looking for a book, I direct them back to their Books to Read List and encourage them to select a book that meets their needs and goals. Over time, I want students to rely on my recommendations less and trust themselves more. Beyond school, students can use their lists when visiting the public library or bookstores. We have all experienced the inability to retrieve the name of a book we want when we are standing in a bookstore. Carrying a list reminds us.

. . .

Wild readers develop their own reading plans and set reasonable goals for following through on them. They read for their own purposes, reflect on their reading experiences, and set goals that expand and strengthen their reading lives. Students who set their own independent reading goals take ownership of their reading beyond school and develop self-efficacy and motivation that doesn't depend on the expectations or guidelines of individual teachers or school reading programs. Motivated by their self-identified needs, students who make reading plans become self-actualized, independent readers.

# Building a Personal Canon

*We don't need to have just one favorite. We keep adding favorites. Our favorite book is always the book that speaks most directly to us at a particular stage in our lives. And our lives change. We have other favorites that give us what we most need at that particular time. But we never lose the old favorites. They're always with us. We just sort of accumulate them.*

—Lloyd Alexander

SINCE THE BEGINNING of the year, Don and I have been sorting and culling our book collection. Our thirteen bookcases groan under double-stacked rows in the best of times, but life events last year worsened the situation. Our home flooded in October, and we packed most of our personal books so contractors could replace our wood floors, baseboards, and bookcases. When we moved back into our home, unpacking and shelving our books took three weekends. Random boxes of books are still sitting in the garage.

Determined to get rid of more books than we buy this year, Don and I decided to downsize our book hoard. Taking books to my kids at school and donating a few boxes to charity wasn't going to cut it. We had to get serious.

It wasn't difficult to find readers who wanted our books. We sent boxes of books to colleagues and their students. Our older daughter, Celeste, took stacks of picture books and early readers for her preschool class and our two granddaughters. When Sarah's friends visit, we invite them to dig through the stack of young adult books in our dining room. Don dutifully hauls books to the local mailing center or Half Price Books, a popular used-book store, every week. Three months into our book reduction project, we see progress. We can walk in our back hallway without fearing an avalanche.

Three bookcases in our book room remain untouched. Reliquaries of our reading lives, the books that live on these shelves live in our hearts, too. Don and I don't need to go through these books because we won't be getting rid of any of them. These shelves hold our personal canon, the books that have shaped and defined us. To an outsider, these shelves store a hodgepodge of thrift-store paperbacks, children's picture books, and best sellers from the past twenty years. A lavish edition of *The Odyssey*, purchased when we moved into our first apartment, sits next to *A Confederacy of Dunces*, John Kennedy Toole's southern classic that we picked up during our New Orleans honeymoon. Robert Heinlein's *Stranger in a Strange Land*, the book Don and I discussed on our first date, sits next to William Goldman's *The Princess Bride*. We use words and phrases from these treasured books (and many others) in our daily conversations. We call groceries "grocs," and Don whispers "As you wish" whenever I ask him to perform onerous tasks around the house. Our shared reading experiences weave through our married life, binding us to each other as husband and wife and as readers.

Don and I share books in our life canons, but many titles hold individual significance. My beloved copy of *Bread and Jam for Frances* lives next to Don's volume of *Curious George* stories—two books that mark our different personalities. I think George is annoying and

Don thinks Frances is too fussy. On our worst days—we *are* Frances and George. On our best days, we are Griffin and Sabine (one shelf higher). When Don and I stew in separate corners, we are both probably reading. That's what matters.

We don't have to agree on every book to appreciate each other. How boring life would be if we did. I often think about Don and me and our overlapping reading lives when I think about my students and me. Our reading lives overlap, too. My students and I swap books back and forth every day, but I don't limit my students' reading lives to the books that matter to me.

While the Common Core text exemplars collect a list of worthy literature that all students should read, I question the premise that any reading list meets the needs of all readers. Creating a list, anchored in a time or viewpoint driven by one group's opinion of what literature is meaningful, marginalizes the personal aspect that we bring to what we read. Ultimately a canon grows from our individual experiences as well as our shared ones.

When we lead students to great works, we offer them a transformative experience, but only the readers themselves can define how reading a text affects them. When I pass *The Diary of Anne Frank* into Ashley's hands, I know that she will find another girl who is struggling with the same questions and has the same need to carve out an identity and purpose. When I sit with Reed, discussing Patrick Ness's dystopian epic, *Monsters of Men*, we weep for the Spackle, indigenous beings destroyed by a colonizing army—a tale as old as humanity. Anne Frank's diary appears on the Common Core list. Ness's Chaos Walking series, a recent work that also captures eternal themes, does not. Only the reader decides which book carries personal value.

It is our charge as more experienced readers to lead children to reading, first as enjoyment and then as a place to understand themselves and the world we must live in together, and ultimately as an appreciation for the power of stories to capture what Thomas Foster calls "the one story, the ur-story, [which] is about ourselves, about what it means to be human" (2003).

What children read shapes the men and women they will become, but what I want most for my students is the discovery that reading is a well that never runs dry. Beyond the confines of a traditional education, often designed by entities outside the readers themselves, lies a vast lifetime of reading and learning. Who can say what books will mark my students' lives? It's not my journey, but I am happy to walk alongside them for a few miles. Perhaps a few of the books I invite my students to read will become part of their personal canons. I hope they find many more without me.

# CHAPTER 5

# Wild Readers Show Preferences

*Sometimes, you read a book so special that you want to carry it around for months after you've finished just to stay near it.*

—Markus Zusak,
*The Book Thief*

R L. LAFEVERS's young adult fantasy, *Grave Mercy*, took over my life. Following seventeen-year-old Ismae's journey from damaged child to empowered assassin for Death enthralled me. I spent every free moment reading the book and burned through all 549 pages in four days. Few other books I have read this year captivated me like *Grave Mercy*, but I recognize why I enjoyed it so much. Beyond the wonderful writing, *Grave Mercy* possesses the qualities I enjoy most in books.

I like lengthy books with extensive storylines spanning years. I gravitate toward fantasy tomes like *The Lord of the Rings* or historical fiction epics like Edward Rutherfurd's *Sarum*. I enjoy books that include complex relationships and plot lines between large casts of primary and secondary characters. I like strong women and rakish bad boys with noble hearts. I fancy a good battle or tasteful love scene, but nothing too explicit, please. For me, *Grave Mercy* perfectly suits my tastes.

As a teenager, I read popular historical works like Alex Haley's *Roots*, E. L. Doctorow's *Ragtime*, and *Lonesome Dove* by Larry McMurtry, along with horror novels like Ann Rice's *Interview with a Vampire* and Stephen King's *The Stand*. My sister, Abbie, and I walked a mile to the public library every Saturday. Unable to carry an armload of books home, I discovered James Michener and John Irving while scanning the shelves for a book that looked long enough to last me an entire week. I kept an emergency stash of paperbacks in my closet just in case I finished my library book before the next Saturday.

These days, a glimpse at my nightstand reveals my diverse reading interests and purposes. I typically have two or three books going at a time. I am slowly reading Peter Johnston's *Opening Minds*, stopping often to reflect on his ideas. Reading one brilliant essay each day in *The Essential Don Murray* inspires me to write. I listen to audio books in the car during my long commute. Chad Harbach's best seller, *The Art of Fielding*, is my current choice. Bored with the young adult paranormal romance craze, I am reading Justine Larbalestier's and Sarah Rees Brennan's vampire romance satire, *Team Human*. I think my daughter, Sarah, might like it next. If not, I will pass it along to my high school colleagues.

Shaped by decades of reading, my preferences grew from thousands of reading experiences. I know what I like in a book and I know why. Open-minded and always looking for another great book, I will try almost anything, but when I feel restless and dissatisfied with a few books in a row, I wander back to the same sorts of books I read when I was sixteen. I am a middle-aged English teacher from Texas, but in my dreams, I am Eowyn, shieldmaiden of the Rohan.

## Wild Readers Chime In

"I try to model going outside of my comfortable genres by asking students for their suggestions. I've discovered many new 'favorites' that way. When they know that I take their suggestions seriously, I think that they're much more willing to listen to mine in turn."

## *Wild Readers' Favorites*

Our Wild Reader Survey respondents exhibit a staggering array of reading preferences. Since the majority of our respondents work with children and teachers in classrooms, libraries, or children's publishers, Susie and I were not surprised that almost 100 percent of participants shared our love for children's and young adult literature. These wild readers did not limit their reading solely to children's books, however. Respondents read a lot of everything—indicating a breadth of reading experiences that included books published for adults, professional texts, and books for younger audiences.

Asking survey participants to identify their favorite authors challenged and dismayed more than one reader who claimed, "You really know how to hurt a person," or, "I have stared at the screen for four minutes and I can't decide." Over a thousand titles from all age ranges and genres appear on our Wild Readers' list of favorites, from classics like *A Wrinkle in Time* and *Wuthering Heights*, to modern best sellers like *The Art of Racing in the Rain* and *Twilight*, to professional and nonfiction titles like *The Outliers* and *Readicide*. The complete list of wild readers' favorites can be found on my Slideshare page at www .slideshare.net/donalynm.

> ## Wild Readers Chime In
>
> "Ask me next week and my favorite books and/or authors will change. I'm a reader who prefers not to re-read titles, so it's often what I have recently read that stays vivid. But I do have good memories of lots of books, without wanting to re-visit them."

Wild readers named eight hundred authors among their favorites—a staggering list of literary greats and popular writers. It's hard to imagine another list that includes both Russian novelist Leo Tolstoy and Jeff Kinney, the author of the Diary of a Wimpy Kid series. Several participants named poets, playwrights, and short story authors like Shakespeare, Langston Hughes, and Edgar Allen Poe, as well as book authors.

Although every genre received hundreds of votes, our Wild Reader Survey respondents prefer realism over fantasy—selecting realistic fiction, historical fiction, biographies, and nonfiction as their favorites in greater numbers than fantasy, science fiction, and traditional literature such as mythology, legends, and fairytales. Many readers suggested their own categories for books when they found our survey choices too limiting—naming travel guides, self-help books, and devotionals on their lists of favorites in addition to our genre categories.

No part of our Wild Reader Survey provoked more manipulation and additional commentary from participants than the preferences section. Over two hundred respondents crammed the comment field of every question with personal remarks—contributing their own genres, offering testimonials about their favorite books and authors, or chiding Susie and me for asking them to identify a few favorites in the first place. It seems wild readers' broad reading tastes and experiences defy neat categorization, which compelled respondents to bend our survey to fit their definitions.

Examining avid adult readers' favorites led Susie and me to investigate our students' reading preferences. Given an opportunity to develop common definitions for genres and lead students' discussions of their favorites before asking them to complete a survey yielded more reliable results than our free-wheeling adult readers did. Asking students to examine and share their reading preferences created a reflective opportunity that celebrated their reading accomplishments and growth, while providing Susie and me with insight into the types of books our students read and enjoy. Now we consider students' preferences when designing genre requirements, planning units of study, making book recommendations to students and colleagues, and purchasing books for our classroom libraries.

## *Students' Favorites*

When asked to select their favorite genre, our students showed narrower preferences in the books they like to read than our Wild Reader Survey participants. Three genres—traditional literature, biographies, and nonfiction texts—received only a handful of votes, and fantasy and science fiction were overwhelming favorites. Science-fiction fans declared that they enjoyed reading about "a future where anything could be possible" or they liked "the cool gadgets and technology." Fantasy aficionados found that these stories were "usually the most interesting and unique" and "there are no limits to what can happen." Both fantasy and science-fiction readers reported that these genres "have a lot of action" and allow readers "to let you see into someone else's imagination."

### Wild Readers Chime In

"My favorite titles and authors would change depending on when you asked me."

Many of our students enjoy reading realistic fiction books, a preference shared by the majority of the adults we surveyed. Asked to explain why she prefers realistic fiction, Courteney said, "I like realistic fiction because I can relate to the situations, and sometimes if it is the right book, I can actually get some tips for what I'm going through because the character is going through the same situation." Several students felt that realistic fiction is "relatable" to their lives, and they connected to the characters and their problems. A few students remarked that they liked "everything" and couldn't choose a favorite genre, while three students indicated that they enjoyed reading romance stories in any genre. Zoe admitted, "I love to read about love."

Determining students' reading preferences helps teachers match books with readers. Valuing their tastes shows our students that we trust them to make their own decisions about what they read. Students' preferences should hold as much sway in the classroom community as ours. When three students asked to poll their classmates about their favorite books for a reading door display, I admit that I was not enthusiastic about some of the winning titles. It didn't matter whether I liked these books. My students' choices were celebrated (figure 5.1). It is easy to connect with students who like the same books we do, but we cannot let our personal reading preferences become biases that limit students' reading. We must push ourselves to read widely in order to best serve our students—as role models who read for diverse purposes and reading advisors who know a lot about books that appeal to all types of readers. The more widely we read, the more expertise we offer to our students.

Expressed preferences reveal a lot about students' reading experiences and book knowledge and provide us with information about whether students have read much in the past, but preferences are not always informed opinions. True preferences come from wide reading and lots of positive encounters with books. Sometimes students' stated preferences reveal they haven't read much. When Hunter, one of my students, expresses his reading preferences in vague generalizations like "scary books" or "funny

FIGURE 5.1: *Students polled classmates about their favorite books.*

books," I know he lacks reading experience and may struggle when self-selecting books. Conversely, when Eric tells me he reads "fantasy series like Percy Jackson and Harry Potter," his preferences show some familiarity with books, series, authors, or genres that inform future book choices. Some students rattle off specific authors, genres, or titles, but deeper discussion reveals they haven't read these books. No matter what our conversations with students reveal about their reading tastes, we gain insight into their reading experiences.

Students' preferences provide a starting point for building positive reading relationships between us and our students. At first, we can build students' confidence by offering books that meet their tastes. As the school year progresses, deeper knowledge about each student's reading experiences and abilities helps us stretch students beyond their comfort zones and offer a wider menu of books, genres, and writing styles. Sarah, our daughter, showed a distaste for science-fiction books in elementary school because she didn't want to read about robots and aliens—her perception of the genre. After sampling books like *Divergent* and *Rot and Ruin,* her appreciation for science fiction evolved as her genre knowledge expanded. Wild readers' preferences become more valuable, reliable, and accurate the more they read.

## *Community Conversations*

Thinking about my students, I see one hundred individuals with their own likes and dislikes. Cole eats crunchy snacks every day. Anthony plays football during recess. Kaitlin likes pink, but Sarah detests it. My students' reading tastes represent their individual personalities and experiences, too. Reading preferences guide wild readers when selecting books—helping readers identify, preview, and evaluate books they might like to read. Secure in their preferences, wild readers possess confidence and self-efficacy, using their knowledge of books and vast reading experiences to evaluate new reading material using information from texts they enjoyed in the past.

## Types of Reading Preferences

Preferences are not fixed. Wild readers move between different types of reading material depending on their needs and interests at any given time. As readers and texts become more sophisticated, tastes may change. Connecting to particular authors or subject matter shapes readers' preferences, too. While wild readers express diverse preferences in what they like to read, certain trends in reading tastes emerge that apply to many. You will undoubtedly recognize readers you know when considering these types of reading preferences.

### *A Preference for Reading Deeply from One Genre or One Author*

Wild readers develop attachments to beloved authors and types of stories, returning to the same sorts of books again and again. Finishing Lisa Graff's *Umbrella Summer,* a tender story about a girl moving on after her brother's death, Parker asks me, "Why do you always recommend sad books to me, Mrs. Miller?"

I answer, "Because you like them."

Parker smiles sheepishly and says, "Yeah, I guess I do."

I know that Parker enjoys realistic fiction stories about children suffering great losses like death and heartbreak. Recognizing her preferences helps me suggest books that value her fondness for sad books and introduce her to authors and stories she might not discover on her own. When she asks for recommendations, I suggest Leslie Connor's *Waiting for Normal* and Sonya Sones's *One of Those Hideous Books Where the Mother Dies*, encouraging her to seek out new writing styles and formats. Over the year, Parker branches into more historical fiction and poetry—feeding her preferences while expanding her reading experiences.

Expand students' reading repertoire while acknowledging the preferences they already express. Offer readers with strong genre preferences read-alike titles with similar themes or storylines and suggest authors who write books in multiple genres.

### A Preference for Fiction over Nonfiction or Vice Versa

Every year I have a few students who obsessively read nonfiction at the expense of everything else. Cleaning lockers after winter break, Kenna, our class locker captain, reports that Kinsey, whose locker is next to hers, has library books spilling out of his locker. Walking down the hall to investigate, I help Kinsey stack books and determine whether each title belongs to the school library, our classroom library, or his personal collection. As Kinsey removes each book from his locker, he recites the title or topic, "Lizards, Solar System, cars, trains, Vietnam War . . . "

Listening to Kinsey's litany, I notice that every book is nonfiction. Through my conferences with Kinsey, I know that he doesn't have much tolerance for stories and enjoys reading to increase his knowledge about the vast list of topics that consume his interests. When making book recommendations, I suggest historical fiction titles like Walter Dean Myer's *Fallen Angels* and

*Letters from Wolfie* by Patti Sherlock—books that expand his knowledge of the Vietnam War. I continue to offer nonfiction texts—introducing Kinsey to nonfiction authors like Jim Murphy and Sy Montgomery, which increases his ability to find more books to read.

## A Preference for Series

Many readers feed their reading lives through popular series, following characters and storylines through several books. Series provide support to developing readers and help ambitious readers read deeply—developing expertise and competence. Struggling to connect Abbie with books, I decided that Lisi Harrison's Clique series was a perfect fit. Abbie was a queen bee who loved designer clothes and dominated her girlfriends. Harrison's mean girl characters helped Abbie work through some of the personal friendship drama she encountered during the year and improved her reading engagement and ability along the way.

## A Preference for Graphic Novels, Magazines, or Internet Content

If we value all readers, we must value all reading. While I do not include magazines in our class reading requirements, I discuss with my students the magazines and websites they read and offer magazines like *Muse* and *Kids Discover* for them to read. I admit that my appreciation for graphic novels took time. Ignorant of the format, I categorized graphic novels as light reading that didn't provide the rigor or depth that full-length books do. In fact, light reading holds surprising benefits and often launches wild reading habits. As Stephen Krashen and Joanne Ujiie (2005) assert, "Many people are fearful that if children engage in 'light reading,' if they read comics and magazines they will stay with this kind of reading forever, that they will never go on to more 'serious' reading. The opposite appears to be the case. The evidence suggests that light reading provides the competence and motivation to continue reading and to read more demanding texts" (p. 6).

In the past, I recommended graphic novels to students who did not enjoy reading or possess the stamina for longer texts. Unwilling to see graphic novels as anything more than compromise offerings for students who wouldn't read, I felt that reading graphic novels was better than not reading at all.

Working with Armann in my class changed my mind. Armann did not enjoy reading when he began sixth grade. His mother expressed concern during Meet the Teacher night and agreed that she was willing to do "whatever it takes" to get Armann to read more. Although I plied Armann with books in the early days of the school year, he expressed little interest or enthusiasm. Spying a stack of new graphic novels on my desk, Armann asked about Kazu Kibuishi's Amulet series, a popular choice with my students. I loaned Armann the first four titles, and he began flipping through them. Two days later, he returned the books, declared them to be "awesome," and asked for more graphic novels. He read entire series like Bone by Jeff Smith and Babymouse by Jennifer and Matt Holm.

As the school year progressed, Armann moved on to more challenging titles like Gareth Hinds's *Beowulf* and *The Odyssey*. Other students began consulting Armann about different titles, and he became our resident graphic novel expert, engaging in sophisticated conversations about the artwork and storylines of numerous titles. I realized that every lesson I taught about reading and writing, Armann applied to the graphic novels he read. His skills reading more traditional text improved because he practiced what he learned with his beloved graphic novels every day.

By the end of the year, Armann was trekking to the library and the bookstore to find graphic novels we didn't have in our school library and recommending titles to our school librarian and me. He introduced me to Carla Jablonski's World War II graphic novel, *Resistance*, and Hope Larson's *Mercury*, two titles I bought, read, and added to our class library. Because of Armann's passion and expertise, I became more knowledgeable about graphic novels and found more reasons to use them in our classroom. Armann's confidence in himself and his reading skills grew. Armann became a wild reader because of graphic novels, and I became a better teacher because of him.

Dedicated to learning more about the format, I spent that summer reading every book on the YALSA's Great Graphic Novels for Teen lists (http://www.ala.org/yalsa/ggnt). Admitting my ignorance about what defined an exemplary graphic novel, I relied on those who possessed greater knowledge—librarians and scholars who study the format. It was like taking an art appreciation class. This focused study helped me evaluate and appreciate graphic novels and share them with students.

In a 2011 guest post on my *Book Whisperer* blog (http://blogs .edweek.org/teachers/book_whisperer/2011/08/making_room _for_graphic_novels.html), Terry Thompson, author of *Adventures in Graphica,* identified numerous ways that graphic novels support readers:

- *Motivation:* Evidenced by increased library traffic, long check-out wait lists, and a phenomenally growing popularity, graphic novels grab readers' attentions and drive them to read more.

  - Engaging graphics make the text more accessible and support readers in the act of making meaning.

  - Since readership in other countries is high compared to the United States, the medium may offer cultural significance to a variety of English language learners.

  - Popular themes with current topics invite readers to keep reading.

  - Connections to entertainment trends and the quality of the graphic design appeal to some of our most disinterested readers.

  - The medium's unconventional nature attracts readers who feel disenfranchised.

  - The innovative style and delivery entice readers who are indifferent to other media or genres.

- *Scaffolding:* Inherent in their design is the way graphic novels merge text with visible representations of meaning that scaffold students as they navigate through the pages. Since the text and the pictures are interdependent, their effects become synergistic.

- Comprehension strategies such as inferring, summarizing, and synthesis are accentuated through supportive graphics and design features.

- Creative teams intentionally design panels and pages to guide readers in determining importance.

- Even though graphic support may require less visualization, readers are immersed in experiences that fill their mental stores with what strong mental images can look like.

- Fluency is represented visibly through word art, speech bubbles, thought bubbles, and facial expressions.

- Picture support frees readers to practice a particular instructional focus such as plot, characterization, and theme.

- English language learners find illustrative support for unusual idioms and colloquial phrases that often confuse them in traditional texts.

- Embedded graphics can offer symbolic representations of concepts from content areas such as history, government, and science.

- Readers take on new vocabulary words they might otherwise skip because their meanings are often illustrated alongside their written form.

Teachers often ask how to use graphic novels instructionally, wondering if there's some special trick to it. There isn't. The simple truth is that you can apply graphic novels to any situation where you'd normally use traditional texts.

I no longer see graphic novels as simply gateway reading material for unmotivated readers. After all, *Maus*, Art Spiegelman's harrowing Holocaust tale, won a Pulitzer. Gene Yuen Lang's *American Born Chinese* was short-listed for the National Book Award and won the Printz Award. Vertigo's *Sandman* garnered a Hugo Award. These literary accolades recognize graphic novels as valuable literature. Since my year with Armann, I have added graphic novels to our class reading requirements, expecting all students to explore at least one example of the format. Even the most proficient readers reported learning something new about reading and storytelling through this exploration.

## A Preference for Rereading Favorite Books

Every other year, during winter break, I reread The Lord of the Rings trilogy. I enjoy the books and consider revisiting Tolkien's florid ramblings about forest glades and tree elves a reading marathon. The sheer length of the series demands reading stamina and attention to detail. Besides, my Elvish gets rusty. I reread *To Kill a Mockingbird* every few years, too. I think I am a different person every time I read Harper Lee's classic. Connecting with Scout when I was younger, I gravitate to Atticus now because he is the parent and adult I aspire to be.

Adult readers revisit beloved favorites and reread books on occasion, but some teachers and parents forbid children from rereading books or won't allow children to reread books for class assignments or reading requirements. In fact, rereading books increases comprehension and enjoyment (Millis, Simon, & tenBroek, 1998; Pressley, 2000; Newkirk, 2011). Talking with my student, Jordan, about rereading the Harry Potter series, he admits that he "discovers new things" when he revisits the books and "sees plot clues" that hint at future events he didn't notice during his first reading.

Students reread books for three main reasons: they want to absorb a treasured story into their skin, they want to cement their knowledge of topics and ideas, or they don't know what else to read. When working with young readers, it is important to determine why they want to reread a text. If a student rereads the same books over and over because he or she can't find anything else engaging to read, help him or her find other books that match a similar storyline or genre. If students want to develop their content expertise, provide books that expand their knowledge. If they reread books because they love them, I say let them. We want to develop students' ownership of reading. When we tell students they can't reread a book they love, we put our goals in front of theirs.

## Genre Avoidance

For several years, my middle school students have identified fantasy and science fiction as their favorite genres, yet fewer adults in our Wild Reader Survey designated these genres as favorites. Not only do my students prefer fantasy to realism, many report that historical fiction, biographies, autobiographies, memoirs, and nonfiction of all types, selected by adult wild readers as among their favorite genres, are their least favorite books to read.

### Historical Fiction and Biographies

Investigating this disconnect between my students' preferences and wild readers' preferences, I asked my students why they claim to dislike books related to history or notable people's lives. Over-whelmingly, they say that historical fiction and biographies are boring. Lynnsey announced, "I have only abandoned two books in [the past] two years and both were historical fiction." Other responses reflect students' emotional and social development, largely anchored in the present and influenced by an egocentric worldview and limited life experiences. Explaining why historical fiction was her least favorite genre, Alicia said, "I don't really like looking back, I like looking into the future." Rose dislikes biographies because "I don't really like learning about someone's life, I just want to live my own." Ethan, editing his remarks for school, proclaimed, "I don't give a _____ about your life." Several students expressed similar sentiments asking, "Why learn about other people's lives when still living yours?"

Perhaps as adults we reflect more about the past, recognize our connections to other people, and find personal relevance when reading about the accomplishments and challenges of eminent individuals. As parents, teachers, and librarians, we shouldn't shy away from our responsibility to expand students' knowledge of the world and their place in it. Historical fiction and biographies offer readers a lens into the lives of people whose circumstances differ from ours and anchor us in a time line of human experiences that reaches into the past and extends into the future.

What are the implications for our teaching when we consider that teachers and librarians may prefer different genres from the children they serve? How can we bridge this divide between the value we see in historical works and many students' ambivalence or downright dislike for it? Considering our students' reading experiences and the books themselves offers insights and opportunities to change students' negative mind-set. Students identify two main reasons they don't like historical texts:

- *Overanalysis of historical fiction and biographies during whole class novel units and classroom instruction.* In an effort to integrate social studies content into language arts class, teachers often select historical fiction titles and biographies for whole class reading. Using these titles as textbook supplements reduces students' interest in reading them. When promoting and reading historical fiction, biographies, autobiographies, and memoirs in class, consider whether the text is well written or chosen for its curricular links. Using overtly didactic texts turns kids off reading and studying history and notable people.

- *Biographies written for children about the lives of adults sanitize the subject to the degree that kids no longer connect to the subject as a real person.* The best historical works reveal the humanity of their subjects. For obvious reasons, you find little mention of John Kennedy's love life, Isaac Newton's fascination with alchemy, or Virginia Wolff's depression in biographies geared to children. Glossing over more scandalous or personal aspects of notable people's lives reduces them to flat, one-dimensional saints, creating biographies that become nothing more than lists of dates and major accomplishments. It is hard for students to connect with them.

Talented nonfiction authors like Kathleen Krull, Deborah Heiligman, Shana Corey, Kadir Nelson, and others have dedicated their writing careers to humanizing eminent historical figures and making them interesting to children. By reading aloud more engaging historical and biographical works, introducing students to noteworthy authors, and encouraging students' interest in weird, unique, or fascinating information, we increase their interest and build background knowledge for further study.

## Dead Presidents and Whales

Open-minded about books and willing to read almost anything, Ashley typically read four or five books a week. By early spring, she had read over a hundred. When I looked at Ashley's reader's notebook and examined her genre requirements graph (an accountability tool that helps students track how many books they read from each genre), it was clear that she had not read a single nonfiction book all year. (See appendix A for a blank form for this graph.) Recognizing this deficit as an opportunity for Ashley to stretch herself as a reader, I suggested that we look for a few nonfiction books she might like to read.

"I hate nonfiction, Mrs. Miller. It's so boring. It's all about dead presidents and whales," she said.

Trying not to laugh, I asked, "Why do you say that, Ashley?"

"The only time you need a nonfiction book is when you are researching a report. I don't like to read those books for fun."

I was surprised that several students at Ashley's table expressed similar disinterest in reading nonfiction. My experiences raising daughters led me to believe that most young children thoroughly enjoyed nonfiction. During the "Why?" years of early childhood, preschool and primary-age children love to read nonfiction texts, begging to read science-related books like Gail Gibbon's *The Moon*

*Book* and Steve Jenkins's *Actual Size* or David Adler's Picture Book Biography series. When I mentioned these titles to Ashley and her classmates, they remember reading and enjoying similar titles when they were younger. What changed as they grew older?

In many primary and elementary school classrooms, students spend the entire day with one teacher, who provides instruction in every subject. Teachers are more likely to use nonfiction trade books in content-area lessons—reading various texts that connect to science, social studies, and math. Children read, share, and discuss more nonfiction texts as a natural part of learning. As they progress through school, courses become departmentalized as children travel among several teachers who provide instruction in specific content areas.

Pressured to teach extensive content in shorter class periods, content-area teachers depend more on textbooks to deliver information and find fewer opportunities for students to read trade nonfiction. Language arts teachers, who share and provide more of students' reading material at school, focus on their own content demands and read less nonfiction with students, too. For the most part, we expect students to read nonfiction only for class work when assigning research reports—Ashley's dead presidents and whales. And increasingly, we encourage students to conduct research online and short-cut reading nonfiction books at all.

Without much exposure, access, or experience reading nonfiction in their classes, it's not surprising that older students read less of this genre. As with any other type of text, we must look for meaningful ways to incorporate nonfiction material in our classrooms if we want children to read more of it.

The quality and diversity of children's nonfiction have improved dramatically over the years. Nonfiction books include more text features like color photographs, illustrations, glossaries, and captions that support and engage young readers. Students can find nonfiction books about topics that interest them: athletes, artists, musicians, arts and crafts, cars, fashion, and animals. Moving away from mass-produced library sets churned out by commissioned writers, children's publishers regularly offer well-written and

CHILDREN'S AND YOUNG ADULT NONFICTION BOOK AWARDS AND REVIEW SOURCES

- National Council of Teachers of English Orbis Pictus Award for Outstanding Nonfiction for Children, http://www.ncte.org/awards/orbispictus/
- Association for Library Services to Children, Robert F. Sibert Informational Book Medal, http://www.ala.org/alsc/awardsgrants/book media/sibertmedal/
- Young Adult Library Services Association Award for Excellence in Nonfiction for Young Adults, http://www.ala.org/yalsa/nonfiction/
- National Council for the Social Studies Notable Trade Books for Young People, http://www.socialstudies.org/notable
- National Science Teachers Association Outstanding Science Trade Books for Students K–12, http://www.nsta.org/publications/ostb/
- The Nonfiction Detectives Blog, http://www.nonfictiondetectives.com/

well-researched nonfiction from outstanding nonfiction authors like Candace Fleming, Sy Montgomery, Nic Bishop, Jim Murphy, and Russell Freedman, who understand their audience and know how to engage children.

With heightened interest in reading nonfiction throughout the school day, teachers need effective, easy-to-implement ways to increase students' nonfiction reading skills, access, and motivation for reading it. Consider these activities for using nonfiction texts in your classroom:

• *Add more nonfiction to book talks.* Adding nonfiction books and magazines to our daily book commercials introduces students to books they might read and increases their title awareness for the types of books available. Personally recommending nonfiction books communicates to students that we value nonfiction and find it interesting to read. When promoting books, consider that some students may prefer nonfiction over fiction. Value all readers by endorsing nonfiction alongside fiction, poetry, graphic novels, and other texts.

• *Read-aloud nonfiction texts.* Regularly reading nonfiction picture books, poetry, articles, excerpts, and online websites like Wonderopolis (at www.wonderopolis.com) increases students' background knowledge and provides engaging opportunities to explore content. Ask your school librarian for nonfiction materials that align with upcoming curriculum content or work with grade-level or department colleagues to locate nonfiction materials. My students enjoy fact and trivia books like *Every Day on Earth* by Steve Murrie and *100 Most Awesome Things on the Planet* by Anna Claybourne. It's easy to read a few facts each day while you are waiting in line or during class transitions. When choosing longer read-alouds, I alternate novel selections with nonfiction books like Philip Hoose's *Moonbird: A Year on the Wind with the Great Survivor B95.*

• *Use nonfiction as mentor texts.* While nonfiction texts provide students with authentic models for organizing and presenting information, well-written nonfiction texts like Kathleen Krull's *Big Wig: A Little History of Hair* and Joyce Sidman's *Ubiquitous: Celebrating Nature's Survivors* provide rich examples of descriptive writing, figurative language, and imagery—concepts historically taught using fiction models. When you design units of study or lesson plans, include nonfiction texts in the mix.

• *Pair fiction texts with nonfiction on related topics.* Offering non-fiction materials that supplement fiction works encourages students to explore real-world connections and contributes to their under-standing of historical and technical references they encounter while reading fiction. My students enjoy reading nonfiction texts like Susan Campbell Bartoletti's *Hitler Youth* and Jim Murphy's *American Plague* after exploring the same topics in historical fiction books like *The Boy Who Dared* (also by Bartoletti) and Laurie Halse Anderson's *Fever 1793.*

• *Provide students frequent opportunities to preview, read, and share nonfiction.* Include nonfiction books when recommending books, and encourage students to browse nonfiction titles in the class and school libraries (figure 5.2). Collect a range of nonfiction texts that relate to curriculum content and invite students to skim and scan these materials every day as warm-up or introductory activities in science and social studies classes. Encourage students to locate text features like maps, charts, photographs, and glossaries. Ask students to share interesting facts and visuals that they discover during these

FIGURE 5.2: *Offer students a range of nonfiction texts, and encourage browsing.*

daily previews. I often notice students returning to the same book day after day during these short scanning sessions, eventually reading nonfiction books they might not have self-selected.

As with any other genre they avoid, when my students claim they dislike reading nonfiction, I assume they lack positive reading experiences. In addition to teaching students how to preview, locate, and identify key information in nonfiction texts, teachers should expose students to a variety of engaging nonfiction and promote awareness of the text types available. Through wide nonfiction reading, students build background content knowledge, increase confidence, and discover authors and topics that feed further reading and independent investigations.

# *Conferring Points*

It's useful to examine a complete picture of students' progress toward internalizing wild reading behaviors. At least once a grading period, Susie and I meet formally with students to examine their reader's notebooks and discuss their reading engagement and long-term commitment. During these reading habits conferences, we gain deeper understanding of how each reader has grown and the wild reading habits each one still needs to develop. While chatting with students about their reading takes place all day every day in our classroom, I want focused, scheduled opportunities to talk with each child about their progress toward wild reading behaviors. As we put the final piece into place—reading preferences—we can consider how each of the wild reading habits discussed in this book come together when looking at individual readers.

## Reading Habits Conference

I record notes from students' independent reading conferences on a reading habits conference chart (see appendix C for a blank version of this form). I use one sheet for each table group and transcribe my observations and students' comments into individual students' conference logs stored in Evernote. I take photographs of students' reading records and save them into Evernote, too. Rereading and copying my notes provides me with an opportunity to reflect and compare notes from current conferences with past observations; you may prefer to keep one form on each student and track progress over time on one sheet of paper.

My reading habits conference chart shows my evolution as a teacher. Every box on the form reveals reflection and decision making about how I see my students, what I want to know about their reading lives, and what we value as a classroom reading community.

I confer with students during our independent reading block. Mindful that talking with me means that students aren't reading, I interrupt them as little as possible during this time. In the past, I realized that students spent part of their reading time watching me fill out conference notes instead of reading, so I begin independent reading conferences by examining a student's reading notebook first.

I collect as much information as I can by analyzing a reader's genre requirements graph, reading lists, to-read lists, and other record-keeping tools. I also reflect on what I know about each child based on daily conversations, class work, and independent reading observations. After jotting down as many observations as I can on my own, I chat with each student—sharing my observations and seeking his or her input. By waiting to interrupt students until I need their input, I communicate that their reading matters more than my paperwork.

## Reading Habits: Reader

After reading Peter Johnston's *Choice Words: How Our Language Affects Children's Learning* (2004), I am more intentional when designing forms, creating anchor charts, and providing written feedback to my students. As Johnston reminds us in his work, the way we talk to children becomes part of the narrative they tell about themselves. Constantly looking for ways to bridge the divide between school reading and life reading, I changed the term "student" or "name" on every form to "reader" or "writer" as the task suited. First and foremost, I want my students to see themselves as readers and writers. Listing each student's name as a reader serves as a concrete reminder to both the child and me that everyone in our class is a reader—even if we are at different stages in our reading development.

Underneath the children's names, I record their independent reading levels. According to district guidelines, I assess every student three times a year using the Qualitative Reading Inventory. The data from these assessments provide me with every student's reading level, but I don't always look these up and record the hard numbers on my conference forms because they aren't necessary. My conference records are for my students and me to use. I don't see the point in transcribing QRI scores onto my conference form when I can look them up later. I usually jot down "at, above, or below grade level" during the conference based on previous assess-ments and working knowledge of each student's reading ability.

## Reading Habits: Preferences

Looking through students' reading lists, I try to identify preferences based on the types of books they read. Does the reader enjoy historical fiction or poetry? Is the reader currently following a series? How diverse are the reader's choices? While some readers select a little of everything, skipping from genre to genre may indicate a lack of clear preferences. Wide reading is the goal, but some children bounce from book to book because they cannot find what they like. Choosing the same genre or storylines over and over may reveal a reading rut—indicating that I need to suggest different books. When many readers in a class are reading the same books, looking at preferences reveals how much influence the reading community has on students' book choices, too.

I also document each reader's current book and access my knowledge of children's literature to determine whether the book aligns with the child's independent reading level. While I haven't memorized the reading levels of every book, I do know the levels of the most commonly read books in our class library. I do not obsess on a book-by-book basis about whether my students read books that match their reading levels at all times, but I do consider trends in reading choices. If students continuously select books that are too easy or too hard for them, I consider this when making book recommendations. Given free choice, lots of books, and reading advisory, most readers advance themselves up a ladder of reading difficulty on their own (Lesesne, 2010). As long as students under-stand and appreciate the books they self-select for independent reading, I don't intervene unless they fail to make progress.

## Reading Habits: Engagement

When assessing reading engagement, I record whether my students fall into their books and fully invest in reading when given the time to read. While it takes a few minutes to settle into class each day, readers who wander around the classroom, fidget, or pretend to read aren't engaged. Again, I consider trends in students' reading behaviors over time. If I notice that certain students won't focus during independent reading time, I counsel them to select different books or reflect on other factors that prevent them from engaging with what they read.

I also consider how many books students have completed. Readers who have finished few books by certain points in the school year may reveal a lack of consistent engagement with what they read. When tallying book totals, though, I take into account the types of books students read. There is a big difference between a reader who has finished all four books in the Eragon series—a staggering two-thousand-page accomplishment—and a reader who has finished four books in the Guardians of Ga'hoole series—shorter, lower-reading level books. These reading events may carry equal challenge and value to each reader. Comparing sheer numbers of books completed does not reveal a complete picture of students' reading accomplishments. We must consider other factors when assessing individual children and their progress toward personalized reading goals. We should never compare book tallies between children or create competitive conditions among them.

After reflecting on my personal observations of readers' engagement in class, I ask each child about his or her at-home reading habits. My students admit to me when they aren't reading outside school. I use these conversations to reinforce the importance of home reading and work with each child to identify opportunities when they can find more time to read. (I discussed this process in chapter 1.)

### Reading Habits: Record Keeping

I expect my students to keep track of their reading lives by recording the books they read and their impressions of them using the various record-keeping tools discussed throughout this book: genre requirements graphs, reading lists, to-read lists, and response entries. We also post reading recommendations and reviews, links to book trailers and author websites, and other reading-related responses to our class Edmodo page and blog. When I assess their independent reading habits, I consider how well students participate in these activities and to what degree they record and reflect on their reading lives. Documenting our reading activities provides my students and me with information for reflection purposes and goal setting. For example, students use their reading lists to consider the books they have read and create book recommendation lists for future students (figure 5.3). I stress to students that my ability to help them progress as readers depends on their willingness to provide snapshots of their reading activities. Although I make note of how well students keep their reading records, I do not grade them down if they have sloppy or incomplete records. I use this information as one more piece in determining their reading habits and ownership for reading.

I have learned that the most avid readers often keep the worst records of their reading activities. They don't care about listing every book they read and cannot be bothered with documenting

FIGURE 5.3: *Students reflect on their favorite books to share with next year's class.*

their reading lives for my course requirements. I encourage these readers to use online websites like Goodreads and show them how these tools can help them develop a deeper understanding of themselves as readers over time. On more than one occasion, I have spent an entire reading conference helping someone go back and fill in her reading lists. My students understand that I must hold them accountable for their reading, but the more they read, the less my school-based tools seem to matter. I suppose that is the point.

Recognize that readers with pristine, carefully documented reading lists and genre graphs may be your most dependent readers. They fill out these forms because you expect it. I rely on conferences, personal observations, and reading responses, as well as reader's notebook records, to tell me what I want to know about my students' reading behaviors (figure 5.4).

## Reading Habits: Commitment

Abandoning books from time to time is a natural reading behavior for many wild readers. I expect students to record the books they abandon as well as the titles they finish because I want to observe trends. Ditching a book now and then indicates self-awareness of personal preferences and engagement. However, students who abandon lots of books in a row or stick with books they don't enjoy or understand require intervention and support.

Examining the books that students abandon helps me determine their commitment to reading in general and identify their consistent success in self-selecting books. Readers who can't finish the books they start require additional reading advisory, short reading goals, and gentle pressure for completing books.

## Reading Habits: Selection

Readers use various resources when finding out about books they would like to read. Assessing students' independent reading habits, I consider how they discover books and which methods they employ work best. While it is acceptable for me to provide book

| Reading Habits Conference | | | Date 12-2-11 | Grading Period | 1  2  ③  4  5  6 |
|---|---|---|---|---|---|
| **Reader** | **Preferences** | **Engagement** | **Record Keeping** | **Commitment** | **Selection** |
| TRISTEN | difficult to see clear preferences / seems to select books at random | reads in class / school | accurate genre graph & reading list (matched and completed) | No More Dead Dogs / abandoned | covers / Ethan S. / me |
| at/below reading level | at/below text level | Sometimes: TV, friends, homework / home | | no plan / plan | other |
| Currently reading: | Eleventh Plague | | What number book is this for the year?  8 | | |
| ALEX | science fiction / fantasy / series | reads in class "sneak reader" / school | incomplete reading list: titles, authors or dates missing | "Why would I do that?" / abandoned | series / 15-year-old brother / me / recommendations |
| above reading level | at/above text level | "Every night before I go to sleep." / home | | Mockingjay, Burning Bridge / plan | other |
| Currently reading: | Catching Fire | | What number book is this for the year?  14 | | |
| ALICIA | realistic fiction / fantasy / "hates historical fiction" | reads in class / school | accurate genre graph and reading list (matched, completed, color-coded) | Nerd Girls / abandoned | book order / book commercials / me / Kenna |
| at reading level | at text level | "30 minutes every day when I get home." / home | | to-read list titles / plan | other |
| Currently reading: | Watsons Go to Birmingham | | What number book is this for the year?  17 | | |
| ABBY | realistic fiction / Informational non-fiction | sometimes reads in class / school | accurate genre graph and reading list (matched and completed) | none / abandoned | me / Lisa / Natalie / recommendations |
| at/below reading level | at/below text level | "reads every night" / home | | to-read list / plan | other |
| Currently reading: | Calligraphy | | What number book is this for the year?  16 | | |

| | |
|---|---|
| *Preferences* | *Does the student show preferences for genres, authors, series? What is the text difficulty of the books he/she reads?* |
| *Engagement* | *How engaged is the student during reading time? Is the student reading at home?* |
| *Record Keeping* | *Is the student using his/her reader's notebook to keep accurate reading records?* |
| *Commitment* | *Does the student abandon books? What is the student's plan for future reading?* |
| *Selection* | *How does the student primarily choose his or her books?* |

FIGURE 5.4: *Students' reading habits conferences.*

recommendations, I should not be students' only source of book information. I encourage them to use online websites, library and bookstore displays, and other tools to learn more about books they might read. Most of all, I reinforce the importance of building relationships with other readers—in class and elsewhere. I look for opportunities to connect students with each other as much as possible.

Occasionally students rely on peers for book recommendations that don't suit them. If students take book suggestions from friends but don't enjoy the books they select from these conversations, I counsel them to take more ownership of their book choices and reflect on why these book recommendations didn't work. Good friends don't always share the same tastes in books.

Conferring about their independent reading habits keeps my students and me focused on our long-term goals—internalizing wild reading behaviors and developing the self-reflection skills necessary to maintain lifelong reading. Through these conversations, I gain deeper understanding into my students' reading lives and they build a greater appreciation for why reading matters to them.

## Keeping Track of Your Reading Life

As they sample texts from poetry, nonfiction, and fiction genres, students develop deeper understanding of themselves as readers and the types of texts that speak to them. As they read widely throughout the school year, preferences emerge that students and teachers might not recognize when examining individual reading events. Identifying students' reading tastes helps students determine the books they gravitate toward and the genres they avoid and guides teachers as they work with students.

I invite my students to read forty books across various genres during the school year (Miller, 2009). Students self-select their own books but must sample a few books in every genre. They then document how many books they read on a genre requirements graph kept in their notebooks (figure 5.5). The $y$-axis marks how many books a student reads, and the $x$-axis designates genre. As students finish books, they shade in a box in the genre column. A dotted line in each genre column indicates the class requirement for that genre. While Susie and I want students to try every genre, we include eleven self-selected genre choices in our forty-book invitation. Including open genre choices allows students freedom to read deeply in a favorite genre, dive into a long series, or explore a favorite author's work.

A quick scan of students' genre graphs during student conferences shows their progress toward reading goals, reveals their preferences, and indicates which genres they don't read as much as others. Avery's genre graph shows that she obviously prefers fantasy

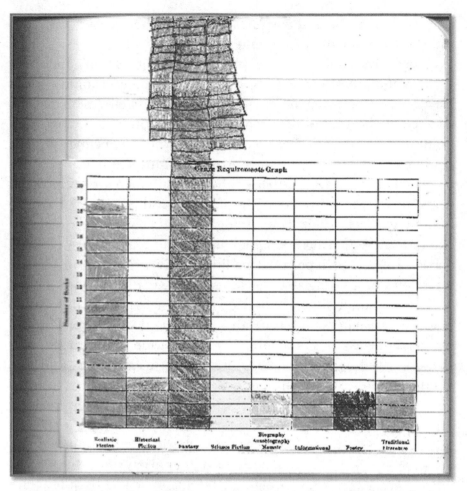

FIGURE 5.5: *Avery's notebook reveals her strong preference for fantasy books.*

and realistic fiction. She created her own boxes when she filled up the fantasy column of her genre graph. While Avery completed the class requirements for every genre, she read the minimum number of poetry books that Susie expected her fifth graders to read—only three. Avery admits that poetry is her least favorite genre.

During conferences, I often cross-check readers' genre graphs against their reading lists to determine if they have correctly identified the genres of what they read. If they cannot identify a book's genre, this may indicate that they didn't comprehend the book, don't fully understand genre characteristics, or read a text that was difficult to categorize. Such mismatches provide opportunities for further discussion and assessment.

The genre requirements graph helps students identify their preferences and areas of growth by documenting their reading choices over time. Recognizing their reading preferences helps them develop an accurate portrait of themselves as readers with specific likes and dislikes. They refer to their genre graphs when reflecting on their reading experiences and setting goals for future reading.

Whether students read all of their requirements or appreciate every genre doesn't matter. The main reason Susie and I expect students to try a little bit of everything is so that they can find what they like to read. Acquiring enough experience to make informed book choices and find their personal reading identities remains our primary intention when asking students to read forty books or more.

Determining readers' expressed preferences in what they like to read helps teachers connect with students and value their individual reading tastes. These preferences provide a foundation for building reading relationships and offer insight into students' needs—inviting us to offer books that match their interests, as well as books that can expand their reading experiences. Wild readers develop authentic preferences through wide reading and heightened awareness of the variety of texts available. Encouraging students to read what they want while exposing them to high-interest, engaging, quality texts of all kinds fosters their engagement and provides the diverse experiences they need to find texts that will meet their reading interests and needs both today and tomorrow.

• • •

By the end of the school year, our students have practiced all of the lifelong reading habits in our classrooms, they have reflected on their personal reading behaviors, and they have developed the tools and skills they need to

### The Forty-Book Requirement

| Genre | Number |
| --- | --- |
| Realistic fiction | 5 |
| Historical fiction | 4 |
| Fantasy | 3 |
| Science fiction | 2 |
| Biography/ autobiography/ memoir | 2 |
| Nonfiction | 5 |
| Poetry | 4 |
| Traditional literature | 3 |
| Graphic novels | 1 |
| Choice | 11 |

*Source:* Miller (2009).

become independent readers without our support. Dedicating time to read, self-selecting books, building relationships with other readers, making reading plans, and developing their own reading preferences, our students feel empowered and capable enough to continue reading away from school. Their reading lives belong to them, and they don't need us. They are wild readers now.

# Coda

*From that time on, the world was hers*
*for the reading.*

—Betty Smith,

*A Tree Grows in Brooklyn*

ALLISON WAS NOT much of a reader at the beginning of the school year. Compliant and a teacher pleaser, Allison faked an interest in books because I expected it from her, but we both knew that she wasn't an enthusiastic reader. She abandoned more books than she completed, declaring each one "boring" or "not her type" of book. She frequently went to the school library or asked me if I needed help around the classroom instead of reading. When I talked to her about reading at home, she admitted she didn't read there. Allison wanted to be a reader. She tried. She just couldn't commit to reading and told me that she felt overwhelmed.

Discarding titles almost daily, Allison spent most of our independent reading time previewing stacks of books that I hand-selected for her. Some books I suggested, like Leslie Connor's *Waiting for Normal,* worked. Others, like *No Passengers Beyond This Point* by Gennifer Choldenko, didn't. For every book she finished, she ditched two or three. I worried that previewing books with me had become her newest reading avoidance activity. Nevertheless, Allison slowly developed fledgling reading confidence and more stamina—finishing several books and self-selecting books on occasion. Her level of engagement waxed and waned from book to book, though. If she wasn't captivated with her choice, she slid back into her nonreading habits again.

Allison's best friend in class was Lynnsey. Unlike Allison, Lynnsey read three or four books a week—tearing through series and constantly seeking new books to read. As their friendship grew, Lynnsey, who seemed unaware of Allison's reading reluctance, recommended the Twilight series to her. Lynnsey adored *Twilight* and promoted the series so passionately to other readers in the class that she convinced even *boys* to read it. Allison, who was just as accommodating a friend as she was a student, borrowed Lynnsey's copy of *Twilight.* I was not optimistic that Allison would finish the book, and I worried that she wouldn't abandon *Twilight* if she didn't enjoy it because she didn't want to offend Lynnsey. Allison had never read a book as long as *Twilight,* and I knew that the book's plot bogged down in places—not the best situation for a developing reader. I kept my misgivings hidden because I wanted it to work.

A week into reading *Twilight,* Allison announced to me that she loved it. I celebrated with her, and we discussed where she was in the book, her predictions about the love triangle of Edward, Jacob, and Bella; her opinions about Bella; and her thoughts about vampires and werewolves. When Allison finished *Twilight,* she moved on to *New Moon,* then *Eclipse.* Pleased that Allison had finally found several books in a row that she enjoyed, I squashed my lukewarm feelings about the series and stopped by her desk often to talk about the books with her.

When Allison was halfway through the final book in the Twilight series, *Breaking Dawn,* I conferred with her about her future reading plans: "What do you plan to read when you finish *Breaking Dawn?*"

Allison seemed surprised: "I haven't really thought about what I would like to read next."

As exciting as it was that Allison had finally found a series she could stick with and complete, I knew that if she didn't find another book soon, she might quickly slip back into her nonreading habits. Assessing Allison's inconsistent reading experiences, I couldn't see clear preferences that would inform future book choices. She did like the Twilight series, though, so it was a place to start. I asked her, "What fascinates you about the Twilight series? Is it the vampires? Is it the romance?"

Allison shrugged, "I am not really sure. I know that Bella and Edward's relationship keeps me interested in the story. I have to keep reading the series to see if they stay together or someone dies. I was worried that the books would be scary, but they aren't."

I replied to Allison, "If you can decide what appeals to you about the Twilight series, that information can lead you to more books you might enjoy reading. Think about it while you're reading *Breaking Dawn* and let me know what you think the next time we talk."

When I stopped to confer with Allison the next day, she told me that she liked the Twilight series because of the romance, not the vampires and werewolves. Armed with this knowledge, I considered what books to suggest next that would keep her reading momentum going. Sarah Dessen was the perfect choice of an author for her because she writes prolifically and her books are relatively tame compared to other teen romance offerings—a good fit for Allison. I asked Zoe, our resident romance book expert, to recommend the best title for someone trying Sarah Dessen's work for the first time. Zoe wholeheartedly suggested *Lock and Key*, a recommendation that other romance readers in class approved as well.

Allison breezed through *Lock and Key* in a few days and read the other Sarah Dessen books on our mature shelf. Carrying an armload of books, Allison bounded into our classroom one Monday morning, "Mrs. Miller, my dad was so surprised that I wanted to go to the bookstore this weekend that he bought me four books! I bought some Sarah Dessen books that you don't have." Allison's announcement drew a crowd of other readers who began passing the books, reading the jacket copy, comparing covers, and jotting titles into their notebooks.

Conferring with students later, I noticed Allison and Lynnsey chatting and looking at Allison's new books. At one point, Allison retrieved *Lock and Key* from a bookcase and gave it to her friend. Smiling, Allison—formerly dependent on book recommendations from others—was suggesting books to one of the wildest readers in our class.

When Allison finished her Sarah Dessen collection, she found other books to read—discovering them in the library, asking friends for recommendations, and reading reviews online. She teased me when she discovered that I didn't enjoy Twilight or romance novels that much: "You sure know a lot about those books when you don't really like them."

I laughed, "Allison, I need to read a little bit of everything, so I can help you find what *you* like."

Learning more about books and authors, reading every day, developing relationships with other readers like Lynnsey and Zoe, committing to a long series like Twilight, and reflecting on her developing preferences and experiences gave Allison greater confidence and self-efficacy. Through her successes, Allison began to see herself as a reader as much as any other student in our class. No longer dependent on my book recommendations, our class library, or conferring with me to keep her motivated, Allison acquired tools to sustain her reading habits. She became a wild reader in sixth grade.

On the last day of school, Allison hugged me and said, "Who knew, Mrs. Miller? Who knew that reading would be something I was good at?"

Teary-eyed, I gave her a squeeze: "I knew, Allison, I always knew. And now you know it, too."

# Appendix A: Reader's Notebook Sheets

## Form A.1 Genre Requirements Graph

| Number of Books | Realistic Fiction | Historical Fiction | Fantasy | Science Fiction | Biography Autobiography Memoir | Nonfiction | Poetry | Traditional Literature | Graphic Novels |
|---|---|---|---|---|---|---|---|---|---|
| 1 | | | | | | | | | |
| 2 | | | | | | | | | |
| 3 | | | | | | | | | |
| 4 | | | | | | | | | |
| 5 | | | | | | | | | |
| 6 | | | | | | | | | |
| 7 | | | | | | | | | |
| 8 | | | | | | | | | |
| 9 | | | | | | | | | |
| 10 | | | | | | | | | |
| 11 | | | | | | | | | |
| 12 | | | | | | | | | |
| 13 | | | | | | | | | |
| 14 | | | | | | | | | |
| 15 | | | | | | | | | |
| 16 | | | | | | | | | |
| 17 | | | | | | | | | |
| 18 | | | | | | | | | |
| 19 | | | | | | | | | |
| 20 | | | | | | | | | |

## My Reading List

Choose a book to read. Record the title, author, and the date you begin reading it.
When you finish the book, record the date you finished and assign the book a star rating.
If you abandon the book, record an (A) in the genre column.

| Title | Author | Genre | Date Started | Date Finished |
|---|---|---|---|---|
| | | | | |

| Star Rating | How did you choose this book? |
|---|---|
| ☆ ☆ ☆ ☆ ☆ | |

| Title | Author | Genre | Date Started | Date Finished |
|---|---|---|---|---|
| | | | | |

| Star Rating | How did you choose this book? |
|---|---|
| ☆ ☆ ☆ ☆ ☆ | |

| Title | Author | Genre | Date Started | Date Finished |
|---|---|---|---|---|
| | | | | |

| Star Rating | How did you choose this book? |
|---|---|
| ☆ ☆ ☆ ☆ ☆ | |

| Title | Author | Genre | Date Started | Date Finished |
|---|---|---|---|---|
| | | | | |

| Star Rating | How did you choose this book? |
|---|---|
| ☆ ☆ ☆ ☆ ☆ | |

| Title | Author | Genre | Date Started | Date Finished |
|---|---|---|---|---|
| | | | | |

| Star Rating | How did you choose this book? |
|---|---|
| ☆ ☆ ☆ ☆ ☆ | |

| Title | Author | Genre | Date Started | Date Finished |
|---|---|---|---|---|
| | | | | |

| Star Rating | How did you choose this book? |
|---|---|
| ☆ ☆ ☆ ☆ ☆ | |

| Title | Author | Genre | Date Started | Date Finished |
|---|---|---|---|---|
| | | | | |

| Star Rating | How did you choose this book? |
|---|---|
| ☆ ☆ ☆ ☆ ☆ | |

| Title | Author | Genre | Date Started | Date Finished |
|---|---|---|---|---|
| | | | | |

| Star Rating | How did you choose this book? |
|---|---|
| ☆ ☆ ☆ ☆ ☆ | |

| Title | Author | Genre | Date Started | Date Finished |
|---|---|---|---|---|
| | | | | |

| Star Rating | How did you choose this book? |
|---|---|
| ☆ ☆ ☆ ☆ ☆ | |

| Title | Author | Genre | Date Started | Date Finished |
|---|---|---|---|---|
| | | | | |

| Star Rating | How did you choose this book? |
|---|---|
| ☆ ☆ ☆ ☆ ☆ | |

| Title | Author | Genre | Date Started | Date Finished |
|---|---|---|---|---|
| | | | | |

| Star Rating | How did you choose this book? |
|---|---|
| ☆ ☆ ☆ ☆ ☆ | |

| Title | Author | Genre | Date Started | Date Finished |
|---|---|---|---|---|
| | | | | |

| Star Rating | How did you choose this book? |
|---|---|
| ☆ ☆ ☆ ☆ ☆ | |

| Title | Author | Genre | Date Started | Date Finished |
|---|---|---|---|---|
| | | | | |

| Star Rating | How did you choose this book? |
|---|---|
| ☆ ☆ ☆ ☆ ☆ | |

| Title | Author | Genre | Date Started | Date Finished |
|---|---|---|---|---|
| | | | | |

| Star Rating | How did you choose this book? |
|---|---|
| ☆ ☆ ☆ ☆ ☆ | |

| Title | Author | Genre | Date Started | Date Finished |
|---|---|---|---|---|
| | | | | |

| Star Rating | How did you choose this book? |
|---|---|
| ☆ ☆ ☆ ☆ ☆ | |

| Title | Author | Genre | Date Started | Date Finished |
|---|---|---|---|---|
|  |  |  |  |  |

| Star Rating | How did you choose this book? |
|---|---|
| ☆ ☆ ☆ ☆ ☆ |  |

| Title | Author | Genre | Date Started | Date Finished |
|---|---|---|---|---|
|  |  |  |  |  |

| Star Rating | How did you choose this book? |
|---|---|
| ☆ ☆ ☆ ☆ ☆ |  |

| Title | Author | Genre | Date Started | Date Finished |
|---|---|---|---|---|
|  |  |  |  |  |

| Star Rating | How did you choose this book? |
|---|---|
| ☆ ☆ ☆ ☆ ☆ |  |

| Title | Author | Genre | Date Started | Date Finished |
|---|---|---|---|---|
|  |  |  |  |  |

| Star Rating | How did you choose this book? |
|---|---|
| ☆ ☆ ☆ ☆ ☆ |  |

| Title | Author | Genre | Date Started | Date Finished |
|---|---|---|---|---|
|  |  |  |  |  |

| Star Rating | How did you choose this book? |
|---|---|
| ☆ ☆ ☆ ☆ ☆ |  |

| Title | Author | Genre | Date Started | Date Finished |
|---|---|---|---|---|
|  |  |  |  |  |

| Star Rating | How did you choose this book? |
|---|---|
| ☆ ☆ ☆ ☆ ☆ |  |

| Title | Author | Genre | Date Started | Date Finished |
|---|---|---|---|---|
|  |  |  |  |  |

| Star Rating | How did you choose this book? |
|---|---|
| ☆ ☆ ☆ ☆ ☆ |  |

| Title | Author | Genre | Date Started | Date Finished |
|---|---|---|---|---|
|  |  |  |  |  |

| Star Rating | How did you choose this book? |
|---|---|
| ☆ ☆ ☆ ☆ ☆ |  |

| Title | Author | Genre | Date Started | Date Finished |
|---|---|---|---|---|
| | | | | |

| Star Rating | How did you choose this book? |
|---|---|
| ☆ ☆ ☆ ☆ ☆ | |

| Title | Author | Genre | Date Started | Date Finished |
|---|---|---|---|---|
| | | | | |

| Star Rating | How did you choose this book? |
|---|---|
| ☆ ☆ ☆ ☆ ☆ | |

| Title | Author | Genre | Date Started | Date Finished |
|---|---|---|---|---|
| | | | | |

| Star Rating | How did you choose this book? |
|---|---|
| ☆ ☆ ☆ ☆ ☆ | |

| Title | Author | Genre | Date Started | Date Finished |
|---|---|---|---|---|
| | | | | |

| Star Rating | How did you choose this book? |
|---|---|
| ☆ ☆ ☆ ☆ ☆ | |

| Title | Author | Genre | Date Started | Date Finished |
|---|---|---|---|---|
| | | | | |

| Star Rating | How did you choose this book? |
|---|---|
| ☆ ☆ ☆ ☆ ☆ | |

| Title | Author | Genre | Date Started | Date Finished |
|---|---|---|---|---|
| | | | | |

| Star Rating | How did you choose this book? |
|---|---|
| ☆ ☆ ☆ ☆ ☆ | |

| Title | Author | Genre | Date Started | Date Finished |
|---|---|---|---|---|
| | | | | |

| Star Rating | How did you choose this book? |
|---|---|
| ☆ ☆ ☆ ☆ ☆ | |

| Title | Author | Genre | Date Started | Date Finished |
|---|---|---|---|---|
| | | | | |

| Star Rating | How did you choose this book? |
|---|---|
| ☆ ☆ ☆ ☆ ☆ | |

| Title | Author | Genre | Date Started | Date Finished |
|---|---|---|---|---|
|  |  |  |  |  |

| Star Rating | How did you choose this book? |
|---|---|
| ☆ ☆ ☆ ☆ ☆ |  |

| Title | Author | Genre | Date Started | Date Finished |
|---|---|---|---|---|
|  |  |  |  |  |

| Star Rating | How did you choose this book? |
|---|---|
| ☆ ☆ ☆ ☆ ☆ |  |

| Title | Author | Genre | Date Started | Date Finished |
|---|---|---|---|---|
|  |  |  |  |  |

| Star Rating | How did you choose this book? |
|---|---|
| ☆ ☆ ☆ ☆ ☆ |  |

| Title | Author | Genre | Date Started | Date Finished |
|---|---|---|---|---|
|  |  |  |  |  |

| Star Rating | How did you choose this book? |
|---|---|
| ☆ ☆ ☆ ☆ ☆ |  |

| Title | Author | Genre | Date Started | Date Finished |
|---|---|---|---|---|
|  |  |  |  |  |

| Star Rating | How did you choose this book? |
|---|---|
| ☆ ☆ ☆ ☆ ☆ |  |

| Title | Author | Genre | Date Started | Date Finished |
|---|---|---|---|---|
|  |  |  |  |  |

| Star Rating | How did you choose this book? |
|---|---|
| ☆ ☆ ☆ ☆ ☆ |  |

| Title | Author | Genre | Date Started | Date Finished |
|---|---|---|---|---|
|  |  |  |  |  |

| Star Rating | How did you choose this book? |
|---|---|
| ☆ ☆ ☆ ☆ ☆ |  |

| Title | Author | Genre | Date Started | Date Finished |
|---|---|---|---|---|
|  |  |  |  |  |

| Star Rating | How did you choose this book? |
|---|---|
| ☆ ☆ ☆ ☆ ☆ |  |

| Title | Author | Genre | Date Started | Date Finished |
|---|---|---|---|---|
| | | | | |

| Star Rating | How did you choose this book? |
|---|---|
| ☆ ☆ ☆ ☆ ☆ | |

| Title | Author | Genre | Date Started | Date Finished |
|---|---|---|---|---|
| | | | | |

| Star Rating | How did you choose this book? |
|---|---|
| ☆ ☆ ☆ ☆ ☆ | |

| Title | Author | Genre | Date Started | Date Finished |
|---|---|---|---|---|
| | | | | |

| Star Rating | How did you choose this book? |
|---|---|
| ☆ ☆ ☆ ☆ ☆ | |

| Title | Author | Genre | Date Started | Date Finished |
|---|---|---|---|---|
| | | | | |

| Star Rating | How did you choose this book? |
|---|---|
| ☆ ☆ ☆ ☆ ☆ | |

| Title | Author | Genre | Date Started | Date Finished |
|---|---|---|---|---|
| | | | | |

| Star Rating | How did you choose this book? |
|---|---|
| ☆ ☆ ☆ ☆ ☆ | |

| Title | Author | Genre | Date Started | Date Finished |
|---|---|---|---|---|
| | | | | |

| Star Rating | How did you choose this book? |
|---|---|
| ☆ ☆ ☆ ☆ ☆ | |

| Title | Author | Genre | Date Started | Date Finished |
|---|---|---|---|---|
| | | | | |

| Star Rating | How did you choose this book? |
|---|---|
| ☆ ☆ ☆ ☆ ☆ | |

| Title | Author | Genre | Date Started | Date Finished |
|---|---|---|---|---|
| | | | | |

| Star Rating | How did you choose this book? |
|---|---|
| ☆ ☆ ☆ ☆ ☆ | |

| Title | Author | Check When Completed |
|---|---|---|
|  |  |  |
|  |  |  |
|  |  |  |
|  |  |  |
|  |  |  |
|  |  |  |
|  |  |  |
|  |  |  |
|  |  |  |
|  |  |  |
|  |  |  |
|  |  |  |
|  |  |  |
|  |  |  |

*Source:* Reprinted with permission from Irene Fountas and Gay Su Pinnell, *Guiding Readers and Writers (Grades 3–6): Teaching Comprehension, Genre, and Content Literacy.* Portsmouth, NH: Heinemann, 2001.

## Form A.4  Status of the Class

| Date | Title | Page Number | I am at the part where . . . |
|------|-------|-------------|------------------------------|
|      |       |             |                              |
|      |       |             |                              |
|      |       |             |                              |
|      |       |             |                              |
|      |       |             |                              |
|      |       |             |                              |
|      |       |             |                              |
|      |       |             |                              |
|      |       |             |                              |
|      |       |             |                              |
|      |       |             |                              |
|      |       |             |                              |
|      |       |             |                              |
|      |       |             |                              |
|      |       |             |                              |
|      |       |             |                              |
|      |       |             |                              |

*Appendix B: Reading Habits Reflections*

## Form B.1  My Reading Itinerary

Beginning Date: _____

Ending Date: _____

Keep a list of your reading travels this week. Record every place you read and how much time you spend reading.

---

Date/Day: _____

Place: _____

| Amount of Time | 1–15 min. | 16–30 min. | 31–45 min. | 46–60 min. | other |
|---|---|---|---|---|---|

---

Date/Day: _____

Place: _____

| Amount of Time | 1–15 min. | 16–30 min. | 31–45 min. | 46–60 min. | other |
|---|---|---|---|---|---|

---

Date/Day: _____

Place: _____

| Amount of Time | 1–15 min. | 16–30 min. | 31–45 min. | 46–60 min. | other |
|---|---|---|---|---|---|

Date/Day: _____

Place: _____

| Amount of Time | 1–15 min. | 16–30 min. | 31–45 min. | 46–60 min. | other |
|---|---|---|---|---|---|

Date/Day: _____

Place: _____

| Amount of Time | 1–15 min. | 16–30 min. | 31–45 min. | 46–60 min. | other |
|---|---|---|---|---|---|

Date/Day: _____

Place: _____

| Amount of Time | 1–15 min. | 16–30 min. | 31–45 min. | 46–60 min. | other |
|---|---|---|---|---|---|

Date/Day: _____

Place: _____

| Amount of Time | 1–15 min. | 16–30 min. | 31–45 min. | 46–60 min. | other |
|---|---|---|---|---|---|

Date/Day: _____

Place: _____

| Amount of Time | 1–15 min. | 16–30 min. | 31–45 min. | 46–60 min. | other |
|---|---|---|---|---|---|

Date/Day: _____

Place: _____

| Amount of Time | 1–15 min. | 16–30 min. | 31–45 min. | 46–60 min. | other |
|---|---|---|---|---|---|

Date/Day:  _____

Place:  _____

| Amount of Time | 1–15 min. | 16–30 min. | 31–45 min. | 46–60 min. | other |
|---|---|---|---|---|---|

Date/Day:  _____

Place:  _____

| Amount of Time | 1–15 min. | 16–30 min. | 31–45 min. | 46–60 min. | other |
|---|---|---|---|---|---|

Date/Day:  _____

Place:  _____

| Amount of Time | 1–15 min. | 16–30 min. | 31–45 min. | 46–60 min. | other |
|---|---|---|---|---|---|

## Form B.1  My Reading Itinerary (continued)

Review your reading travels this week and answer the following questions.

Where do you spend the most time reading?

_____

_____

_____

What appeals to you about reading in this place?

_____

_____

_____

Do you read more during or outside of school? Why?

_____

_____

_____

Do you think that finding time to read is easy or hard for you? Why?

_____

_____

_____

Describe in detail your perfect reading place.

_____

_____

_____

What did you learn about your reading habits this week?

_____

_____

_____

## Form B.2 My Selection Reflection

Reader: _____

List the last five books you have chosen to read. Include the book you are currently reading or any books that you have abandoned. Describe how you chose each book.

Title: _____

Author: _____

How did you choose
this book? _____

|  | It was amazing. | It was good. | It was boring. | I am still reading it. | Abandoned |
|---|---|---|---|---|---|
| Rate this book: |  |  |  |  |  |

Title: _____

Author: _____

How did you choose
this book? _____

|  | It was amazing. | It was good. | It was boring. | I am still reading it. | Abandoned |
|---|---|---|---|---|---|
| Rate this book: |  |  |  |  |  |

Title: _____

Author: _____

How did you choose
this book? _____

Rate this book:  It was amazing.  It was good.  It was boring.  I am still reading it.  Abandoned

---

Title: _____

Author: _____

How did you choose
this book? _____

Rate this book:  It was amazing.  It was good.  It was boring.  I am still reading it.  Abandoned

---

Title: _____

Author: _____

How did you choose
this book? _____

Rate this book:  It was amazing.  It was good.  It was boring.  I am still reading it.  Abandoned

Answer the following questions about your book choices.

How do you find out about books that you would like to read?

_____

_____

_____

When you see a book or hear about it, how do you decide that it is a book you would or would not like to read?

_____

_____

_____

Do you ever abandon a book? Why or why not?

_____

_____

_____

Are you successful in choosing your own books to read? Why or why not?

_____

_____

_____

## Form B.3  My Reading Influences

Reader _____

Think about the other readers that you know and how you share books. Answer the following reflection questions about your reading influences.

List readers that you know who talk to you on a regular basis about books and reading.

_____    _____

_____    _____

_____    _____

Think about how you share books and reading with other readers. Provide an example for each one that applies to you.

Take book recommendations

_____

_____

Give book recommendations

_____

_____

Loan your personal books

_____

_____

Borrow another reader's personal books

_____

_____

Talk to other readers about what you are reading

_____

_____

Book Commercials

_____

_____

Write book reviews

_____

_____

Post comments to online sites

_____

_____

How have the other readers you know influenced your reading?

_____

_____

_____

How have you influenced other readers?

_____

_____

_____

Is it important for you to have other readers to talk to about books and reading? Explain why or why not.

_____

_____

_____

# Appendix C: Reading Habits Assessments

**Independent Reading Time Observation**     Reader: _____

| Date_____ Start Time _____ End Time_____ | | |
| --- | --- | --- |
| **Minute** | **Reading** | **Other Observed Behaviors** |
| 1 | Yes  No | |
| 2 | Yes  No | |
| 3 | Yes  No | |
| 4 | Yes  No | |
| 5 | Yes  No | |
| 6 | Yes  No | |
| 7 | Yes  No | |
| 8 | Yes  No | |
| 9 | Yes  No | |
| 10 | Yes  No | |

| Date_____ Start Time _____ End Time_____ | | |
| --- | --- | --- |
| **Minute** | **Reading** | **Other Observed Behaviors** |
| 1 | Yes  No | |
| 2 | Yes  No | |
| 3 | Yes  No | |
| 4 | Yes  No | |
| 5 | Yes  No | |
| 6 | Yes  No | |
| 7 | Yes  No | |
| 8 | Yes  No | |
| 9 | Yes  No | |
| 10 | Yes  No | |

| Date_____ Start Time _____ End Time_____ | | |
| --- | --- | --- |
| **Minute** | **Reading** | **Other Observed Behaviors** |
| 1 | Yes  No | |
| 2 | Yes  No | |
| 3 | Yes  No | |
| 4 | Yes  No | |
| 5 | Yes  No | |
| 6 | Yes  No | |
| 7 | Yes  No | |
| 8 | Yes  No | |
| 9 | Yes  No | |
| 10 | Yes  No | |

My reflection:

_____

_____

_____

Reader's reflection:

_____

_____

_____

Our plan:

_____

_____

_____

Taken from *Reading in the Wild*, by Donalyn Miller and Susan Kelley, copyright © 2014 Donalyn Miller and Susan Kelley. Used with permission.

**Form C.2**

### Reading Habits Conference Chart

Date _____ Grading Period 1 2 3 4 5 6

| Reader | Preferences | Engagement | Record Keeping | Commitment | Selection |
|---|---|---|---|---|---|
| reading level | text level | school / home | | abandoned / plan | recommendations / other |

Currently reading: _____ What number book is this for the year? _____

| | Preferences | Engagement | Record Keeping | Commitment | Selection |
|---|---|---|---|---|---|
| reading level | text level | school / home | | abandoned / plan | recommendations / other |

Currently reading: _____ What number book is this for the year? _____

| | Preferences | Engagement | Record Keeping | Commitment | Selection |
|---|---|---|---|---|---|
| reading level | text level | school / home | | abandoned / plan | recommendations / other |

Currently reading: _____ What number book is this for the year? _____

Preferences: Does the student show preferences for genres, authors, series? What is the text difficulty of the books he/she reads?
Engagement: How engaged is the student during reading time? Is the student reading at home?
Record Keeping: Is the student using his/her reader's notebook to keep accurate reading records?
Commitment: Does the student abandon books? What is the student's plan for future reading?
Selection: How does the student primarily choose his or her books?

# Appendix D: Reading Habits Surveys

## Form D.1  Wild Reader Survey

1. Do you consider yourself an avid reader—someone who chooses to read often?

   _____

2. On average, how much time do you spend reading each week?

   _____

3. How do you find out about books you would like to read? (Choose all answers that apply.)

   ☐ Authors' blogs or websites
   ☐ Book award lists
   ☐ Book club
   ☐ Book review blogs or websites
   ☐ Book vendor websites and publications
   ☐ Bookstore displays
   ☐ Library websites and publications
   ☐ Periodicals
   ☐ Professional book review publications

   ☐ Publishers' catalogues or websites
   ☐ Randomly chosen
   ☐ Recommendations from colleagues and/or librarians
   ☐ Recommendations from family, friends, and/or students
   ☐ Social networking sites (Facebook, Twitter, Goodreads, Shelfari, etc.)
   ☐ Workshop presentations

   Other (please specify) _____

   _____

4. How do you share books and reading with other readers? (Choose all answers that apply.)

   ☐ Do not share books and reading with others
   ☐ Donate books or give as gifts
   ☐ Give spontaneous testimonials
   ☐ Lend or trade books

   ☐ Novel or author studies with children or students
   ☐ Participate in a book club
   ☐ Post to blogs or websites

☐ Post to social networking sites (Facebook, Twitter, Goodreads, Shelfari, etc.)

☐ Read-alouds with children or students

☐ Share reading with children or students

☐ Write reviews

Other (please specify) _____

_____

5. How do you plan for future reading? (Choose all answers that apply.)
   ☐ Book club lists
   ☐ Do not plan for future reading
   ☐ Follow book award announcements
   ☐ Follow new releases by favorite authors
   ☐ Follow new releases in a series
   ☐ Keep a to-read list
   ☐ Keep a to-read stack of books
   ☐ Preorder new releases
   ☐ Reserve books at the library

Other (please specify) _____

_____

6. What types of books do you commonly read? (Choose all answers that apply.)

| Genre | Fiction | Nonfiction | Poetry |
|---|---|---|---|
| Picture books | ☐ | ☐ | ☐ |
| Early Elementary (K–3) | ☐ | ☐ | ☐ |
| Middle Grade (4–6) | ☐ | ☐ | ☐ |
| Young Adult (7–12) | ☐ | ☐ | ☐ |
| Adult books | ☐ | ☐ | ☐ |
| Professional books | ☐ | ☐ | ☐ |

Other (please specify) _____

7. List your three favorite books.

_____

_____

_____

8. List your three favorite authors.

_____

_____

_____

9. What are your favorite genres?
   ☐ Realistic Fiction
   ☐ Historical fiction
   ☐ Fantasy
   ☐ Science fiction
   ☐ Poetry
   ☐ Traditional literature (myths, legends, folktales/fairy tales)
   ☐ Nonfiction (biography, autobiography, memoir)
   ☐ Nonfiction (informational)

Other (please specify) _____

_____

_____

10. What is the greatest obstacle that prevents you from reading as much as you would like?
    ☐ Assigned reading for work or school
    ☐ Few opportunities to share books and reading with other readers
    ☐ Lack of information about books
    ☐ Nothing stands in my way
    ☐ Too busy

    Other (please specify) _____
    _____

11. Please provide additional information about your reading experiences that you would like to include.

    _____

    _____

    _____

    _____

    _____

    _____

    _____

    _____

## Form D.2  End-of-Year Reading Habits Survey

Thank you for participating in this survey about your reading habits. Your comments will help future students!

**Reader's Name** _____

### Do you like to read?

☐ Yes
☐ No

### How well do you think you read?

☐ below grade level
☐ average
☐ above grade level

### How much time do you spend reading during an average week?

☐ 0–3 hours
☐ 4–6 hours
☐ 7–10 hours
☐ more than 10 hours

### What is the greatest obstacle that prevents you from reading?

☐ not enough time
☐ nothing to read that interests me
☐ no one to share books with or talk to about reading
☐ nothing stands in my way

**Where are your favorite places to read?**

1. _____

2. _____

3. _____

**How many books have you read this year?** _____

**Have you read more or less than last year?**

☐ More
☐ Less
☐ About the same

If less, explain why:

_____

_____

**How do you find books you would like to read? (check all that apply)**

☐ teachers' recommendations
☐ librarians' recommendations
☐ friends' recommendations
☐ family members' recommendations
☐ book commercials
☐ library visits
☐ book order forms
☐ bookstores
☐ series
☐ authors
☐ randomly chosen
☐ Other (please specify)

_____

_____

# Rank the parts of our class environment that help you as a reader.

| | Tenth | Ninth | Eighth | Seventh | Sixth | Fifth | Fourth | Third | Second | First |
|---|---|---|---|---|---|---|---|---|---|---|
| class reading time | | | | | | | | | | |
| home reading time | | | | | | | | | | |
| classroom library | | | | | | | | | | |
| school library | | | | | | | | | | |
| genre requirements | | | | | | | | | | |
| teacher who reads | | | | | | | | | | |
| classmates who read | | | | | | | | | | |
| assignments that relate to reading (Hero's Journey, Newbery) | | | | | | | | | | |
| discussions about books | | | | | | | | | | |
| read-alouds | | | | | | | | | | |

**What was the best book you read this year?**

_____

**What made this book so good?**

_____

**List 5 books you plan to read over the summer.**

1. _____

2. _____

3. _____

4. _____

5. _____

**List any books you look forward to reading when they are published.**

1. _____

2. _____

3. _____

4. _____

5. _____

**How did you surprise yourself as a reader this year?**

_____

_____

_____

## Form D.3  End-of-Year Reading Preferences Survey

Thank you for participating in this survey about your reading preferences. Your suggestions will help future readers!

**Reader's name:** _____

**List your favorite books.**

1. _____

2. _____

3. _____

4. _____

5. _____

**List your favorite authors.**

1. _____

2. _____

3. _____

4. _____

5. _____

**List any series that you have completed in your lifetime.**

1. _____

2. _____

3. _____

4. _____

5. _____

## List any series that you are currently reading or following.

1. _____
2. _____
3. _____
4. _____
5. _____

## What is your favorite genre?

☐ traditional literature
☐ poetry
☐ realistic fiction
☐ historical fiction
☐ fantasy
☐ science fiction
☐ mystery
☐ biography, autobiography, memoir
☐ informational (nonfiction)
☐ Other (please specify) _____

## Why is this genre your favorite? _____

_____

_____

## What is your LEAST favorite genre?

☐ traditional literature
☐ poetry
☐ realistic fiction
☐ historical fiction
☐ fantasy
☐ science fiction
☐ mystery
☐ biography, autobiography, memoir
☐ informational (nonfiction)
☐ Other (please specify) _____

## Why is this genre your least favorite? _____

_____

_____

## List any nonfiction topics that you enjoy reading about.

1. _____

2. _____

3. _____

4. _____

5. _____

# Appendix E: Students' Favorite Titles and Series

THESE LISTS OFFER STUDENTS' FAVORITE titles and series reported on their end-of-year preferences surveys for the 2010–2011 and 2011–2012 school years. An asterisk indicates the first book in a series or the existence of companion titles. The titles represent a wide range of genres, formats, reading levels, and content.

## Realistic Fiction

*13 Little Blue Envelopes*
    by Maureen Johnson*

*Airhead* by Meg Cabot*

*Alabama Moon* by Watt Key

*Anything But Typical*
    by Nora Raleigh Baskin

*Blindsided*
    by Priscilla Cummings

*Bluefish* by Pat Schmatz

*Boys Are Dogs* by Leslie Margolis*

*Boys without Names*
    by Kashmira Sheth

*Bridge to Terabithia*
    by Katherine Paterson

*Bronx Masquerade*
    by Nikki Grimes

*Capture the Flag*
    by Kate Messner*

*Chasing Redbird*
    by Sharon Creech

*Chicken Boy*
    by Frances O'Roark Dowell

*The Clique* by Lisi Harrison*

*Close to Famous* by Joan Bauer

*A Crooked Kind of Perfect*
    by Linda Urban

*Curveball: The Year I Lost My Grip*
    by Jordan Sonnenblick

*Deadline* by Chris Crutcher

*The Diary of a Wimpy Kid*
    by Jeff Kinney*

*Doodle Bug: A Novel in Doodles*
    by Karen Romano Young

*Drums, Girls, and Dangerous Pie*
    by Jordan Sonnenblick*

*Eight Keys* by Suzanne LeFleur

*Flipped*
    by Wendelin Van Draanen

*Flying Solo* by Ralph Fletcher

*Football Genius* by Tim Green

*The Fourth Stall*
    by Chris Rylander*

*Ghetto Cowboy* by G. Neri

*Great Wall of Lucy Wu*
    by Wendy Wan-Long
    Shang

*Guys Read: Funny Business*
    by Jon Scieszka*

*Hatchet* by Gary Paulsen

*Heart of a Shepherd*
    by Rosanne Parry

*Heat* by Mike Lupica

*The Heist Society* by Ally Carter*

*Hoot* by Carl Hiaasen

*Hound Dog True*
    by Linda Urban

*How to Survive Middle School*
    by Donna Gephart

*Hurt Go Happy* by Ginny Rorby

*If I Stay* by Gayle Forman*

*Keeper* by Mal Peet

*Kissed by an Angel*
    by Elizabeth Chandler*

*Leepike Ridge* by N. D. Wilson

*Lock and Key*
    by Sarah Dessen

*The London Eye Mystery*
    by Siobhan Dowd

*A Long Walk to Water*
    by Linda Sue Park

*A Mango-Shaped Space*
    by Wendy Mass

*Millicent Min: Girl Genius*
    by Lisa Yee*

*Ninth Ward* by Jewell Rhodes

*No More Dead Dogs*
    by Gordon Korman

*Notes from a Midnight Driver*
 by Jordan Sonnenblick

*One for the Murphys*
 by Lynda Mullaly Hunt

*Out of My Mind* by Sharon Draper

*The Outside of a Horse*
 by Ginny Rorby

*The Outsiders* by S. E. Hinton

*Peak* by Roland Smith

*Pie* by Sarah Weeks

*The Princess Diaries*
 by Meg Cabot*

*Red Kayak* by Priscilla Cummings

*Riding Invisible*
 by Sandra Alonzo

*Rivals* by Tim Green

*Ruby Holler* by Sharon Creech

*Rules* by Cynthia Lord

*The Rules of Survival*
 by Nancy Werlin

*The Running Dream*
 by Wendelin Van Draanen

*The Schwa Was Here*
 by Neal Shusterman*

*See You at Harry's* by Jo Knowles

*Shiloh* by Phyllis Reynolds
 Naylor*

*So B. It* by Sarah Weeks

*Someone Like You*
 by Sarah Dessen

*Stargirl* by Jerry Spinelli*

*The Storm Runners*
 by Roland Smith*

*The Strange Case of Origami Yoda*
 by Tom Angleberger

*Stupid Fast* by Geoff Herbach*

*The Summer I Turned Pretty*
 by Jenny Han*

*Swindle* by Gordon Korman*

*Touch Blue* by Cynthia Lord

*Trash* by Andy Mulligan

*Travel Team* by Mike Lupica

*True ( . . . Sort Of)*
 by Katherine Hannigan

*ttfn* by Lauren Myracle*

*Twisted* by Laurie Halse
 Anderson

*Umbrella Summer* by Lisa Graff

*Waiting for Normal*
 by Leslie Connor

*Walk Two Moons*
 by Sharon Creech

*Ways to Live Forever*
 by Sally Nichols

*Wild Things* by Clay Carmichael

*Wonder* by R. J. Palacio

*Zach's Lie* by Roland Smith*

## Historical Fiction

*A Long Way from Chicago*
  by Richard Peck*

*Al Capone Does My Shirts*
  by Gennifer
  Choldenko*

*Alchemy and Meggy Swann*
  by Karen Cushman

*Bamboo People* by Mitali Perkins

*Between Shades of Gray*
  by Ruta Sepetys

*The Black Stallion*
  by Walter Farley*

*Blood Red Horse* by K. M. Grant*

*Bloody Jack: Being an Account of
  the Curious Adventures of
  Mary "Jacky" Faber, Ship's
  Boy* by L. A. Meyer*

*The Book Thief* by Markus Zusak

*Boy at War* by Harry Mazer*

*Breaking Stalin's Nose*
  by Eugene Yelchin

*The Brooklyn Nine*
  by Alan Gratz

*Bud, Not Buddy* by Christopher
  Paul Curtis

*Chains* by Laurie Halse
  Anderson*

*Code Talker: A Novel about the
  Navajo Marines of World War
  Two* by Joseph Bruchac

*Countdown* by Deborah Wiles*

*Crispin: A Cross of Lead* by Avi*

*Dead End in Norvelt*
  by Jack Gantos

*The Devil's Arithmetic*
  by Jane Yolen

*The Earth Dragon Awakes: The
  San Francisco Earthquake of
  1906* by Laurence Yep

*Elephant Run* by Roland Smith

*Eliza's Freedom Road*
  by Jerdine Nolan

*Fever 1793* by Laurie Halse
  Anderson

*The Friendship Doll*
  by Kirby Larson

*Green Glass Sea* by Ellen Klages*

*Hattie Big Sky* by Kirby Larson*

*Homeless Bird* by Gloria Whelan

*I Survived: The Sinking of the Titanic, 1912* by Lauren Tarshis*

*Island of the Blue Dolphins* by Scott O'Dell

*Jason's Gold* by Will Hobbs

*Lay That Trumpet in Our Hands* by Susan McCarthy

*May B* by Caroline Rose Starr

*Nory Ryan's Song* by Patricia Reilly Giff*

*Number the Stars* by Lois Lowry

*One Crazy Summer* by Rita-Williams Garcia*

*The Ravenmaster's Secret: Escape from the Tower of London* by Elvira Woodruff

*Saving Zasha* by Randi Barrow*

*Secret Keeper* by Mitali Perkins

*Soldier X* by Don Wuffson

*Soldier's Heart* by Gary Paulsen

*Thunder from the Sea* by Joan Hiatt Harlow

*Trouble Don't Last* by Shelley Pearsall

*The True Confessions of Charlotte Doyle* by Avi

*Turtle in Paradise* by Jennifer Holm

*War Horse* by Michael Morpurgo

*The Water Seeker* by Kimberly Willis Holt

*Watsons Go to Birmingham—1963* by Christopher Paul Curtis

*The Wednesday Wars* by Gary Schmidt*

*Where the Red Fern Grows* by Wilson Rawls

*Wonderstruck* by Brian Selznick

*Woods Runner* by Gary Paulsen

## Fantasy and Traditional Literature

*100 Cupboards* by N. D. Wilson*

*11 Birthdays* by Wendy Mass*

*The Alchemyst* by Michael Scott*

*Alice in Wonderland*
   by Lewis Carroll

*Artemis Fowl*
   by Eoin Colfer*

*The Bad Beginning*
   by Lemony Snicket*

*Beastly* by Alex Flinn

*Bigger Than a Breadbox*
   by Laurel Snyder

*The Book of Three*
   by Lloyd Alexander*

*Breadcrumbs* by Anne Ursu

*Breathe* by Clif McNish

*The Capture: Guardians of Gahoole*
   by Kathryn Lasky*

*The Children of the Lamp*
   by P. B. Kerr*

*Coraline* by Neil Gaiman

*A Curse Dark as Gold*
   by Elizabeth Bunce

*D'Aulaires' Book of Greek Myths*
   by Edgar and Ingri
   D'Aulaire

*The Demon King*
   by Cinda Williams Chima*

*The Dragon's Tooth*
   by N. D. Wilson*

*Elsewhere* by Gabrielle Zevin

*The Emerald Atlas*
   by John Stephens*

*Eragon* by Christopher Paolini*

*Fablehaven* by Brandon Mull*

*Fake Mustache*
   by Tom Angleberger

*False Prince* by Jennifer Nielsen*

*The Fellowship of the Ring*
   by J.R.R. Tolkien*

*The Fire Within*
   by Chris D'Lacey*

*The Goose Girl* by Shannon Hale

*Graceling* by Kristin Cashore*

*Grave Mercy: His Fair Assassin*
   by R. L. LaFevers

*The Graveyard Book*
   by Neil Gaiman

*Gregor the Overlander*
   by Suzanne Collins*

*Harry Potter and the Sorcerer's
   Stone* by J. K. Rowling*

*The Hobbit* by J.R.R. Tolkien

*Hold Me Closer, Necromancer*
   by Lish McBride*

*Holes* by Louis Sachar

*How to Ditch Your Fairy*
   by Justin Larbelestier

*The Indian in the Cupboard*
by Lynne Reid Banks*

*Inkheart* by Cornelia Funke*

*Keeper* by Kathi Appelt

*Killer Pizza* by Greg Taylor*

*Leven Thumps and the Gateway
to Foo* by Obert Skye*

*The Lightning Thief*
by Rick Riordan*

*The Lion, the Witch, and the
Wardrobe* by C. S. Lewis*

*The Lost Hero* by Rick Riordan*

*Malice* by Chris Wooding*

*Matilda* by Roald Dahl

*Merlin and the Making of the King*
by Margaret Hodges

*Miss Peregrine's Home for Peculiar
Children* by Ransom Riggs*

*Mister Monday* by Garth Nix*

*A Monster Calls* by Patrick Ness

*Mrs. Frisby and the Rats of NIMH*
by Robert O'Brien

*Oh My Gods! A Look-It-Up Guide to
Greek Mythology*
by Megan Bryant*

*The Once and Future King*
by T. H. White

*The One and Only Ivan*
by Katherine Applegate

*Peter Nimble and His Fantastic Eyes*
by Jonathan Auxier

*The Phantom Tollbooth*
by Norton Juster

*Princess Academy*
by Shannon Hale

*The Red Pyramid*
by Rick Riordan*

*Redwall* by Brian Jacques*

*The Ruins of Gorlan*
by John Flanagan*

*The Scorpio Races*
by Maggie Stiefvater

*The Sea of Trolls*
by Nancy Farmer*

*Shiver* by Maggie Stiefvater*

*Skeleton Creek*
by Patrick Carman*

*Skullduggery Pleasant*
by Derek Landy*

*A Tale Dark and Grimm*
by Adam Gidwitz*

*The Tale of Despereaux*
by Kate DiCamillo*

*The Thief Lord*
by Cornelia Funke

*Treasury of Greek Mythology*
by Donna Jo Napoli

*Twilight* by Stephenie Meyer*

*Unwitting Wisdom: An Anthology
of Aesop's Fables*
by Helen Ward

*Wait 'Til Helen Comes*
by Mary Downing Hahn

*The Warrior Heir*
by Cinda Williams Chima*

*Warriors: Into the Wild*
by Erin Hunter*

*The White Giraffe*
by Lauren St. John*

*Wildwood* by Colin Meloy*

*Winterling* by Sarah Prineas*

*Wolf Brother* by Michelle Paver*

*The Wonderful Wizard of Oz*
by L. Frank Baum*

## Science Fiction

*Among the Hidden* by Margaret
Peterson Haddix*

*The Beasties* by William Sleator

*The Boy at the End of the
World*
by Greg Van Eekhout

*Bruiser* by Neal Shusterman

*The City of Ember*
by Jeanne DuPrau*

*The Cryptid Hunters*
by Roland Smith*

*Delirium* by Lauren Oliver*

*Divergent* by Veronica Roth*

*Double Identity* by Margaret
Peterson Haddix

*Ender's Game*
by Orson Scott Card*

*The Enemy* by Charlie Higson*

*Everlost* by Neal Shusterman*

*The Extraordinary Adventures of
Alfred Kropp* by Rick Yancey*

*The Giver* by Lois Lowry*

*Gone* by Michael Grant*

*HIVE: Higher Institute of
Villainous Education*
by Mark Walden*

*The Hunger Games*
by Suzanne Collins*

*The Invention of Hugo Cabret*
by Brian Selznick

*The Knife of Never Letting Go*
by Patrick Ness*

*Leviathan* by Scott Westerfeld*

*Life As We Knew It*
by Susan Beth Pfeffer*

*Matched* by Ally Condie*

*Maximum Ride: The Angel
Experiment*
by James Patterson*

*The Maze Runner*
by James Dashner*

*NERDS: National Espionage,
Rescue, and Defense Society* by
Michael Buckley*

*No Passengers beyond This Point*
by Gennifer Choldenko

*Rot and Ruin*
by Jonathan Maberry*

*The Seems: The Glitch in the Sleep*
by John Hulme*

*Ship Breaker*
by Paolo Bacigalupi*

*Stormbreaker*
by Anthony Horowitz*

*Uglies* by Scott Westerfeld*

*Unwind* by Neal Shusterman*

*When You Reach Me*
by Rebecca Stead

*A Wrinkle in Time*
by Madeline L'Engle*

## Nonfiction

*13 Planets: The Latest View of the
Solar System* by David Aguilar

*1st and 10: Top Ten Lists of
Everything Football* by Sports
Illustrated for Kids*

*Amelia Lost: The Life and
Disappearance of Amelia
Earhart* by Candace Fleming

*An American Plague: The True
and Terrifying Story of the*

*Yellow Fever Epidemic of 1793*
by Jim Murphy

*A Black Hole Is Not a Hole*
by Carolyn Cinami
Decristofano

*The Book of Blood: From Legends
and Leeches to Vampires and
Veins* by H. P. Newquist

*Can We Save the Tiger?*
by Martin Jenkins

*Car Science*
by Richard Hammond

*The Case of the Vanishing Golden
Frogs: A Scientific Mystery*
by Sandra Markle

*Dewey the Library Cat: A True Story*
by Vicki Myron

*The Diary of Anne Frank*
by Anne Frank

*DK Eyewitness: Spy*
by Richard Platt*

*Don't Touch that Toad and Other
Strange Things Adults Tell You*
by Catherine Rondina

*The Elements: A Visual Exploration
of Every Known Atom in the
Universe* by Theodore Gray

*Far from Shore: Chronicles of an
Open Ocean Voyage*
by Sophie Webb

*Guinea Pig Scientists: Bold
Self-Experimenters in
Science and Medicine*
by Mel Boring

*Guts* by Gary Paulsen

*Helen Keller: A Photographic Story
of a Life* by Leslie Garrett

*Hitler Youth: Growing Up in
Hitler's Shadow* by Susan
Campbell Bartoletti

*The Hive Detectives: Chronicle of a
Honey Bee Catastrophe*
by Loree Griffin Burns

*How Angel Peterson Got His Name*
by Gary Paulsen

*How They Croaked: The Awful
Ends of the Awfully Famous*
by Georgia Bragg

*Human Body: A Book with Guts*
by Simon Basher*

*Jimmie Johnson: Racing Champ*
by Marty Gitlin*

*Kakapo Rescue: Saving the World's
Strangest Parrot*
by Sy Montgomery

*Knucklehead: Tall Tales and
Almost True Stories of Growing
Up* by Jon Scieszka

*My Life in Dog Years*
by Gary Paulsen

*National Geographic Kids
Everything: Big Cats*
by Elizabeth Carney*

*Oh Rats! The Story of Rats and
People* by Albert Marrin

*On the Court with LeBron James*
by Matt Christopher*
(sports hero series)

*Outbreak: Plagues That Changed
History* by Bryn Barnard

*Phineas Gage: A Gruesome but True Story about Brain Science* by John Fleischman

*Raptor: A Kid's Guide to Birds of Prey* by Christyna Laubach

*Rescuing Rover: Saving America's Dogs* by Raymond Bial

*Saving the Baghdad Zoo: A True Story of Hope and Heroes* by Kelly Milner Halls

*Sharkpedia* by Nancy Elwood

*Shelter Dogs: Amazing Stories of Adopted Strays* by Peg Kehret

*Small Steps: The Year I Got Polio* by Peg Kehret

*Soul Surfer* by Bethany Hamilton

*Space, Stars, and the Beginning of Time: What the Hubble Telescope Saw* by Elaine Scott

*Spilling Ink: A Young Writer's Handbook* by Ellen Potter and Anne Mazer

*Tales of the Cryptids: Mysterious Creatures That May or May Not Exist* by Kelly Milner Halls

*The Tarantula Scientist* by Sy Montgomery

*Temple Grandin: How the Girl Who Loved Cows Embraced Autism and Changed the World* by Sy Montgomery

*TIME for Kids Big Book of How* by Time Magazine*

*Titanic: Voices from the Disaster* by Deborah Hopkins

*Trapped: How the World Rescued Thirty-Three Miners from 2,000 Feet below the Chilean Desert* by Marc Aronson

*Wolves* by Seymour Simon*

*World without Fish* by Mark Kurlansky

## Poetry and Novels in Verse

*A Writing Kind of Day: Poems for Young Poets* by Ralph Fletcher

*All the Small Poems and Fourteen More* by Valerie Worth

*Amazing Faces* by Lee Bennett Hopkins

*Comets, Stars, the Moon and Mars: Space Poems and Paintings* by Douglas Florian

*Countdown to Summer: A Poem for Every Day of the School Year* by J. Patrick Lewis

*Dark Emperor and Other Poems of the Night* by Joyce Sidman

*Diamond Willow* by Helen Frost

*Dirty Laundry Pile: Poems in Different Voices* by Paul Janeczko

*Dizzy in Your Eyes: Poems about Love* by Pat Mora

*The Dream Keeper and Other Poems* by Langston Hughes

*Falling Down the Page: A Book of List Poems* by Georgia Heard

*Forgive Me, I Meant to Do It: False Apology Poems* by Gail Carson Levine and Matthew Cordell

*Hailstones and Halibut Bones: Adventures in Poetry and Color* by Mary O'Neill

*Hate That Cat* by Sharon Creech*

*Hoop Kings* by Charles Smith*

*I Never Said I Wasn't Difficult* by Sara Holbrook

*Inside Out and Back Again* by Thanhha Lai

*Joyful Noise: Poems for Two Voices* by Paul Fleischman

*Knock at a Star: A Child's Introduction to Poetry* by X. J. Kennedy

*Lemonade and Other Poems Squeezed from a Single Word* by Bob Raczka

*A Light in the Attic* by Shel Silverstein

*Locomotion* by Jacqueline Woodson*

*Love That Dog* by Sharon Creech*

*Mirror Mirror: A Book of Reversible Poems* by Marilyn Singer

*Neighborhood Odes* by Gary Soto

*The New Kid on the Block* by Jack Prelutsky

*Out of the Dust* by Karen Hesse

*Pieces: A Year in Poems and Quilts* by Anna Grossnickle Hines

*A Pizza the Size of the Sun* by Jack Prelutsky

*Poetry for Young People: William Carlos Williams* edited by Christopher McGowan*

*Poetry Speaks Who I Am: Poems of Discovery, Inspiration,*

*Independence, and Everything Else* by Elise Paschen

*The President's Stuck in the Bathtub: Poems about the Presidents* by Susan Katz and Robert Neubecker

*Put Your Eyes Up Here* by Kalli Dakos

*Requiem: Poems of the Terezin Ghetto* by Paul Janeczko

*Toasting Marshmallows: Camping Poems* by Kristine O'Connell George

*Ubiquitous: Celebrating Nature's Survivors* by Joyce Sidman

*UnBEElievables: Honeybee Poems and Paintings* by Douglas Florian

*The Watch That Ends the Night: Voices from the Titanic* by Allan Wolf

*Water Sings Blue: Ocean Poems* by Kate Coombs

*What My Mother Doesn't Know* by Sonya Sones

*Where the Sidewalk Ends* by Shel Silverstein

*The World According to Dog: Poems and Teen Voices* by Joyce Sidman

## Graphic Novels, Manga, and Comics

*Adventures of Tintin* by Herge*

*American Born Chinese* by Gene Luen Yang

*Amulet #1: The Stonekeeper* by Kazu Kibuishi*

*Anya's Ghost* by Vera Brosgol

*Astronaut Academy* by Dave Roman*

*Avatar: The Last Airbender* by Gene Yuen Yang*

*Babymouse #1: Queen of the World!* by Jennifer and Matthew Holm*

*Bone* by Jeff Smith*

*Cardboard* by Doug TenNapel

*The Complete Calvin and Hobbes* by Bill Watterson*

*Drama* by Raina Telgemeier

*Excalibur* by Tony Lee

*Flight* by Kazu Kibuishi*

*Gettysburg: The Graphic Novel* by C. M. Butzer

*Ghostopolis* by Doug TenNapel

*Giants Beware!* by Jorge Aguirre

*Knights of the Lunch Table: The Dodgeball Chronicles* by Frank Cammuso*

*Lunch Lady and the Cyborg Substitute* by Jarrett Krosoczka*

*Maximum Ride: The Manga* by James Patterson*

*Meanwhile* by Jason Shiga

*Mercury* by Hope Larson

*Missile Mouse: Star Crusher* by Jake Parker*

*The Odyssey* by Gareth Hinds (based on Homer's epic poem)

*Outlaw: The Legend of Robin Hood* by Tony Lee

*Rapunzel's Revenge* by Shannon Hale*

*Resistance* by Carla Jablonski*

*Robot Dreams* by Sara Varon

*Secret Science Alliance and the Copycat Crook* by Eleanor Davis*

*Sidekicks* by Dan Santat

*Smile* by Raina Telgemeier

*Squish #1: Super Amoeba* by Jennifer and Matthew Holm*

*Tales from Outer Suburbia* by Shaun Tan

*The Storm in the Barn* by Matt Phelan

*To Dance: A Ballerina's Graphic Novel* by Siena Siegal

*Trickster: Native American Tales* by Matt Dembicki

*Zeus: King of the Gods* by George O'Connor*

*Zita the Spacegirl* by Ben Hatke

# References

Adams, M. J. (1994). *Beginning to read: Thinking and learning about print.* Cambridge, MA: MIT Press.

Allen, N. L., Carlson, J. E., & Zelenak, C. A. (2000, October 19). *The National Assessment of Education Progress 1996 technical report.* Retrieved from http://nces.ed.gov/pubsearch/pubsinfo.asp?pubid=1999452

Allington, R. L. (2006). *What really works for struggling readers: Designing research-based programs.* Boston, MA: Pearson, Allyn & Bacon.

Allington, R. L., & McGill-Franzen, A. E. (2013). *Summer reading: Closing the rich/poor achievement gap.* New York, NY: Teachers College Press.

Anderson, J. (2005). *Mechanically inclined: Building grammar, usage, and style into writer's workshop.* Portland, ME: Stenhouse.

Applegate, A., & Applegate, M. (2004). The Peter effect: Reading habits and attitudes of preservice teachers. *Reading Teacher, 57,* 554–563.

Atwell, N. (2007). *The reading zone.* New York, NY: Scholastic Teaching Resources.

Baker, P. J., & Moss, R. K. (1993). Creating a community of readers. *School Community Journal, 3,* 319–334. Retrieved from http://www.adi.org/journal/ss01/chapters/Chapter23-Baker&Moss.PDF

Bennett, S., & Kalish, N. (2006). *The case against homework: How homework is hurting our children and what we can do about it.* New York, NY: Crown.

Carter, B. (2000). Formula for failure: Reading levels and readability formulas do not create lifelong readers. *School Library Journal, 46*(7), 34–37. Retrieved from http://www.schoollibraryjournal.com/article/CA153046.html

Chilton, M. (2012, September 7). Children "embarrassed to read" is an issue that should worry us all. *Guardian.* Retrieved from http://www.telegraph.co.uk/culture/9527793/Children-embarrassed-to-read-is-an-issue-that-should-worry-us-all.html

Clark, C. (2012). *Children's reading today: Findings from the National Literacy Trust's annual survey.* London, UK: National Literacy Trust. Retrieved from http://www.literacytrust.org.uk/assets/0001/4450/Young_people_s_reading_FINAL_REPORT.pdf

Commeyras, M., Bisplinghoff, B. S., & Olson, J. (2003). *Teachers as readers: Perspectives on the importance of reading in teachers' classrooms and lives.* Newark, DE: International Reading Association.

Cunningham, A. E. (2005). Vocabulary growth through independent reading and reading aloud to children. In E. H. Hiebert & M. L. Kamil (Eds.), *Teaching and learning vocabulary: Bringing research to practice* (pp. 45–65) Mahwah, NJ: Erlbaum.

Cunningham, A. E., & Stanovich, K. E. (1998, Spring/Summer). What reading does for the mind. *American Educator, 1*–8. Retrieved from http://www.keithstanovich.com/Site/Research_on_Reading_files/Cunningham_Stano_Amer_Educator_1998.pdf

Dewey, J. (1933) *How we think: A restatement of the relation of reflective thinking to the educative process* (rev. ed.) Boston: D. C. Heath.

Dolin, A. K. (2010). *Homework made simple: Tips, tools, and solutions for stress-free homework.* Washington, DC: Advantage Books.

Dreher, M. J. (2002). Motivating teachers to read. *Reading Teacher, 56*(4), 338–340. Retrieved from http://www.drradloff.com/documents/motivating-teachers-to-read-2002.pdf

Foster, T. C. (2003). *How to read literature like a professor: A lively and entertaining guide to reading between the lines.* New York, NY: HarperCollins.

Fountas, I. C., & Pinnell, G. S. (2001). *Guiding readers and writers (grades 3-6): Teaching comprehension, genre, and content literacy.* Portsmouth, NH: Heinemann.

Francis, B. H., Lance, K. C., & Lietzau, Z. (2010). *School librarians continue to help students achieve standards: The third Colorado study.* Denver: Colorado State Library, Library Research Service.

Gallagher, K. (2009). *Readicide: How schools are killing reading and what you can do about it.* Portland, ME: Stenhouse.

Gambrell, L. B. (1996). Creating classroom cultures that foster reading motivation. *Reading Teacher, 50,* 14–25.

Gambrell, L. B., Palmer, B. M., Codling, R. M., & Mazzoni, S. A. (1996). Assessing motivation to read. *Reading Teacher, 49,* 518–533.

Gewertz, C. (2010, March 24). NAEP reading results deemed disappointing. *Education Week.* Retrieved from http://www.edweek.org/ew/articles/2010/03/24/27naep.h29.html?tkn=OQZFCTLC2v4g7b7fe8iw1juZ1b/Q0/oRvFdo&cmp=clp-edweek

Green, J. (2011, November). Keynote speech presented at the Assembly on Literature for Adolescents Annual Conference, Chicago, IL.

Guthrie, J. (2008). *Engaging adolescents in reading.* Thousand Oaks, CA: Corwin Press.

Guthrie, J., & Wigfield, A. (2000). Engagement and motivation in reading. In M. Kamil, P. Mosenthal, D. Pearson, & R. Barr (Eds.), *Handbook of reading research* (pp. 518–533) Mahwah, NJ: Erlbaum.

Iyengar, S., & Ball, D. (2007). *To read or not to read: A question of national consequence.* Washington, DC: National Endowment for the Arts, Office of Research and Analysis. Retrieved from http://www.nea.gov/research/ToRead.pdf

Jacobs, A. (2011). *The pleasure of reading in an age of distraction.* New York, NY: Oxford University Press.

Johnson, D., & Blair, A. (2003). The importance and use of student self-selected literature to reading engagement in an elementary reading curriculum. *Reading Horizons, 43*(3), 181–202.

Johnston, P. (2004). *Choice words: How our language affects children's learning.* Portland, ME: Stenhouse.

Kelley, M., & Clausen-Grace, N. (2010). R5: A sustained silent reading makeover that works. In E. Hiebert & R. Reutzel (Eds.), *Revisiting silent reading: New directions for teachers and researchers.* Newark, DE: International Reading Association.

Kim, J. S. (2006). Effects of voluntary summer reading intervention on reading achievement: Results from a randomized field trial. *Educational Evaluation and Policy Analysis, 28*(4), 335–355.

Kittle, P. (2012). *Book love: Developing depth, stamina, and passion in adolescent readers.* Portsmouth, NH: Heinemann.

Kohn, A. (2006a). *The homework myth: Why our kids get too much of a bad thing.* Cambridge, MA: Da Capo Press.

Kohn, A. (2006b). Abusing research: The study of homework and other examples. *Phi Delta Kappan, 88*(1), 9–22.

Kohn, A. (2012, November 25). *Homework: New research suggests it may be an unnecessary evil.* Retrieved from http://www.huffington post.com/alfie-kohn/homework-research_b_2184918.html

Kralovec, E., & Buell, J. (2000). *The end of homework: How homework disrupts families, overburdens children, and limits learning.* Boston, MA: Beacon Press.

Krashen, S. D. (2004). *The power of reading: Insights from the research* (2nd ed.). Portsmouth, NH: Heinemann.

Krashen, S. D., & Ujiie, J. (2005). Junk food is bad for you, but junk reading is good for you. *Journal of Foreign Language Teaching, 1*(3), 5–12.

Lance, K. 2004. The impact of school library media centers on academic achievement. In C. Kuhlthau (Ed.), *School Library Media Annual* (pp. 188–197) Westport, CT: Libraries Unlimited.

Larson, J., (2012). *CREW: A weeding manual for modern libraries. Texas State Library and Archives Commission.* Retrieved from https://www.tsl.state.tx.us/sites/default/files/public/tslac/ld/ld/pubs/crew/crewmethod12.pdf

Larson, K. (2013, February 5). *Beach combing for books.* Retrieved from http://nerdybookclub.wordpress.com/2013/02/05/searching-for-treasure-by-kirby-larson/

Lesesne, T. S. (2010). *Reading ladders: Leading students from where they are to where we'd like them to be.* Portsmouth, NH: Heinemann.

London, C. A. (2011, December 13). *Books build.* Retrieved from http://nerdybookclub.wordpress.com/2011/12/13/books-build/

McKool, S. S., & Gespass, S. (2009). Does Johnny's reading teacher love to read? How teachers' personal reading habits affect instructional practices. *Literacy Research and Instruction, 48,* 264–276.

McQuillan, J., & Conde, G. (1996). The conditions of flow in reading: Two studies of optimal experience. *Reading Psychology: An International Quarterly, 17,* 109–135.

Miller, D. (2009). *The book whisperer: Awakening the inner reader in every child.* San Francisco, CA: Jossey-Bass.

Millis, K. K., Simon, S., & tenBroek, N. S. (1998). Resource allocation during the rereading of scientific texts. *Memory and Cognition, 26,* 232–246.

Morrison, T. G., Jacobs, J. S., & Swinyard, W. R. (1999). Do teachers who read personally use recommended literacy practices in their classrooms? *Reading Research and Instruction, 38*(2), 81–100.

National Center for Education Statistics. (1996). *The NAEP report.* Washington, DC: Author.

Newkirk, T. (2011). *The art of slow reading: Six time-honored practices for engagement.* Portsmouth, NH: Heinemann.

New York Comprehensive Center. (2011). *Informational brief: Impact of school libraries on student achievement.* New York: New York Comprehensive Center. Retrieved from http://www.nysl.nysed.gov/libdev/nyla/nycc_school_library_brief.pdf and http://www.nysl.nysed.gov/libdev/nyla/nycc_school_library_brief.pdf

Pearl, N. (2003). *Book lust: Recommended reading for every mood, moment, and reason.* Seattle, WA: Sasquatch Books.

Pressley, M. (2000). What should comprehension instruction be the instruction of? In M. L. Kamil, P. B. Mosenthal, P. D. Pearson, & R. Barr (Eds.), *Handbook of reading research* (Vol. 3, pp. 545–561). Mahwah, NJ: Erlbaum.

Ranganathan, S. R. (1963). *The five laws of library science.* Bombay, India: Asia Publishing House.

Schunk, D. H. (2003). Self-efficacy for reading and writing: Influence of modeling, goal-setting, and self-evaluation. *Reading and Writing Quarterly, 19,* 157–172.

Sparks, S. D. (2011, May 30). Panel finds few gains from the testing movement. *Education Week.* Retrieved from http://www.edweek .org/ew/articles/2011/05/26/33academy.h30.html?tkn= ULTFtJf0KzhX1WoYBwa7Fno9JPFBN1wbfCeV&intc=bs

Thompson, T. (2008). *Adventures in graphica: Using comics and graphic novels to teach comprehension.* Portland, ME: Stenhouse.

Tovani, C. (2013, January). *TCTELA Conference Workshop* at the 2013 Texas Council of Teachers of English Language Arts Annual Conference, Dallas, TX.

University of Oxford. (2011, April 8). *Reading at 16 linked to better job prospects.* Retrieved from http://www.ox.ac.uk/media/news _stories/2011/110804.html

Worthy, J., & McKool, S. (1996). Students who say they hate to read: The importance of opportunity, choice, and access. In D. J. Leu, C. K. Kinzer, & K. A. Hinchman (Eds.), *Literacies for the 21st century: Research and practice: 45th yearbook of the National Reading Conference* (pp. 245–256) Chicago, IL: National Reading Conference.

Worthy, J., & Roser, N. (2010). Productive sustained reading in a bilingual class. In E. Hiebert & R. Reutzel (Eds.), *Revisiting silent reading: New directions for teachers and researchers.* Newark, DE: International Reading Association.

# *Acknowledgments*

MY STUDENT JOSH asked me, "Why would anyone read the acknowledgments? The author just mentions his family and stuff."

I explained, "Well, sometimes a reader can learn about authors' writing processes or discover interesting things about their lives."

He seemed unimpressed: "Hmm. I think that it's just a list of people's names I don't know."

Josh is probably right. Casual readers skip the acknowledgments. Since this book explores the habits of wild readers, though, I know that some of you will read the acknowledgments because you are completists. Like me, you read every word in a book. I read dedications, forewords, afterwords, authors' notes, and acknowledgments because I find writers and writing fascinating. Walking through a book from beginning to end requires listening to the author babble on a bit.

I can never fully express my gratitude to the folks at Jossey-Bass, my publisher, for taking a big chance on me with *The Book Whisperer* four years ago and waiting patiently for me to complete *Reading in the Wild*. In particular, I thank Kate Bradford, my editor, and Dimi Berkner, the marketing director, for helping me bring this book to publication in spite of my many professional and personal challenges the past three years. I also appreciate copyeditor Bev Miller for her sense of humor and shared love for reading, which made wading through my mistakes bearable.

Thank you to the hundreds of teachers, librarians, parents, and readers who participated in our Wild Reader Survey. Your honest comments and willingness to share your reading lives with all of us provided the foundation for this book and profoundly influenced my teaching.

I spent six wonderful years at Trinity Meadows Intermediate School in Keller Independent School District in Keller, Texas. A special thanks to the Nile River team—Dana Allison, Maria Collins, Matt Quattlebaum, Sara Hutson, Ashleigh Robertson, Vicki Arrington, and Karen Nichols. Working with you was the best experience of my teaching career. I appreciate my wonderful principals, Ron Myers and Susan Mackey, for embracing my wild ideas like reading doors and summer library hours. Teachers thrive when they work with administrators who support them and offer autonomy and trust.

Jumping into Twitter four years ago, I could not have predicted how much it would add to my life. I have built professional relationships with incredible colleagues. My tweeps and fellow Nerdy Book Club members are the wild readers who sustain and teach me every day: Paul Hankins, John Schumacher, Cindy Minnich, Mary Lee Hahn, Karen Terlecky, Tony Keefer, Kate Messner, Cynthia Alaniz, Niki Barnes, Beth Shaum, Alyson Beecher, Cathy Blackler, Susan Dee, Brian Wyzlic, Jillian Heise, Mindi Rench, Teresa Kravtin, Jen Vincent, Sherry Gick, Karin Perry, Kristin McIlhagga, Dawn Little, Lee Ann Spillane, Sarah Andersen, and Laura Komos. Special thanks to Amber White and Heather Jensen from the Michigan Reading Association, who invited me to give my first keynote speech and keep inviting me to Michigan. It has become a second home.

I learned a lot about being a professional author from Jeff Anderson and Terry Thompson, who call me to see if I'm writing and answer my non sequitur text messages about reading, writing, and teaching at all hours. Terry provided pivotal support in the early stages of this book and helped me find clarity when I was mired down in parts that didn't matter. Someday a major publisher will figure out what a great editor he is. Jeff is my Obi-Wan, providing me with invaluable advice and support over the years. I have watched Jeff lead staff development scores of times, and I always learn something new. Thank you, gentlemen. I know your prom dates had a great time.

During a conference in Denver, Penny Kittle and Franki Sibberson helped me find the structure of this book when I couldn't see it. Thank you for the laughs and wisdom, ladies. You are brilliant.

I am blessed with four rare and precious "red sea glass" friends (K. Larson, 2013)—Colby Sharp, Katherine Sokolowski, Teresa Bunner, and Teri Lesesne—who read the manuscript during its creation and provided me with encouragement and critical feedback when I needed it. I am sure they are thrilled the book is done so I won't send them any more insecure 3:00 a.m. e-mails. Colby called this "his book" and asked me often when I was going to finish it for him. Katherine read individual paragraphs at some points, researched hiking terms for two hours when I went off on a wild reader tangent, and texted me about *The Raven Boys* by Maggie Stiefvater when I needed a break. Teresa provides great advice. I should follow it more often. Thank you for being my confidantes and role models. You lift everyone around you with your enthusiasm and love for young people and their rights to positive school and reading experiences. I am especially honored that Teri Lesesne agreed to write the foreword for this book. Thank you, Teri, for your leadership and friendship.

My dear friend and mentor Susie Kelley agreed to join me in researching lifelong readers and used her classroom as a laboratory for two years. Susie has taught me more about teaching than anyone else. I am blessed to learn from her. Susie compiled all of the data for *Reading in the Wild* and combed through hundreds of student samples and Wild Reader Survey responses to select the quotes and examples that appear in this book. She improved my life. She improved my teaching. And she certainly improved this book with her contributions.

I became a teacher because of my daughters, Celeste and Sarah, and I continue striving to improve reading classrooms for all children because of them. They taught me a lot about what young readers want and need. As a preschool teacher and mother of two toddlers, Celeste reads with small children all day. She knows how much reading matters. Celeste, I am sorry I sent *Dragons Love Tacos* and *Chicken Butt* home. It's a grandmother's job to send silly books home. Thank you for reading them hundreds of times. Sarah is our Wild Reading poster child. She insists to her boyfriend that he read and pleads with her English teacher for more reading time. Thank you, Sarah, for waiting two extra years for me to finish this book. We can play Skyrim now.

Without my husband, Don, I couldn't write a single word. He reads research so he can talk to me about the beehive of ideas in my brain, he looks the other way when towers of books arrive at our house, and he makes my lunch every day of the school year. Honey, I am the envy of the teachers' lounge because of you. Most of all, Don understands my book and reading obsessions because we share them. Marrying another wild reader was the best decision I ever made.

I have been blessed to work with many remarkable children and become part of their families for a year or longer. I am a better teacher because you taught me how. I appreciate your families who agreed to participate in this book. I know that your thoughts about reading and your classroom experiences will influence many. Yes, Josh, this includes you. Are you still reading?

—Donalyn Miller

• • •

I thank Donalyn for inviting me to help with *Reading in the Wild.* I am humbled that she values my opinions. In *The Book Whisperer,* Donalyn mentions me as her mentor. Clearly, throughout the years, our roles have reversed. Her enthusiasm for reading has kept me up-to-date on books, and I have had a front-row seat to observe and learn from Donalyn. I am thankful that we had the opportunity to share ideas and grow together as reading professionals. I know our students benefited from our collaboration.

—Susie Kelley

# About the Authors

**Donalyn Miller** has worked with a wide variety of upper elementary and middle school students and currently teaches fifth grade at O. A. Peterson Elementary in Fort Worth, Texas. In her popular book *The Book Whisperer*, she reflects on her journey to become a reading teacher and describes how she inspires and motivates her middle school students to read forty or more books a year. She currently facilitates a community blog, The Nerdy Book Club, and cowrites a monthly column for Scholastic's *Principal-to-Principal Newsletter*. Her articles about teaching and literacy have appeared in publications such as *Reading Teacher, Educational Leadership*, and the *Washington Post*.

• • •

**Susan Kelley** teaches fifth-grade language arts at Trinity Meadows Intermediate in Keller, Texas. She has taught in rural and urban areas at various grade levels for thirty-seven years. Throughout her career, she has developed reading and writing workshops that inspire students to love all aspects of written language. Weaving best practices with her experiences, she has shared her techniques and enthusiastic results with other educators. She acknowledges that at the end of the school year, her students proudly announce, "I am a reader. I am an author."

# *About the Sponsor*

E DUCATION WEEK PRESS is the book division of Editorial Projects in Education, the nonprofit publisher of *Education Week*, American education's newspaper of record. The press was launched in 2002 to further its mission of elevating awareness and understanding of important educational issues among professionals and the public. Education Week Press publishes books, including e-books, and digital resources on a wide range of issues affecting K–12 schooling. For more information, go to edweek.org/go/books.

# Index